OREGON
WINE + FOOD
THE COOKBOOK

Danielle Centoni & Kerry Newberry

PHOTOGRAPHY BY JOHN VALLS

Figure 1

Vancouver / Toronto / Berkeley

For the impossible dreamers who risked it all to turn craggy hillsides and old pig farms into a world-class wine industry.

For the hard-working talents who believe in the power of community, embrace the unpredictable, and continue raising the bar.

For all those who enjoy the stories behind the food and wine that bring us together around the table. May this book inspire you to make something special to share with the people you love.

And finally, for Maria, whose unflagging support, diligence, generosity, and vision embodied the very virtues that define Oregon wine country itself.

Cataloguing data is available from Library and Archives Canada
ISBN 978-1-77327-194-1 (hbk.)

Cover design by Teresa Bubela and Naomi MacDougall
Interior design by Teresa Bubela
Photography by John Valls
Food styling by Andrea Slonecker

Editing by Michelle Meade
Copy editing by Pam Robertson
Proofreading by Renate Preuss
Indexing by Iva Cheung

Printed and bound in China by Printplus Ltd., Hong Kong
Distributed internationally by Publishers Group West

Figure 1 Publishing Inc.
Vancouver BC Canada
www.figure1publishing.com

Figure 1 Publishing works in the traditional, unceded territory of the xʷməθkʷəy̓əm (Musqueam), Sḵwx̱wú7mesh (Squamish), and səl̓ilwətaɬ (Tsleil-Waututh) peoples.

RECIPE NOTES

Unless stated otherwise:

Butter is unsalted.

Citrus juices are freshly squeezed.

Eggs are large.

Herbs are fresh.

Parsley is flat-leaf (Italian).

Produce is medium-sized.

Salt is kosher.

CONTENTS

INTRODUCTION

MORE THAN FIFTY YEARS AGO, an eclectic crew brought their big dreams to an offbeat state. In a region mostly known for its vast forests, volcanic peaks, verdant valleys, and rain—so much rain—they wanted to plant grape vines. Despite a choir of skeptics from more established wine regions, this fearless collective of academics, scientists, cowboys, and artists stayed true to their vision. Now their stories are told around the table, renegade winemakers charting history.

Back then, winemaking in Oregon took a relentless spirit; a drive to experiment, invent, and adapt with no guide or map or manual for growing grapes here on the razor's edge. It took faith, hoping each year that the grapes would ripen, because there was no guarantee. And it took grit, a willingness to push past the failures and learn from the mistakes. But the payoff? Wines with ethereal beauty and an extraordinary expression of place. A place that, quite frankly, was very much off the radar.

An often-told tale recounts those early years, when the wine pioneers would haul their best bottles to international competitions or national tastings, and inevitably had to point to where Oregon was on the map. Today, wine connoisseurs point to that same spot on the map as a top wine destination they want to visit.

Oregon, it turns out, is climatically one of the best places to grow grapes on the planet. According to Dr. Greg Jones, one of the leading climatologists in wine, Oregon's northern latitude and geographic surroundings provide for ideal growing season lengths, low risk from weather extremes, and some of the largest diurnal temperature ranges during ripening of anywhere in the world. What does this mean? During the peak ripening period (generally May through September), the days are long and warm, allowing the grapes to develop beautiful and concentrated flavors. At night, the extreme drop in temperature slows down the maturation, helping to preserve the natural acidity. This leads to the balanced and food-friendly wines that Oregon is so revered for. Add in ancient geological drama, including volcanic eruptions and the epic Missoula floods, and Oregon also has a magnificent and varied terroir that is found in pockets across the state from the Willamette Valley to the Rogue Valley.

The geography, the climate, the soil—and of course, that dogged spirit—are a few of the many reasons Oregon wine is synonymous with quality today, and why labels consistently earn top scores in every major wine publication. But despite the accolades and growth, a defining ethos perseveres that keeps Oregon wine distinctive. It's still a little

maverick, it still draws outside the lines, and, well, there's still all that damn rain.

That's why upstart winemakers still flock here. They seek out that unpredictability. They embrace the unknown of a region still on the rise. What prevailed then remains true today—wine in Oregon is emotion. Whether you uncork a bottle of Pinot Noir or Picpoul, that wine represents a risk-taking spirit. It's pushing boundaries, it's the pursuit of quality, and it's innovating with purpose.

When you talk to winemakers here, they want to move people with their wine. They want to connect you to the spirit of this place. They want to capture the purest expression of the soil, the seasons, the sense of wonder found in something shaped by nature.

This deep connection to the environment defined the industry from the beginning and the state has long been a leader in environmental stewardship. Early on, the industry adopted sustainability as a core tenet, seeking out third-party certifications with the highest standards such as Demeter Certified Biodynamic, USDA Certified Organic, and Salmon-Safe. In fact, Oregon is home to some of the largest biodynamic vineyards in the country (page 150 and page 178) and has the largest percentage of certified vineyards nationally.

That is why you can spot sheep munching weeds in vineyards, nest boxes for songbirds as a form of natural pest management, and beehives for pollination. A commitment to building biodiversity in the vineyard and regenerative agriculture has also taken root. Most recently, Oregon had the second winery in the world to achieve the Regenerative Organic certification (page 214) and is one of the only states in the U.S. with a bee-friendly wine trail.

Ask any Oregon winemaker, from the pioneer to the upstart, what they think sets the state's wine industry apart and one word always rises to the top: collaboration. You can see it during harvest when winemakers are working around the clock. Here's a common scenario: It's dark outside and probably raining and the neighboring winery has a tractor break down. No problem, another winery will lend them one and bring a batch of cookies, too (page 174).

Or it's 6 AM and a few vineyard sheep have escaped the fence—yes, it's raining sideways— and the first truck that encounters the sheep is a neighbor and a winemaker on the way to work. They park, and begin to corral the sheep, texting an update. But the vineyard manager had already had a call about his wayward sheep and when he meets up with his colleague, he gives him an espresso. That's collaborative spirit. And that's Oregon.

You also see it in the winemaking collectives popping up across the state—a model where upstart winemakers share a facility and equipment and expertise as they grow their craft. Here, there are no secrets. Only rising tides. In this culture, innovation thrives. It's why you find small plots of obscure varieties like Trousseau Noir and Vermentino flourishing. Or why you find a high school art teacher turned winemaker building massive handmade clay amphorae for aging wine, resurrecting an ancient tradition that's embraced by winemakers across the state.

In Oregon, the sense of fearlessness that sparked the industry lives in the next generation in new ways, building a bridge between the past and the future. A bridge also exists between the wine and food worlds, with delicious creations. There's Brigid's Bender, a semi-firm cheese washed in red wine from Briar Rose Creamery in the Willamette Valley's Dundee Hills. And the world-famous Rogue River Blue from Rogue Creamery in Southern Oregon that's wrapped in Syrah leaves soaked in pear brandy.

Wine and food are the great connectors. That's something you'll read in many of the winemaker profiles in this book. It's a big reason many of them pursued a career in wine—to connect to soil, to seasons, to friends and family, to other cultures, to humanity. For many in this book, wine is a universal language. An expression of time and place and memories best shared around the dinner table.

And that's what this book is all about. It's a culmination of stories from Oregon's beautiful wine country that we hope you share around the table. The recipes focus on ingredients abundant in the Pacific Northwest—fresh seafood, seasonal vegetables, native plants, wild mushrooms—that can be enjoyed and procured by home cooks everywhere. Some recipes are personal favorites shared by the winemakers themselves, others come from a kindred group of chefs who are just as dedicated to celebrating and preserving the bounty of the region. We hope these recipes bring you to the heart of Oregon wine country, where the scent of evergreens, the sound of rain, and the sense of possibility is ever-present. Where the stargazers and game changers and eternal optimists know that with every vintage you are rolling the dice. But they do it anyway. Because when you get it right—it's magic.

OREGON WINES: FACT SHEET

National rank: Third-largest premium wine producer in the U.S.

Number of appellations: 23

Varieties produced: 100+

Wine production: Approximately 5.3 million cases annually

 Average hours of summer sunlight: 16 hours per day (Oregon has longer days with more sunlight than California's prime growing region.)

 Annual rainfall (by region):

North (Willamette Valley): 40 to 50 inches

South: 20 to 30 inches

Columbia River Gorge: 40 inches

Eastern Oregon (Columbia Valley, Walla Walla, and the Rocks District): 10 to 15 inches

GRAPES HARVESTED IN 2021: 114,677 TONS
LEADING VARIETIES:

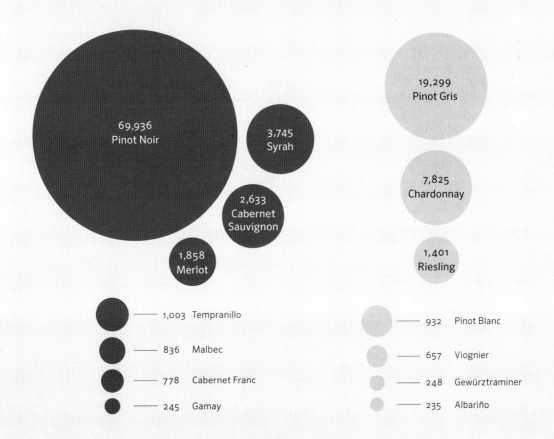

69,936 Pinot Noir

3,745 Syrah

19,299 Pinot Gris

2,633 Cabernet Sauvignon

7,825 Chardonnay

1,858 Merlot

1,401 Riesling

1,003 Tempranillo

932 Pinot Blanc

836 Malbec

657 Viognier

778 Cabernet Franc

248 Gewürztraminer

245 Gamay

235 Albariño

NUMBER OF WINERIES IN OREGON

2021	2020	2019	2018	2017	2016	2015	2014	2013
1,058	995	908	793	769	725	702	676	605

A TIMELINE

MEANINGFUL PEOPLE, PLACES, AND MOMENTS IN OREGON WINE

1961 AND SO IT BEGINS: Richard Sommer pioneers Oregon's wine industry and plants the first post-prohibition vinifera grapes, including Pinot Noir, in the state at HillCrest Vineyard in the Umpqua Valley.

1965 David Lett, a winemaking legend also known as "Papa Pinot," plants the Willamette Valley's first Pinot Noir cuttings.

1972 Dick Erath (page 122) produces 216 cases of commercial wine—the first official wine production in the now famous Dundee Hills.

1977 Nick's Italian Café in McMinnville opens and becomes the wine country's first destination restaurant and the de facto hangout for Oregon's winemakers. The standard order: wood-fired pizza, local Pinot, and a game of pool.

1982 Classic Wines Auction launches and becomes one of the longest-running charity wine auctions in the U.S. over the following decades.

1987 Rollin Soles founds Argyle Winery with the purpose of growing and making world-class sparkling wine in the cool climate of Oregon's Willamette Valley (page 62). ▶ Domaine Drouhin Oregon is established by Maison Joseph Drouhin, one of the most prestigious domaines in Burgundy, France. Set on 100 acres in the Dundee Hills, this investment brings international recognition to the region.

1989 The state's first shareholder-owned and publicly traded winery, Willamette Valley Vineyards (page 226), opens in Turner.

1991 Oregon winemakers and Tuality Healthcare professionals join together to launch ¡Salud!, a charity auction to raise funds to support the health care needs of the Oregon wine industry's seasonal workers, the first of its kind in the country.

1994 Higgins opens in downtown Portland, the city's original farm-to-table restaurant. Chef-owner Greg Higgins makes it his mission to work directly with local farmers, foragers, growers, and winemakers. (Recipes on pages 64 and 67.)

1996 Sokol Blosser broadens sustainability efforts with the first Salmon-Safe certified vineyard (page 198). By 2023, more than 350 vineyards are certified by the fish-forward nonprofit organization. ▶ The Czarnecki family opens the Joel Palmer House in Dayton, a nationally renowned restaurant famous for its wild mushroom dishes and extensive cellar of Oregon Pinot Noir.

1999 Cooper Mountain Vineyards (page 84) becomes the first Demeter-certified biodynamic winery in the Pacific Northwest.

2002 King Estate (page 150), Oregon's largest winery at the time, receives organic certification for all 465 acres of its estate vineyards. By 2022, this has grown to 1,033 vineyard acres.

2006 Stoller (page 208) becomes the world's first LEED Gold-certified winemaking facility. ▶ The first annual Oregon Truffle Festival kicks off, celebrating the state's native truffles with truffle forays, dinners, and speakers.

2008 The Durant family (page 116) opens the first and only olioteca in the Pacific Northwest.

2009 The Allison Inn & Spa in Newberg welcomes guests to the first luxury, eco-friendly wine country resort in Oregon, with on-site restaurant JORY named for the region's famed volcanic soil. (See pages 34 and 36 for recipes.)

2011 The inaugural year for the Oregon Chardonnay Celebration, an annual educational event with seminars and tastings. ▸ Red Hills Market opens in Dundee and quickly turns into the go-to spot for winemaker lunches. (Recipe on page 144.)

2014 Fueled by Fine Wine holds its first half marathon in the Dundee Hills, now a popular tradition for Pinot-loving runners.

2015 The Oregon Wine Experience becomes the leading annual fundraising event in Southern Oregon, raising funds and awareness for the Children's Miracle Network and other programs through culinary events and classes.

2016 The International Pinot Noir Celebration (IPNC), an annual event that brings together local chefs, winemakers, and Pinot Noir enthusiasts from around the world, reaches a milestone year with its thirtieth anniversary.

2017 Cowhorn Vineyard & Garden (page 94) is the first winery to achieve Living Building Challenge (LBC) Petal Certification, the world's most rigorous green building standard.

2018 Analemma (page 44) is the first U.S. winery to release Mencia, from the Spanish and Portuguese grape they planted in 2014. ▸ Chehalem Winery (page 80) becomes the sixth B Corp–certified winery in Oregon. Oregon currently has more certified wineries than any other state.

2019 Rogue Creamery's Rogue River Blue Cheese is named World's Best Cheese at the 2019 World Cheese Awards in Bergamo, Italy. ▸ Inaugural year for Women in Wine: Fermenting Change, an event dedicated to empowering and advancing women in the wine industry.

2020 AHIVOY, a nonprofit that supports education and empowerment for Latin and Hispanic vineyard workers, takes root. ▸ Inaugural year for Our Legacy Harvested, an organization working to educate, advance, and empower the wine industry's BIPOC community. ▸ Celebrating Hispanic Roots event launches, led by an alliance of Oregon winery owners and winemakers with heritage from Mexico, South America, Spain, and the Caribbean.

2021 The EU grants the Willamette Valley the coveted Protected Geographical Indication (PGI) status. It is only the second American wine region, after Napa, to receive this recognition. The PGI system protects iconic names of agricultural products, spirit drinks, and wines with a link to their geographical origin.

2022 The Tributary Hotel opens in McMinnville with Okta, an on-site restaurant led by two-Michelin-star chef Matthew Lightner. ▸ Remy Wines (page 190) hosts the world's first Queer Wine Fest.

Oregon is uniquely situated compared to other wine-growing regions of the world—it experiences coastal influences from the Pacific Ocean and long hours of sunlight in the summer growing season without intense heat, making it perfect for wine grapes to slowly ripen and develop highly complex flavors.

In the northern part of the state, you'll find a cool climate that produces fresh and elegant Pinot Noir and Chardonnay. It's also home to the Willamette Valley AVA, the largest in the state with the highest concentration of wineries. As this region slowly grew, winemakers began to notice clusters of vineyards with distinct microclimates, soil, and elevation which led to the creation of sub-appellations. There are currently eleven nested or sub-AVAs inside the larger Willamette Valley AVA. We highlight seven in the book.

As you travel to the southern part of the state, the climate gets warmer, there's less rain, and the geology changes. In this region, grapes like Tempranillo and Syrah can ripen successfully and you'll find more full-bodied and fruit-forward red wines. The overarching Southern Oregon AVA encompasses the Rogue Valley, Umpqua Valley, and their nested AVAs.

With twenty-three official American Viticultural Areas (AVAs) and more than 1,000 wineries producing over 100 varieties of grapes, there's a wonderful world of wine to explore in Oregon. Here's a snapshot of some of the prominent AVAs whose wines are featured in this book.

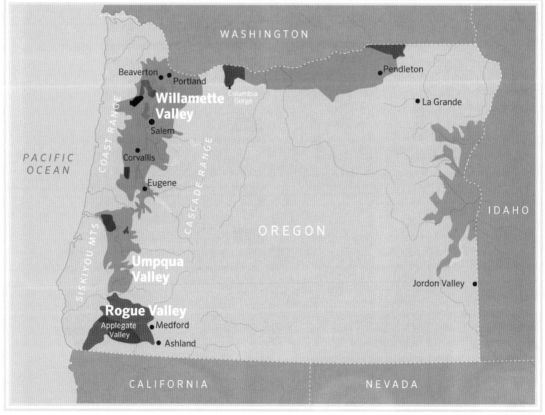

Willamette Valley

ESTABLISHED: 1983

FACT: Located just outside of Portland, this area tops the list for Pinot pilgrimages in the U.S., and is home to more than 700 wineries. It's recognized as one of the premier Pinot Noir–producing areas in the world. The following six AVAs are all in the Willamette Valley.

Chehalem Mountains

ESTABLISHED: 2006

FACT: The only AVA with the Willamette Valley's three dominant soil types: marine sedimentary, volcanic basalt, and wind-blown loess.

Dundee Hills

ESTABLISHED: 2005

FACT: Known for its rich, red volcanic Jory soil, formed by the Columbia River Basalts more than 14 million years ago, Dundee Hills is home to some of the state's most famous vineyards.

Eola-Amity Hills

ESTABLISHED: 2006

FACT: This is the only AVA you can visit by water. Find the Wheatland Ferry, a charming slip of a boat, between the towns of Newberg and Salem.

McMinnville

ESTABLISHED: 2005

FACT: In between wine tasting, you can visit the Evergreen Aviation & Space Museum, home to the Spruce Goose, the largest wooden airplane ever built.

Ribbon Ridge

ESTABLISHED: 2005

FACT: The smallest AVA in Oregon, measuring 3½ miles long by 1¾ miles wide.

Yamhill-Carlton

ESTABLISHED: 2004

FACT: Yamhill-Carlton is home to the first high school viticulture program in the U.S. that includes a commercial vineyard at the school and college-level accreditation for all coursework.

Lower Long Tom

ESTABLISHED: 2021

FACT: Long Tom is a regional name associated with the Kalapuyan people who have lived in the area for more than 10,000 years.

Columbia Gorge

ESTABLISHED: 2004

FACT: Spanning the beautiful Columbia River Gorge National Scenic Area, this AVA is home to over ninety waterfalls and a world of wildflower hikes and mountain bike trails.

Southern Oregon

ESTABLISHED: 2004

FACT: Home to Crater Lake, the state's only national park and the deepest lake in the U.S. The sparkling blue lake draws travelers from around the world. The Southern Oregon AVA includes the Rogue Valley, Umpqua Valley, and their nested AVAs.

Umpqua Valley

ESTABLISHED: 1984

FACT: Named for the renowned fishing river that runs nearby, this AVA is surrounded by pristine wilderness areas and has one of Oregon's more diverse climates. Pack your fly rod and your camping gear!

Rogue Valley

ESTABLISHED: 1991

FACT: Stay in the town of Ashland and you can experience the Tony Award–winning Oregon Shakespeare Festival after wine tasting.

Applegate Valley

ESTABLISHED: 2000

FACT: Jacksonville, a charming historic Gold Rush town, is the perfect hub from which to explore this region. Fifty miles long, this AVA stretches along the Applegate River and is nested in the Rogue Valley AVA.

GRAPE VARIETIES

Oregon's geological and climatic diversity makes for an exhilarating wine region where a remarkable diversity of grapes—from Albariño to Zinfandel—can grow and thrive. Since the first Pinot Noir was planted over fifty years ago, what persists across the state today is the spirit of innovation instilled by the Pinot pioneers. Upstart winemakers, and a new guard eager to innovate, continue to blaze the trail, planting unexpected varieties for expanding palates.

In fact, there's an astonishing number of grape varieties in Oregon, more than 100—racing down hillsides, clinging to rocky cliffs, crisscrossing mountain foothills, and thriving in the state's twenty-three American Viticultural Areas (AVAS). Endless exploration awaits.

Take a road trip through the windswept and waterfall-saturated Columbia River Gorge or down to the mountainous and deeply forested Applegate Valley and you'll find grape growers in these areas cultivating an array of lesser-known varieties, from Mencia (page 44) to Vermentino (page 214). Why? Because winemakers love to experiment and create delicious new wines to try.

Then there are the tribute grapes. Some of this grape diversity hails from dedicated Pinot producers planting one-acre plots as an ode to their heritage. Unexpected and delightful finds, these bottles are usually only available in the tasting rooms. At Montinore, winemaker Rudy Marchesi celebrates his Italian roots with single varieties rarely seen in the United States, such as Lagrein

and Teroldego (page 180). You can also find Tocai Friulano, a crisp, herbal white, at Cooper Mountain Vineyards (page 84) and Furioso Vineyards (page 130).

A kindred spirit is found over at Remy Wines, where Remy Drabkin (page 190) focuses mainly on Italian varieties grown in the Pacific Northwest, including Lagrein, Dolcetto, Sangiovese, and Barbera. And winemakers like Brianne Day of Day Wines, endlessly creative, are always scouting new varieties for passion projects. Part of her joy is instilling a sense of adventure through wine. Her wines on pages 105 and 108 showcase just that.

Even more astounding is that each of these graceful vineyard rows, these intricately planted hillsides, these carefully researched sites, offers a unique and singular taste of place. The French call that terroir, a sublime concept that loosely translates to the taste and flavors imparted on a wine due to factors like soil, topography, and climate.

With all the varieties growing in the state, we decided to focus here on the top eight Oregon grapes featured in the book—but we encourage you to explore all the up-and-coming darlings. (Hint: Malbec and Vermentino are gaining speed.) This chart captures select grapes along with their flavor profile and suggested food pairings.

RED GRAPES

Our most common red grape varieties include Pinot Noir, Syrah, Cabernet Sauvignon, and Merlot, but Cabernet Franc, Grenache, and Tempranillo are rising stars, especially in Southern Oregon. Other underdog grapes with tiny plantings but great cheerleaders behind them include Gamay, Trousseau, and Barbera. In fact, Oregon is home to the annual I Love Gamay Wine Festival, co-founded by Division Wines (page 110).

GAMAY

Winemakers love this underdog grape that produces a light-bodied, fruity red wine similar in taste to Pinot Noir.

WINEMAKER QUOTE: "The beauty of Gamay is its ability to deliciously translate its surroundings directly into the glass. We know this so well through the historical documentation in bottles of the great and distinct vineyards of the Crus of Beaujolais. How exciting it is for us to be able to discover and taste this magical power of Gamay through the lens of Oregon soil, climate, and landscape in real time."—Kate Norris, Division Winemaking Company

FOOD PAIRING: A roast chicken picnic, grilled veggies, or the fabulous Époisses Juicy Lucy Burger (page 113).

TYPICAL FLAVORS

RASPBERRY

CRANBERRY

CURRANT

PINOT NOIR

The state's flagship grape—more than 50 percent of the wine grapes grown in Oregon are Pinot Noir.

WINEMAKER QUOTE: "Thin-skinned and small-clustered, Pinot Noir is the Goldilocks of the wine world. Not too hot and not too cold is when it is happiest. To complicate things, it doesn't do well when it ripens too quickly and excels when it ripens slowly over a long period, late into the fall. Only when the conditions are 'just right' does Pinot Noir provide us with beautiful aromas, an elegant yet rich experience on the palate, and a seductive and complex bouquet. The narrow band of climate and soil conditions that makes our Goldilocks happy is found in few places in the world. Luckily, Oregon is one of them."—Rudy Marchesi, Montinore Estate

FOOD PAIRING: One of the most food-friendly wines you'll find, this lighter-body red pairs perfectly with salmon, mushrooms, risotto, cheese boards, and even dessert (page 89).

TYPICAL FLAVORS

DARK CHERRY

RED CURRANT

MUSHROOM

SYRAH

The No. 2 red grape in Oregon is Syrah, most often planted in Southern Oregon regions including the Umpqua, Rogue, and Applegate Valleys.

WINEMAKER QUOTE: "When grown in cooler climates, as is the case for much of Oregon, Syrah develops more alluring aromatics, elegance, and intriguing savory and peppery characteristics. Under these cooler growing conditions is where the most beautiful, soulful, and transparent expressions of Syrah can be found."—Nate Wall, Troon Vineyard

FOOD PAIRING: Bold flavors call for grilled meats, braised beef, and even an unexpected match like earthy beets (page 216).

TYPICAL FLAVORS

BAKING SPICES

BLACK CHERRY

BLUEBERRY

TEMPRANILLO

The first winery to commercially grow and produce wine from Tempranillo in the Pacific Northwest is Abacela in Southern Oregon.

WINEMAKER QUOTE: "The thick-skinned, deep blue-black berries of Tempranillo are best suited in the Rogue Valley where they can find elegance and complexity."—JP Valot, Valcan Cellars

FOOD PAIRING: Try roasted lamb, hearty meat dishes (like the Lomo Saltado on page 224), paella with chorizo, or a hunk of Manchego cheese with a crusty baguette.

TYPICAL FLAVORS

CHERRY

PLUM

CEDAR

As far as production, most of Oregon's white wines fit into two camps: Chardonnay and Pinot Gris. The state also grows a fair amount of Riesling, Viognier, Sauvignon Blanc, Albariño, and Gewürztraminer. A smattering of other up-and-coming white grapes that produce food-friendly wines include Auxerrois, Pinot Blanc, Muscat, Picpoul, and Vermentino.

CHARDONNAY

A rising star in Oregon, showcasing the beauty and elegance found in cool-climate expressions.

WINEMAKER QUOTE: "Chardonnay is both a mirror and magnifying glass. It reflects the soil and the site from where it is grown while simultaneously revealing the type of vessel in which it is fermented. Transparent and yet mysterious, Chardonnay deserves its status as one the most noble varietals."—Kate Payne Brown, Stoller Family Estate

FOOD PAIRING: An ideal partner for all kinds of fish dishes, from Salmon Rillettes with Crème Fraîche (page 81) to Halibut Tacos with Avocado Dressing (page 175). But for pure bliss, pair this elegant white wine with Dungeness crab. (See page 144 for the ultimate dinner party starter, Dungeness Crab Rolls with Smoked Trout Roe and Hazelnut Dust.)

TYPICAL FLAVORS

LEMON CURD

GREEN APPLE

PEAR

PINOT GRIS

A fruit-forward and food-friendly sipper that's also the most widely planted white grape in Oregon.

WINEMAKER QUOTE: "Oregon's cool climate, especially in Willamette Valley, provides ideal growing conditions for Pinot Gris. The finished wines are known for complex fruit, vibrant acidity, and balance. As a result, Oregon has some of the highest quality and most age-worthy Pinot Gris in the world."—Brent Stone, King Estate Winery

FOOD PAIRING: Think summery dishes: grilled fish, veggies, and salads such as the Spring Salad with Pickled Rhubarb, Strawberries, and Grilled Ham (page 58) and Beet and Burnt Honey Salad (page 152).

TYPICAL FLAVORS

STONE FRUIT

CITRUS

GREEN APPLE

RIESLING

A crisp and aromatic white wine revered for its versatility and ageability.

WINEMAKER QUOTE: "Riesling is delicious in a diversity of styles, all the way from dry to dessert wines. Widely regarded as the most ageable white wine, it's also wildly food-friendly and adapts to a range of growing regions, making it an intriguing grape to taste the world of wine through."—Claire Jarreau, Brooks Wine

FOOD PAIRING: Match this pretty aromatic white wine with seafood, cheese boards, and spicy eats. Find the perfect match on page 75 with the Butter-Poached Shrimp with Wild Mushrooms and Lemon Cream Sauce.

TYPICAL FLAVORS

CITRUS

HONEYSUCKLE/ WHITE BLOSSOMS

STONE FRUIT

SAUVIGNON BLANC

A fun and food-friendly white wine that's a hidden treasure in Oregon.

WINEMAKER QUOTE: "Sauvignon Blanc can be such a polarizing grape depending on where it's grown and how it's made. Thankfully for us, when grown in the rich volcanic soils and under the warm summer sunshine of the Willamette Valley, it shows the ripe and tropical side of the variety, while still maintaining the brisk acidity it's known for."—Brianne Day, Day Wines

FOOD PAIRING: Here's looking at you vegetable lovers—this wine is a great match for a slew of vegetables. Also cheese plates, shellfish, and a delicious kale salad (page 114).

TYPICAL FLAVORS

TROPICAL FRUIT

MELON

STONE FRUIT

THE WINERIES

THE RECIPES

ABBEY ROAD FARM

BLAIR TRATHEN
WINEMAKING DIRECTOR

WILL PREISCH
CHEF AND INNKEEPER

REGION
WILLAMETTE VALLEY

Expect the unexpected at Abbey Road Farm, one of the Willamette Valley's most idyllic epicurean retreats. On this beautiful eighty-two-acre farmstead, the state-of-the-art winery gets as much attention as the cinematic farm crew—goats, pigs, donkeys, llamas, and thirty chickens all named Betty. Meticulous gardens grow everything from Swiss chard to squash to a slew of different microgreens.

Chef and innkeeper Will Preisch found his way to Abbey Road Farm after traveling the world and cooking at renowned farm-to-table restaurants from Manresa in Los Gatos to Lark in Seattle. "Working at a restaurant with an attached garden was always on my culinary bucket list," he says. "I was also drawn to the closeness and connection to the land here."

The garden, orchards, and wild berry patches provide Will inspiration for the five-course

breakfast he cooks at the inn, which has luxury suites ingeniously housed in repurposed grain silos. On weekends, he further flexes his fine-dining chops with Verdant, an elevated and seasonal six-course tasting menu paired with estate wines.

His counterpart in the hospitality program is winemaker Blair Trathen. A New Zealand native, Blair and his wife, also a winemaker, worked their first harvest in Oregon in 2001 at Beaux Frères. "We were immediately taken with the wines, food quality, and close-knit community," he says. After chasing harvests around the globe—along with a few years schussing down premier ski slopes—they beelined

back to the Willamette Valley ready to put down roots.

At Abbey Road Farm, Blair gets to channel his adventurous spirit into the wine program.

Outside of the Willamette Valley's flagship grapes, Pinot Noir and Chardonnay, the property has a diverse array of varieties planted over forty-two acres, including Mencia, Mondeuse, Aligoté, and Trousseau Noir. "The eclectic nature of the estate vineyard plantings is a distinguishing point of difference for Abbey Road Farm," says Blair. "To be able to work with such an esoteric cast of grape varieties is definitely exciting."

SUMMER BEAN SALAD
with Stone Fruits and Peppers

CHEF: WILL PREISCH, ABBEY ROAD FARM

WINE PAIRING: Abbey Road Farm Trousseau Gris Rosé

Serves 4 to 6

This stunner of a summer salad is like a farmers' market on a plate. And since it's a Will Preisch recipe, it has a few hidden surprises, like Japanese yuzu kosho—a fermented yuzu paste that adds bright, funky spice to the sweet stone fruit purée. Abbey Road Farm's Trousseau Gris Rosé is a delightful match to this summery salad, with crisp acidity and hints of peach and melon that play off the stone fruit flavors.

SUMMER BEANS Sort the beans by type. Bring a large saucepan of water to a boil over high heat and salt generously. Set a bowl of ice water nearby. Working with one variety of bean at a time, add to the pan and blanch for 1 to 2 minutes, until tender-crisp. You want the beans to have some snap to them, but not be raw or starchy. Using a slotted spoon or tongs, transfer beans into the ice water to stop the cooking. Drain beans and pat dry.

In a large bowl, combine beans, oil, ginger, and garlic, and toss. Salt to taste and add more oil, ginger, or garlic if desired to make the flavors pop.

STONE FRUIT PURÉE Preheat oven to 450°F. Line a baking sheet with parchment paper.

Add fruit to the prepared baking sheet, drizzle oil on top, and season lightly with salt. Roast for 15 to 20 minutes, until fruit is softened and caramelized in places.

Scrape fruit and all juices and oil from the baking sheet into a blender and purée. Add vinegar and yuzu kosho and blend until smooth.

ASSEMBLY Slice peppers into long strips.

Heat oil in a large skillet over medium heat. Add peppers and sauté for 2 to 3 minutes, until blistered and tender.

Spread ¼ cup of stone fruit purée in the bottom of a wide serving bowl. Arrange beans, peppers, and stone fruit slices on top, spacing them apart so that the salad is plated in a light and airy manner. Garnish with basil leaves and a sprinkle of sesame seeds.

SUMMER BEANS
2 lbs summer beans, such as Romano, wax beans, green beans, purple string beans (the more colors and textures, the better), ends trimmed

2 tsp toasted sesame oil, plus extra to taste

1 tsp grated ginger, plus extra to taste

1 tsp grated garlic, plus extra to taste

Salt

STONE FRUIT PURÉE
2 cups sliced ripe stone fruits, such as peaches, plums, apricots, or nectarines

2 Tbsp vegetable oil

Salt

2 Tbsp apple cider vinegar

2 tsp yuzu kosho (see Note)

ASSEMBLY
1 lb Italian frying peppers, such as Jimmy Nardello, or red bell peppers, seeded and deveined

2 Tbsp extra-virgin olive oil

2 to 3 ripe stone fruits, such as peaches, plums, apricots, or nectarines, pitted and thickly sliced

10 to 20 leaves basil, torn into bite-sized pieces, for garnish

1 Tbsp toasted white and/or black sesame seeds, for garnish

NOTE Yuzu kosho is a Japanese fermented seasoning paste, made with chiles, yuzu peel, and salt. There are two types: tart green, which uses unripe yuzu and chiles, and the more savory red, which uses ripe yuzu and chiles. Either will work in this dish. Look for yuzo kosho at Asian markets.

CHICKEN AND WAFFLES
with Maple-Sherry Glaze and Parmesan

CHEF: WILL PREISCH, ABBEY ROAD FARM

WINE PAIRING: Abbey Road Farm Terry Vineyard Chardonnay

The lucky guests who stay in the grain silos turned guest cottages at Abbey Road Farm get to wake up to dishes like this in the morning. This brunch entrée (just be sure to prep the waffle batter the night before) finds its perfect dancing partner in Abbey Road Farm's Terry Vineyard Chardonnay. The wine pops with crisp apple notes, lively acidity, and plush texture that plays off the sweet and salty flavors of the dish.

CORNMEAL WAFFLES In a large mixing bowl, combine flour, cornmeal, yeast, and sugar.

Heat milk, butter, and salt in a medium saucepan over medium-high heat until it reaches 100°F (warm but not hot) and the butter is fully melted. (If the mixture gets too hot, cool it down to 100°F before proceeding to avoid killing the yeast.)

Mix the warm liquid into the dry ingredients until thoroughly combined. Cover the bowl with plastic wrap or a clean dish towel and rest overnight in a warm place. (Refrigerate if not using within 9 hours.)

Preheat a waffle iron. Whisk eggs and baking soda in a small bowl, then mix into the batter. Cook waffles in the waffle iron according to the manufacturer's instructions. Brush with melted butter. Set aside. (Waffles can also be made a few hours in advance and reheated. When ready to serve, reheat the waffles at 350°F for 2 to 4 minutes until warm and crispy.)

MAPLE-SHERRY GLAZE Add sherry to a small saucepan and bring to a simmer over medium-high heat. Add syrup, sugar, and vinegar. Simmer for 10 to 15 minutes, until reduced by one-third. Makes about ⅔ cup. (Glaze can be made several days ahead and refrigerated; gently reheat before serving.)

Serves 4

CORNMEAL WAFFLES
1¼ cups all-purpose flour
¾ cup coarse-ground cornmeal
2¼ tsp active dry yeast
1 tsp granulated sugar
2 cups whole milk
½ cup (1 stick) butter,
    cut into pieces
½ tsp salt
2 eggs
½ tsp baking soda
¼ cup (½ stick) butter, melted,
    for toasting the waffles

MAPLE-SHERRY GLAZE
⅓ cup sherry (preferably oloroso)
⅓ cup pure maple syrup
⅓ cup packed brown sugar
⅓ cup sherry vinegar

4 boneless, skin-on chicken thighs (about 1½ to 2 lbs), cut into 2-inch chunks

1 tsp salt, plus extra to season

2 cups buttermilk

1 cup rice flour

1 cup Wondra or all-purpose flour

1 cup potato starch

½ cup cornstarch

2 tsp garlic powder

2 tsp ground ginger

1 tsp smoked paprika

Vegetable oil, for frying

Bunch of sage, leaves only

ASSEMBLY

Bunch of chives, finely chopped

1 cup grated Parmesan

FRIED CHICKEN Arrange chicken in a shallow baking dish and sprinkle with the 1 tsp salt. Pour buttermilk over and marinate in the refrigerator for 3 hours. Drain. (Chicken can be refrigerated overnight at this point.)

In a medium mixing bowl, whisk together both flours, potato starch, cornstarch, garlic powder, ground ginger, and smoked paprika. Season with salt.

Heat 3 inches of oil in a deep saucepan set over medium heat to a temperature of 365°F. Line a baking sheet with paper towels and place a rack on another baking sheet. Set them both near the stove.

While the oil is heating, dredge chicken into the flour mixture, one piece at a time, and set on the wire rack. Set aside to rest for 10 to 15 minutes to help the coating adhere. Working in batches, lower 3 to 4 chicken pieces into the hot oil and fry for 5 minutes, until golden brown. Using a slotted spoon, transfer chicken to the paper-towel–lined baking sheet. Season lightly with salt. Repeat with the remaining chicken. (Tip: Let the oil return to 365°F between batches and don't let it fall below 340°F while frying.)

Add sage leaves to the hot oil and fry for 10 seconds, until they stop popping. Drain on paper towels.

ASSEMBLY Place the fried chicken in a bowl and drizzle generously with maple-sherry glaze. Toss to coat, then add chives and toss again.

Place a warm buttered waffle on each plate, spoon chicken on top and drizzle a little extra glaze around the plate and on top of the waffle. Sprinkle with Parmesan and garnish with a few fried sage leaves.

ADELSHEIM VINEYARD

GINA HENNEN
WINEMAKER

REGION
WILLAMETTE VALLEY

When Gina Hennen was a chemistry student, she had no idea those long hours working on her thesis would lead to a career as a winemaker—not because of the subject matter, but because of the generosity of one of her advisors. "She was into wine and she gave me a really nice bottle of champagne," says Gina. "It was my first introduction to exceptional wines."

An appreciation for wine would follow her into her career as an electrical engineer in the semiconductor industry, but it turns out the cubicle life wasn't a great fit. She wanted to get her hands dirty. As she became more immersed in wine appreciation, she found more opportunities to engage in the process of making it. One afternoon spent experiencing a sliver of the grape harvest was particularly memorable. "As I was watching people punching down the fermenters, the physicality of it, the smells . . . it was all so compelling. I love how winemaking engages all of your senses."

No longer able to ignore the lure of the grape, she went back to school to learn the craft. One of her earliest jobs in the industry was at Adelsheim Vineyard, founded by pioneering winemaking family David and Ginny Adelsheim way back in 1971. She liked it so much, she's been there ever since, working her way from cellar hand to winemaker in her fifteen-year tenure. Clearly, winemaking was a perfect fit, blending her creativity with her chemistry degree, and satisfying her itch to make things with her hands and share them with others.

"I like having people over, sharing a bottle of wine, telling stories around the table, and having that community. It's one of my favorite parts of winemaking."

She approaches each vintage with the goal of capturing a time and place in a bottle. Her Breaking Ground Pinot Noir and Staking Claim Chardonnay are prime examples. "They're an exploration, a meditation, on what the Chehalem Mountains AVA is. It's more varied than other AVAs, with many different soil types and niches. Those wines blend grapes from several different vineyards to tap into that."

CORN SOUP

with Dungeness Crab and Roasted Apple Relish

CHEF: CHRIS SMITH, JORY RESTAURANT

WINE PAIRING: Adelsheim Staking Claim Chardonnay

Serves 4

Adelsheim is a cornerstone of the extensive Oregon wine list at the Allison Inn & Spa's restaurant JORY. The winery's Staking Claim Chardonnay inspired executive chef Chris Smith to create a rich and creamy corn soup topped with Dungeness crab that can be served warm or cold. "The wine provides a brightness and acidity that not only balances out the silky soup," says Chris, "but also adds floral and fruity notes that lift the crab and apple components."

CORN SOUP Cut corn kernels off the cobs. Set kernels aside.

Put corn cobs in a stockpot (you can break them in half to fit the pot better) and add just enough water to cover. Bring to a boil and then simmer on medium heat for 30 minutes. Strain corn stock and reserve separately. Discard the cobs.

Melt butter in the same saucepan over medium heat. Add onion, leek, and garlic. Sauté for 7 minutes, or until translucent. Pour in wine, stirring to scrape up the browned bits. Add 1½ quarts of corn stock and bring to a simmer. Add potato and simmer for 5 minutes, until cooked. Stir in corn kernels and simmer for 10 minutes. Remove from heat.

Add cream and purée the soup with an immersion blender until silky smooth. (Alternatively, blend the soup in a traditional blender, puréeing in batches. Be careful not to let steam build up. One way is to keep the lid ajar with a clean dish towel over it to allow steam to escape.) Thin out with more corn stock if desired. Season with salt and sherry vinegar to taste. Keep warm. Or, if you prefer a cold soup, refrigerate until chilled. (Can be made up to 4 days ahead and refrigerated.)

ROASTED APPLE RELISH Preheat oven to 400°F. Roast whole apples on a baking sheet lined with parchment paper for 30 to 45 minutes, until charred and tender. Cool completely. Remove the skin and cores and finely chop.

In a medium bowl, combine roasted apples, shallot, chives, lemon zest, and oil. Season with salt to taste. Refrigerate until ready to serve. (Can be made up to 2 days ahead.)

ASSEMBLY In a bowl, drizzle crabmeat with a little olive oil. Add apple relish and gently mix.

Ladle soup into bowls and divide the crab mixture on top. Drizzle with olive oil to finish.

CORN SOUP

7 ears corn, shucked
½ cup (1 stick) butter
1 large onion, diced
1 leek, white and light green parts only, thinly sliced
6 cloves garlic, finely chopped
1 cup dry white wine
1 large russet potato, peeled and cut into ½-inch cubes
2 cups heavy cream
Salt, to taste
Sherry vinegar, to taste

ROASTED APPLE RELISH

2 Granny Smith apples
1 small shallot, finely chopped
2 Tbsp finely chopped chives
Grated zest of 1 lemon
1 Tbsp extra-virgin olive oil
Salt, to taste

ASSEMBLY

½ lb Dungeness crabmeat, to serve
High-quality extra-virgin olive oil, for drizzling

DASHI WITH WILD MUSHROOMS
and Miso Pork Belly

CHEF: CHRIS SMITH, JORY RESTAURANT

WINE PAIRING: Adelsheim Breaking Ground Pinot Noir

The components in this elegant entrée—from the deeply savory broth and succulent pork to the sweet garlic purée—work together to create a lush bowl layered with complexity. Luckily, each one can be made well ahead of time and they're simple to execute too. A complex Pinot, such as Adelsheim's masterfully crafted Breaking Ground, is a great fit with the rich flavors of this dish.

PORK BELLY Preheat oven to 300°F. Score the fat side of the pork belly in a crosshatch pattern and season with salt and pepper.

Combine remaining ingredients in a roasting pan. Add pork belly, fat-side up, and enough water to almost cover. Cover the dish with aluminum foil. Braise for 3 to 4 hours, or until very tender and edges of the pork are shreddable.

Using tongs, carefully transfer pork belly to a baking dish. Discard the braising liquid. Set another pan, weighted with heavy cans, on top of the pork. Refrigerate for 4 hours, or until thoroughly chilled.

Cut pork into 4 slabs, each about 3 inches wide.

DASHI BROTH In a stockpot, combine all ingredients except the fish sauce, tamari (or soy sauce), and lemon juice (or rice vinegar). Bring just to a simmer over medium-high heat. Remove from heat and cover. Set aside to steep for 30 minutes to 1 hour. Strain broth carefully, leaving any grit from the mushrooms behind, and discard solids.

Return broth to the stockpot and simmer over medium-high heat for 30 minutes, or until reduced by half. Add fish sauce, tamari, and lemon juice to taste. (Can be made up to 5 days ahead and refrigerated.)

Serves 4

PORK BELLY

2 lbs meaty pork belly
Salt and black pepper
4 bay leaves
1 jalapeño, halved lengthwise
1 (2-inch) piece ginger, peeled and roughly chopped (¼ cup)
1 Tbsp black peppercorns
3 cups dry white wine
1 cup Thai sweet chili sauce, such as Mae Ploy brand
1 cup mirin
¼ cup tamari

DASHI BROTH

1 gallon vegetable stock or water
6 oz dried shiitake mushrooms
4 cloves garlic, crushed
2 sweet onions, thinly sliced
1 stalk lemongrass, smashed
1 sheet (1 oz) kombu (dried kelp)
1 (2-inch) piece ginger, peeled and thinly sliced
½ cup bonito flakes
2 Tbsp fish sauce
2 Tbsp tamari or soy sauce
Lemon juice or rice vinegar, to taste

BLACK GARLIC PURÉE

1 cup garlic cloves
½ cup granulated sugar
8 to 12 cloves black garlic
  (see Note)
Juice of ½ lemon, or to taste
Salt, to taste

ASSEMBLY

2 Tbsp white or red miso paste
1 lb wild mushrooms, roughly
  chopped

NOTE Black garlic may look
edgy, but the cloves are
wonderfully sweet and savory,
getting their color from low
and slow gentle roasting until
the cloves are tender, black,
and molasses-like in flavor.
They're easy to find at gourmet
markets, Asian markets, and
online retailers.

BLACK GARLIC PURÉE In a small saucepan, combine the garlic cloves, sugar, and 1 cup water over low heat. Cook for 30 minutes, stirring occasionally, until garlic is golden brown and softened and the water has mostly evaporated.

With a slotted spoon, transfer garlic to a blender or food processor (reserving the cooking liquid). Add black garlic, lemon juice, and a splash of cooking liquid, then purée until smooth. (Can be made up to 5 days ahead and refrigerated.)

ASSEMBLY Preheat broiler.

In a small bowl, mix miso paste and 2 tablespoons water.

In a saucepan, warm the dashi broth. Add wild mushrooms, cover, and simmer for 15 minutes, until tender.

Place pork belly on a parchment-lined baking sheet and brush with the diluted miso paste. Broil pork belly for 3 minutes, just until heated through and miso begins to caramelize.

Divide the dashi broth and mushrooms among bowls, add pork belly, and garnish with a dollop of black garlic purée.

ALEXANA WINERY AND VINEYARD

DR. MADAIAH REVANA

FOUNDER AND PRESIDENT

REGION

WILLAMETTE VALLEY

You don't meet many winery owners who are also renowned cardiologists. But then you don't meet too many winery owners like Dr. Madaiah Revana of Alexana Winery. His passion for wine took root in the early 1990s, when he began collecting first-growth Bordeaux wines.

But it was a trip to Tuscany in 1995 that sparked a serious interest in vineyards. Enamored by their beauty, the trip reminded him of the feeling that a singular piece of land can evoke. "It inspired me to follow my family's farming legacy," says Dr. Revana, who grew up in an agricultural community near Bangalore, India.

A few years later, while attending a medical conference in the Napa Valley, he chanced upon a small plot of prime property in St. Helena. In 1998, he planted his first vineyard there. "Discovering unique parcels of land and developing them into estate vineyards has been a passion ever since," he says.

In 2005, Dr. Revana crossed paths with Oregon winemaker Lynn Penner-Ash. He shared his love of the great wines of Burgundy with her and the two became fast friends. Soon after, he enlisted Lynn to guide his search for the perfect piece of land to produce Pinot Noirs that could rival those from Burgundy. He acquired a pristine eighty-acre estate in Dundee Hills. Over the next year, his team planted select clones of Pinot Noir, along with Chardonnay.

"Wine is an outlet for me," says Dr. Revana, who balances his calling as a cardiologist with creating exceptional wine estates. In 2008, he grew his portfolio with an estate in the Uco Valley, one of the top wine regions in Mendoza, Argentina. "Over the last twenty years, wine has become more than a business or a passion for me," he shares. "It has become part of who I am and an integral part of my journey."

Seared Albacore Tiradito with Mango Relish (p. 40)

SEARED ALBACORE TIRADITO
with Mango Relish

CHEFS: JACO SMITH AND HENRY WHITTIER-FERGUSON, LECHON RESTAURANT

WINE PAIRING: Alexana Signature Chardonnay

For bold and beautiful chile-citrus flavors, you can't beat tiradito. Emblematic of Peru's Japanese-influenced Nikkei cuisine, the dish traditionally combines ceviche and sashimi. Chef Jaco Smith of Portland's LeChon Restaurant switches that up with this popular version using seared albacore. He adds a juniper rub for earthy and floral layers that play off the bright acidity of the *leche de tigre* sauce. Alexana's Signature Chardonnay brings elegance and vibrancy with lingering notes of baked lemon and stone fruit.

MANGO RELISH In a small mixing bowl, combine all ingredients.

JUNIPER RUB Using a spice grinder or mortar and pestle, combine bay leaves, cardamom seeds, garlic powder, coriander seeds, peppercorns, and juniper berries and grind into a fine powder. Transfer to an airtight container and stir in brown sugar and salt. (Rub can be stored in an airtight container at room temperature for several months.)

SEARED ALBACORE Preheat a grill over high heat.

Trim away the thin flap and some of the pointed end from the tuna loin and reserve for the sauce. Coat the loin with juniper rub. Add to the grill and sear on high heat for about 1 minute per side. Immediately transfer to a plate to cool (the center of the loin should remain raw).

Serves 2 to 4

MANGO RELISH
1 ripe mango, peeled and diced (about 1 cup)
½ red onion, diced (about ½ cup)
¼ bunch cilantro, chopped (about 2 Tbsp)
1 tsp salt
Juice of 1 lime

JUNIPER RUB
2 dried bay leaves
1½ Tbsp cardamom seeds
1 Tbsp garlic powder
1 Tbsp coriander seeds
½ Tbsp black peppercorns
½ Tbsp juniper berries
2 Tbsp brown sugar
1 Tbsp salt

SEARED ALBACORE
1 (½- to 1-lb) sashimi-grade albacore tuna loin
¼ cup Juniper Rub (see here)

NOTE Aji amarillo paste and aji panca paste are made from classic Peruvian chiles and can be found at gourmet markets or online retailers.

AJI LECHE DE TIGRE

1 cup orange juice

1 cup lime juice

½ cup grapefruit juice

1 Tbsp grated ginger

1½ tsp finely chopped shallot

2 Tbsp aji amarillo chile paste
(see Note)

1 Tbsp aji panca chile paste (see
Note)

1 Tbsp salt

½ tsp black pepper

½ cup vegetable oil

¼ cup reserved albacore scraps

ASSEMBLY

1 English cucumber, thinly sliced

1 tsp toasted sesame seeds

Cilantro leaves or radish
microgreens

AJI LECHE DE TIGRE Using a blender, combine citrus juices, ginger, shallot, aji amarillo paste, aji panca paste, salt, and pepper. Gradually pour in oil in a thin, steady stream and blend until emulsified. Add the raw fish scraps and blend until puréed and thickened.

ASSEMBLY Spoon a thin layer of the aji leche de tigre sauce onto the plates. Using a sharp knife, cut the cooled albacore into ¼-inch-thick slices and arrange on the plates so the fish is in the sauce but not covered by it. Spoon mango relish on top and garnish with sliced cucumber, sesame seeds, and cilantro (or microgreens). Serve immediately.

BRAISED DUCK LEGS
with Wild Rice

CHEFS: JACO SMITH AND HENRY WHITTIER-FERGUSON, LECHON RESTAURANT

WINE PAIRING: Alexana Revana Vineyard Estate Pinot Noir

This dish features iconic Pacific Northwest ingredients tailor-made for pairing with Pinot Noir—duck, wild rice, mushrooms, and hazelnuts—with a dollop of smoky aji panca chile paste for Peruvian flair. The deeply flavored, meltingly tender duck is served over a bed of wild rice finished with a hazelnut horchata, which gives the rice a delicious nutty creaminess, while a chimichurri cuts through the richness with herbaceous acidity. The Alexana Revana Vineyard Estate Pinot Noir makes an ideal companion with dark cherry aromas, bright acidity, and a silky-smooth texture.

HAZELNUT HORCHATA Preheat oven to 350°F. Arrange hazelnuts in an even layer on a baking sheet and toast for 8 to 10 minutes, until golden. If they have brown papery skins, fold nuts into a clean dish towel while still hot and vigorously rub. Some skins will remain on, which is fine.

Soak hazelnuts and rice in 2 cups water overnight. Transfer nuts, rice, and water to a high-powered blender and blend well. Strain mixture through a cheesecloth, pressing if necessary. The strained liquid should be smooth and milky white. If grainy, strain again until smooth. Refrigerate until ready to use. (Can be made up to 3 days ahead.)

RED WINE–BRAISED DUCK Preheat oven to 350°F.

Heat a Dutch oven or deep cast-iron skillet over medium heat. When hot, add duck legs skin side down. Cook for 10 to 15 minutes, until well browned. Flip duck legs and cook for another 5 minutes, until browned. Transfer to a plate.

Pour off the excess fat in the pan and reserve. Add wine, stirring to scrape up the browned bits. Simmer for 5 minutes, until reduced by half. Add stock, garlic, shallots, thyme, rosemary, chile paste, and salt. Return duck legs skin side up to the pan. Bring to a simmer, then transfer to the oven. Cook, uncovered, for 2 hours, or until the legs are very tender. Carefully transfer legs to a platter and tent with aluminum foil to keep warm. (Discard the flavorful braising liquid or reserve for another use, such as another braise or stew.)

Serves 4

HAZELNUT HORCHATA
1 cup hazelnuts
½ cup jasmine rice

RED WINE–BRAISED DUCK
4 duck legs
1 cup red wine
4 cups chicken or vegetable stock
2 heads garlic
2 shallots, quartered
4 sprigs thyme
Sprig of rosemary
2 tsp aji panca chile paste (see Note)
1 to 2 tsp salt, depending on the saltiness of your stock

> **NOTE** Aji panca chile paste is made from a classic Peruvian chile and can be found at gourmet markets or online retailers.

WILD RICE

1 cup wild rice or wild rice blend, rinsed

½ tsp salt, plus more to taste

2 Tbsp reserved duck fat (divided)

4 oz wild mushrooms (chanterelles, shimejis, maitakes), roughly chopped

¾ cup fresh or frozen corn kernels

4 cloves garlic, finely chopped

½ small shallot, finely chopped

¼ cup Hazelnut Horchata (see here)

1 Tbsp finely chopped tarragon

ORANGE ZEST CHIMICHURRI

¾ cup vegetable oil

2 Tbsp red wine vinegar

Grated zest and juice of ½ orange

Bunch of cilantro

Bunch of Italian parsley

3 cloves garlic

1½ tsp dried oregano

1½ tsp red pepper flakes

¾ tsp salt

½ tsp paprika

½ tsp ground cumin

WILD RICE In a large saucepan, combine wild rice, salt and 2 cups water. Bring to a boil over high heat, then reduce to low. Cover and simmer for 45 minutes, until water is absorbed and rice is tender but not mushy. Spread out rice on a baking sheet to cool.

Heat 1 tablespoon of the reserved duck fat in a large skillet over medium heat. Add mushrooms and sauté about 5 minutes until they release their liquid. Add the corn and sauté about 3 minutes until it begins to brown. Add garlic and shallot and sauté another 2 minutes. Add the remaining tablespoon of duck fat and the cooled rice. Sauté until rice is hot and slightly browned. Turn off heat, then add hazelnut horchata and tarragon. Season with salt.

ORANGE ZEST CHIMICHURRI In a food processor, combine oil, vinegar, orange zest and juice with cilantro, parsley, and garlic. Pulse until finely chopped and blended. Add oregano, pepper flakes, salt, paprika, and cumin and pulse to combine. (Can be made several days ahead and refrigerated.)

ASSEMBLY Spoon a few tablespoons of chimichurri onto plates and place a scoop of rice on top. Place duck legs on top of the rice and serve immediately with remaining chimichurri on the side.

ANALEMMA
WINES

**STEVEN
THOMPSON**
CO-FOUNDER

KRIS FADE
CO-FOUNDER

REGION: COLUMBIA GORGE

Steven Thompson has a deep appreciation for the things we can't see or touch but that move us, change us. They can't be quantified, but you can't deny that they're a force.

"Not everything can be measured by science," he says. "A lot of the most important aspects of our lives can't be measured—love, joy, appreciation, wonder, gratitude. These intangibles are essential. Wine exists in that category. It's a felt experience."

For Steven, most of those intangibles in wine come from the vines—not just the minerals and microbes in the soil, but the way they're part of an ecosystem. And so, more than a winemaker, he considers himself a vigneron. "My mentor said, 'If you want to learn how to make good wine, you have to learn the vineyard.' I've been associated with the vineyards ever since."

Steven worked as a vineyard manager and eventually became assistant vigneron for Christophe Baron at Cayuse in Walla Walla, where he adopted his approach for Analemma: biodynamic farming, planting varieties born for the climate, tending to those vines assiduously, then letting the fruit tell its story. "We like to allow it to express itself the best it can," he says. "We ferment it cleanly, use neutral barrels, and stay out of the way."

Steven and co-founder Kris Fade chose to put down their roots in Mosier in part because it's in a younger AVA, Columbia Gorge, unbound by tradition. When they realized the climate was similar to

Galicia, Spain, they made a point of adding to the Oregon-grown conversation by planting a variety of warm season and Spanish varieties, especially Mencia, which is quickly becoming their calling card.

As for the biodynamic approach, it all comes back to acknowledging the power in things we can't measure. "Biodynamic doesn't neglect the intangible aspects of life," says Steven. "We farm with a strong intention to make things healthier—the soil, the vines, the trees, the microbes. When we're farming with the intention of giving and fostering life, I think that translates to the fruit, and to the wine."

Vanilla Bean Panna Cotta with Balsamic-Roasted Strawberries and Walnut Biscotti (p. 48)

SPRING CHINOOK SALMON

with Fennel-Olive Salad, Rosemary Polenta, and Asparagus

CHEF: MARK DERESTA, RIVERSIDE RESTAURANT

WINE PAIRING: Analemma Mosier Hills Mencia

Serves 4

"Nothing captures the bounty of the Gorge more than the spring run of chinook," says Hood River chef Mark DeResta, who has been cultivating culinary relationships, including with local fishers, for Riverside's locally inspired menu for nearly three decades. Wonderfully rich and fatty, spring chinook is the glory of the Gorge, embodying a connection to place in a dramatic and delectable fashion. Analemma's Mencia, with notes of anise, crushed gravel, and blue fruit, makes a beautiful pairing.

ROSEMARY POLENTA Heat oil in a medium saucepan over medium heat. Add onion and garlic and sauté for 5 minutes, until onion is translucent. If necessary, reduce heat to prevent onion from browning. Add rosemary, salt, and red pepper flakes and sauté for 1 minute, until rosemary is fragrant. Add milk and 2 cups water. Bring to a simmer and slowly stir in polenta until fully incorporated. Reduce heat to low and cook for 8 to 10 minutes, stirring occasionally.

Remove from heat, cover, and set aside to rest on the back of the stove while preparing the rest of the meal (about 20 minutes). When ready to serve, stir in butter and cheese. Add more water if polenta becomes too thick.

FENNEL-OLIVE SALAD In a mixing bowl, combine tomato, garlic, red onion, olives, parsley, anchovy, and thyme. Thinly shave the fennel on a mandoline and then fold into the mixture. Add the vinegar and oil, using a larger amount of vinegar if you prefer the salad more tart. Set aside for 10 minutes at room temperature. Season with salt and pepper to taste.

ROSEMARY POLENTA

2 Tbsp extra-virgin olive oil
½ large onion, diced (1 cup)
2 cloves garlic, thinly sliced
1 tsp finely chopped rosemary
1 tsp salt
Pinch of red pepper flakes
2 cups whole milk
1 cup coarse polenta
1 Tbsp butter
½ cup grated pecorino

FENNEL-OLIVE SALAD

1 large tomato, peeled, seeded, and diced
1 clove garlic, thinly sliced
¼ red onion, diced
¼ cup finely chopped Kalamata olives
¼ cup chopped Italian parsley
1 tsp finely chopped anchovy
1 tsp finely chopped thyme leaves
1 fennel bulb, halved lengthwise
¼ to ½ cup red wine vinegar
½ cup extra-virgin olive oil
Salt and black pepper

3 Tbsp extra-virgin olive oil
(divided)

Bunch of asparagus, bottoms
trimmed, cut into 1-inch slices
on a bias

Salt

4 (4- to 5-oz) skinless spring
chinook (king) salmon fillets

1 tsp fennel pollen

1 Tbsp butter

ASSEMBLY Heat 2 tablespoons oil in a medium skillet over medium-high heat. Add asparagus and sauté for 3 minutes, until cooked through but crunchy. Remove from heat and season with salt to taste.

Season salmon with salt and fennel pollen. Heat the remaining 1 tablespoon oil and the butter in a large cast-iron skillet over medium-high heat. Add salmon, presentation side down, and reduce heat to medium. Cook for 3 to 4 minutes, until opaque about halfway up the sides and the bottom is a caramelized dark brown. Turn over, increase heat to high, and cook for another 2 to 3 minutes.

Place a large spoonful of polenta on four plates. Arrange asparagus next to the polenta. Place a salmon fillet partially over asparagus, then top with a small pile of fennel salad. Spoon a little vinaigrette from the bottom of the bowl over the salad.

VANILLA BEAN PANNA COTTA

with Balsamic-Roasted Strawberries and Walnut Biscotti

CHEF: MARK DERESTA, RIVERSIDE RESTAURANT

WINE PAIRING: Analemma Mosier Hills Petit Manseng

Oregon strawberries, so sweet and red they almost seem candied, become even more intensely jammy when roasted. Chef Mark DeResta smartly pairs this final course with Analemma's Petit Manseng, a varietal from southern France known for both its high sugars and acidity, which gives it a dry finish. The dessert-style wine is gorgeous with anything rich, sweet, and fatty, like foie gras appetizers and, yes, this cloud-like panna cotta.

PANNA COTTA Pour ½ cup of the milk into a small bowl. Sprinkle the gelatin evenly over the top and let sit at least 15 minutes.

Meanwhile, in a small saucepan, combine the remaining 1½ cups milk with the sugar and salt. Split the vanilla bean lengthwise, scrape out the seeds with the back of the knife, and add them to the pan along with the pod. Bring just to a simmer over medium heat, whisking to ensure the sugar dissolves. Remove from heat and allow to steep for 15 minutes.

Discard vanilla pod. (Or rinse, dry, and tuck into a jar of sugar to make vanilla sugar.) Whisk the gelatin mixture into the hot milk until fully dissolved. Strain through a fine-mesh strainer into a shallow baking dish. Allow to cool to room temperature, then refrigerate for 3 hours until cold and jiggly. Stir the panna cotta to create a texture resembling very soft scrambled egg.

Whip cream to firm peaks. Fold the whipped cream into the cooled panna cotta mixture a little bit at a time. Divide among six (6-oz) ramekins or glasses, cover in plastic wrap, and refrigerate. (Can be made several days ahead.)

BALSAMIC-ROASTED STRAWBERRIES Preheat oven to 400°F. In a shallow baking dish, combine strawberries, maple syrup, and vinegar. Roast for 1 hour, until strawberries are dark and sauce is bubbling and slightly syrupy. Allow to cool completely, then refrigerate until cold. (Can be made several days ahead and refrigerated.)

Serves 6

PANNA COTTA
2 cups whole milk (divided)
1½ tsp unflavored powdered gelatin
½ cup granulated sugar
Pinch of salt
1 vanilla bean
1 cup heavy cream

BALSAMIC-ROASTED STRAWBERRIES
1½ lbs strawberries, hulls removed, halved
¼ cup pure maple syrup
¼ cup balsamic vinegar

WALNUT BISCOTTI

1¼ cups all-purpose flour,
    plus extra for dusting

½ tsp baking powder

¼ tsp salt

¼ cup (½ stick) butter, softened

⅔ cup granulated sugar

1 egg

¼ tsp vanilla extract

½ cup walnuts, lightly toasted
    and chopped

ASSEMBLY

High-quality aged balsamic
    vinegar, for drizzling (optional)

WALNUT BISCOTTI Preheat oven to 325°F. Line a baking sheet with parchment paper.

In a small mixing bowl, combine flour, baking powder, and salt.

In a stand mixer with a paddle attachment, cream together butter and sugar for 3 minutes, stopping to scrape down the sides of the bowl as needed. Beat in egg and vanilla. Reduce speed to low, then add in the flour mixture. Add walnuts and mix until fully incorporated.

Divide dough into two balls and place well apart on the prepared baking sheet. Flatten and shape each dough ball into an elongated oval, about 8 inches long and 2 inches wide. Bake for 15 minutes. Rotate pan, then bake for another 15 minutes until firm and lightly browned around the edges. Remove from oven and cool on a wire rack for a few minutes. Keep the oven on.

Cut the biscotti diagonally into ¾-inch-wide slices. Set with a cut side up on the baking sheet and bake for 5 minutes. Turn to the other cut side and bake for another 5 minutes, until dry and crisp. (Cooled biscotti can be stored in an airtight container for 1 week.)

ASSEMBLY Top each panna cotta with balsamic strawberries and drizzle with aged balsamic vinegar, if using. Serve with a walnut biscotti.

ANAM CARA CELLARS

NICK AND SHEILA NICHOLAS
PROPRIETORS

REGION
WILLAMETTE VALLEY

Anam Cara's wines are intensely personal. The grapes come from just one vineyard, the Nicholas Vineyard, so named for owners Nick and Sheila Nicholas who tractored and tended every square inch of the thirty-five-acre property themselves and live steps from the vines they planted.

"We've done it all," says Nick. "This is our one and only vineyard, and it's beautiful."

Their journey to the vineyard started with pizza, of all things. The Nicholases owned a thriving business in California's Napa Valley wine country where local winemakers bartering for pepperoni pies gave them an enviable wine collection and a deep passion for the grape. So they chucked it all in 2001 and headed north, lucking out on an old, run-down orchard in the Chehalem Mountains. "We would hack through the blackberries and find outhouses and more," Sheila recalls. But the potential was there: Jory and loess soils on a southeast-facing slope in a wind tunnel that keeps it cooler in summer and dry in the winter. "We knew what we were getting into," she says.

The plan was to just sell their organically grown grapes—mostly Pinot Noir, plus Chardonnay and Riesling—but, Sheila says, "once you grow them you think, 'Oh I wonder what they taste like.'" And so, Anam Cara Cellars was born. They started at ground zero, just as they did when establishing the vineyard, learning by doing, and tapping into the knowledge of their community.

All the while, Sheila was helping grow the reputation of Oregon wine itself, using her marketing background to serve on a host of committees, including helping to establish the Chehalem Mountains AVA in 2006.

Their DIY diligence has paid off, as Anam Cara's elegant wines—Pinots with a "beautiful dustiness"—add a unique voice to the Oregon wine landscape. "We learned the rhythm of the vineyard," says Nick. "If you're good to the vines, they're good to you."

MISO-MARINATED SOCKEYE
with Crispy Shiitakes and Wilted Spinach

CHEF: ALLEN ROUTT, THE PAINTED LADY

Serves 4

MISO-MARINATED SALMON
2 Tbsp white miso paste
2 Tbsp chicken stock
1 Tbsp pure maple syrup
1 tsp soy sauce
2 Tbsp salt
1½ lbs sockeye salmon
  (four 6-oz fillets)

CRISPY SHIITAKES AND WILTED SPINACH
2 Tbsp peanut oil
2 cups sliced shiitake mushrooms, stems removed (about 5 oz)
Salt and black pepper, to taste
1 clove garlic, finely chopped
2 (10-oz) bags baby spinach

ASSEMBLY
1 Tbsp toasted sesame seeds
Steamed brown rice, to serve

WINE PAIRING: Anam Cara Cellars Nicholas Estate Pinot Noir

Although the Painted Lady is one of Newberg's oldest and most revered fine-dining restaurants, chef Allen Routt's miso-marinated salmon is easy enough for even novice cooks to execute any night of the week. For the most pro-level presentation, don't skip his genius brining technique. It helps break down some of the muscle fibers in the fish so it won't tighten up during cooking and push the white albumin out.

MISO-MARINATED SALMON In a medium bowl, mix miso paste, chicken stock, maple syrup, and soy sauce. If possible, let the mixture sit for 1 to 2 hours to allow flavors to meld.

In another medium bowl, mix salt and 2½ cups cold water. Submerge salmon in the brine for 10 to 30 minutes. Remove salmon, rinse, and pat dry. Coat salmon in the miso mixture and marinate for 1 hour in the refrigerator.

Preheat oven to 325°F. Grease a baking sheet or line with parchment paper.

Remove salmon from the refrigerator and wipe off the excess marinade. Place on the prepared baking sheet. Bake for 15 to 20 minutes, depending on the thickness of the fillets, until medium to medium-rare. (It should flake easily but still be slightly translucent in the center.) If desired, place fish under a broiler for 1 to 2 minutes to caramelize the miso.

CRISPY SHIITAKES AND WILTED SPINACH Meanwhile, heat oil in a large wok or skillet over medium-high heat. Add shiitakes, season with salt and pepper, and sauté for 7 to 10 minutes, until mushrooms are golden and crispy. Add garlic and cook for 1 minute, until toasted. Remove from heat.

When the salmon is nearly done, return the skillet to medium-high heat. Add spinach and sauté until wilted. Season with salt and pepper.

ASSEMBLY Divide shiitakes and spinach among the plates and top with sesame seeds. Place a salmon fillet on top. Serve with steamed brown rice.

Nick's Mint, Coriander, and Fennel
LAMB KEBABS

CHEF: NICK NICHOLAS, ANAM CARA CELLARS

Serves 4

1 Tbsp coriander seeds
1 Tbsp fennel seeds
2 shallots, halved and thinly sliced
1 large clove garlic, finely chopped
3 Tbsp dried mint (see Note)
¼ cup extra-virgin olive oil
¼ cup crushed tomatoes
1 Tbsp soy sauce
1 Tbsp whole grain mustard
2 lbs boneless leg of lamb or lamb
   stew meat, trimmed of fat and
   cut into 1½-inch cubes
Vegetable oil, for grilling
1 (750-ml) bottle Pinot Noir
Warm pitas, to serve
Green salad, to serve

NOTE Look for dried mint in the spice aisle at supermarkets or at Middle Eastern markets. Or you can even cut open a bag of herbal peppermint tea.

WINE PAIRING: Anam Cara Cellars Heather's Reserve Pinot Noir

These lamb kebabs were the centerpiece of the first meal that Nick cooked for Sheila back in 1980 when he lived in London. He must have made a big impression—when Nick returned to the U.S., Sheila followed. As luck would have it, the kebabs go great with Pinot Noir—the varietal Anam Cara Cellars is known for all these years later. For their vegetarian friends, the Nicholases grill portobello mushrooms and shorten the marinating time to just one hour.

Using a spice grinder or mortar and pestle, grind coriander and fennel seeds into a powder. Transfer to a 1-gallon ziptop bag or large mixing bowl, then add shallots, garlic, mint, oil, tomatoes, soy sauce, and mustard. Stir to combine. Add lamb and turn to coat. Marinate in the refrigerator for at least 5 hours or overnight.

Remove meat from the refrigerator about 1 hour before cooking. If using wood skewers, soak them in water for at least 30 minutes.

Preheat a grill over medium heat, to 350°F to 400°F. Scrape the grill grates clean and brush with vegetable oil.

Using a slotted spoon, transfer meat to a new bowl and douse with some of the Pinot Noir to rinse off most of the marinade (save the rest to enjoy with the meal). Thread each skewer with 6 cubes of meat.

Grill skewers for 10 minutes, turning frequently, until meat is charred and cooked through.

Serve with warm pitas and salad.

ANTIQUUM FARM

STEPHEN HAGEN
FOUNDER AND FARMER

REGION
WILLAMETTE VALLEY

At Antiquum Farm, the geese, sheep, chickens, ducks, and even the Kunekune pigs have everything to do with a glass of wine. "Most people are growing wine because they love wine," says Stephen Hagen. "I'm growing wine because I love farming."

On his 140-acre estate set near the coastal foothills in the Willamette Valley, Stephen approaches farming the old-fashioned way, eschewing any outside inputs or fertilizer on the farm and following what he's coined "grazing-based viticulture."

Like a well-tuned symphony, he has the resident farm animals follow intricately planned grazing rotations. At peak season, the varied flock can soar to well over 300 animals—a whirl of mowing and fertilizing the vineyards and the land in a way that maximizes benefits for all.

"It's a more articulate and expressive vineyard, because of the strength of the diversity that we're putting into it," says Stephen. At the core, he sees grazing-based viticulture as an extreme exploration of the concept of terroir. "What happens if we truly farm in a self-contained system and minimize our supply chain footprint?"

Since he's adopted these farming methods, he's seen the Pinot Noir and Pinot Gris grapes begin to genetically change. "The wines have shifted into something utterly distinct, more wild and expressive," he says.

At the end of the day, he can't imagine doing anything else. "Good farming at its core has the ability to reflect some of the best traits and instincts of humanity," says Stephen. "That's what draws me to it as a life and a craft. There's the opportunity every single day to experience humor, peace, and compassion."

Spring Salad with Pickled Rhubarb, Strawberries, and Grilled Ham (p. 58)

SPRING SALAD

with Pickled Rhubarb, Strawberries, and Grilled Ham

CHEF: ISAAC OCEJO, CULINARY PARTNER OF ANTIQUUM FARM

WINE PAIRING: Antiquum Farm Alium Pinot Gris

After a winter of gnarly roots and tubers, springtime at the farmers' market feels like a celebration of all that's green and tender. Chef Isaac Ocejo's beautiful salad for Antiquum Farm takes full advantage of the season's greatest hits—fava beans and radishes, strawberries and rhubarb, and a slab of salty grilled ham for that all-important savory counterpoint. The Antiquum Farm Alium Pinot Gris, with its dense fruit core and rich earthy texture, wraps the transition of winter to spring around each component of the salad.

PICKLED RHUBARB In a large saucepan, combine vinegar, sugar, salt, red pepper flakes, thyme, and 2 cups water and bring to a boil over medium-high heat, stirring continuously.

Place rhubarb in a medium mixing bowl. Pour the hot pickling liquid over the rhubarb and steep for 30 minutes, until it reaches room temperature. (Can be made 1 week ahead and refrigerated.)

DIJON-SHALLOT VINAIGRETTE In a small jar or bowl, combine shallot and vinegar. Set aside for 5 minutes.

In another bowl, mix mustard, oil, salt, and pepper. Strain the vinegar into the mustard mixture and discard the shallot. Whisk until emulsified. (Can be made 1 week ahead and refrigerated.)

Serves 4 to 6

PICKLED RHUBARB
1 cup red wine vinegar
¾ cup granulated sugar
¼ cup salt
Pinch of red pepper flakes (optional)
Sprig of thyme (optional)
2 stalks rhubarb, cut ¼-inch thick on the bias (about 4 cups)

DIJON-SHALLOT VINAIGRETTE
1 shallot, finely chopped
¼ cup red wine vinegar
1 Tbsp Dijon mustard
½ cup Arbequina olive oil
Salt and black pepper, to taste

SPRING SALAD

1 ham steak, 1 inch thick

2 bunches radishes, tops removed

Vegetable oil

Salt and black pepper, to taste

Bunch of mizuna or other tender
    bitter springtime greens

2 pints strawberries, tops removed
    and quartered

2 cups shelled fava beans
    (see Note)

Pickled Rhubarb, drained
    (see here)

Dijon-Shallot Vinaigrette (see here)

4 sprigs mint, leaves only, plus
    extra for garnish

NOTE To prepare fava beans, remove the fuzzy outer pods and cook the beans in a saucepan of salted, boiling water for 30 seconds. Plunge beans into cold water to stop the cooking. Squeeze to slip off the waxy skin and pop out the tender bean inside. Shelled fava beans will keep refrigerated for several days.

SPRING SALAD Preheat a charcoal grill over medium-high heat or a gas grill fitted with a smoker box of soaked wood chips. (You want to impart a smoky flavor to the ham and radishes.) Add ham to the grill and sear about 3 to 4 minutes per side. Transfer ham to a cutting board and cut into rectangular lardons, about 1 inch by ½ inch.

In a medium bowl, toss radishes with just enough oil to coat. Season with salt and pepper. Add radishes to the grill and sear for 2 minutes, until they start to char.

In a large mixing bowl, combine ham, radishes, mizuna (or greens), strawberries, fava beans, and pickled rhubarb. Add vinaigrette and toss to coat.

Thinly slice the mint leaves (do this just before serving because they bruise easily) and toss 1 tablespoon into the bowl. Season with salt and pepper. Garnish with more mint and serve.

MAPLE-BRINED PORK TENDERLOIN
with Parisienne Gnocchi

CHEF: ISAAC OCEJO, CULINARY PARTNER OF ANTIQUUM FARM

WINE PAIRING: Antiquum Farm Passiflora Pinot Noir

Serves 4

What are Parisienne gnocchi? Think tiny gougères. It's the same eggy yet light dough, but boiled instead of baked, and then crisped in a pan. Although this recipe is long, the components are easy and can be made ahead so day-of dinner prep is a breeze.

Antiquum Farm's Passiflora Pinot Noir accentuates this company-worthy dish with flavors of passion fruit, mango, orange rind, ripe raspberry, and blackberry. It sails through the palate, only stopping to make space for each taste of pork, gnocchi, and lentils.

PARISIENNE GNOCCHI Bring a large saucepan of lightly salted water to a boil.

In a medium saucepan, combine butter, salt, and ¾ cup water and bring to a boil over medium heat. Add flour and use a wooden spoon to stir continuously for 2 minutes, until flour is thoroughly incorporated and the dough forms a ball and starts to steam. Remove pan from the heat.

Transfer dough to the bowl of a stand mixer fitted with a paddle attachment. Beat on medium speed for 1 minute, until slightly cooled. Beat in eggs, one at a time. Fold in the cheese, parsley, and thyme.

Transfer dough to a piping bag fitted with a ½-inch round tip. (Alternatively, use a ziptop bag and cut off ½ inch from the corner.) Lightly oil a baking sheet.

Hold the piping bag over the saucepan of boiling salted water and quickly squeeze out a 1-inch length of dough, using scissors or a knife to cut the dough, and let it drop into the water. Repeat until you have about 12 to 20 gnocchi in the water (or however many you can drop in there before a minute is up). Boil for 3 minutes, until puffed and cooked through. Using a slotted spoon, transfer gnocchi to the prepared sheet. Repeat with the remaining dough. (Can be made several days ahead and refrigerated.)

BLACK LENTILS Heat oil in a medium saucepan over medium heat. Add onion and garlic and sauté for 5 minutes until tender. Add lentils and 2½ cups water, then increase heat to medium-high. Simmer for 15 to 20 minutes, until lentils are tender but not mushy. Season with champagne vinegar, salt, and pepper. Cover and keep warm.

PARISIENNE GNOCCHI
½ cup (1 stick) butter
1 tsp salt
1 cup all-purpose flour
4 eggs
½ cup grated Parmesan
¼ cup chopped Italian parsley
1 Tbsp chopped thyme
Olive oil, for greasing

BLACK LENTILS
1 Tbsp vegetable oil
½ large onion, diced (about 1 cup)
3 cloves garlic, thinly sliced
¾ cup black lentils, rinsed
Splash of champagne vinegar
Salt and black pepper, to taste

PICKLED MUSTARD SEED CRÈME FRAÎCHE

⅓ cup champagne vinegar
3 Tbsp mustard seeds
1½ Tbsp salt
1 tsp granulated sugar
½ cup crème fraîche

MAPLE-BRINED PORK TENDERLOIN

⅓ cup pure maple syrup
2 Tbsp salt
1 Tbsp packed brown sugar
1½ lbs pork tenderloins
    (approximately 2 tenderloins)
2 Tbsp butter (divided)
1 fennel bulb, cut into 8 wedges

ASSEMBLY

2 Tbsp butter, plus extra if needed
Bunch of chives, very finely
    chopped, for garnish

PICKLED MUSTARD SEED CRÈME FRAÎCHE Combine vinegar, mustard seeds, salt, sugar, and ¾ cup water in a small saucepan over medium heat and stir to dissolve salt. Simmer for 10 minutes, until most of the liquid has been absorbed into the mustard seeds. Drain mustard seeds through a fine-mesh strainer. Set aside to cool completely.

Fold the mustard seeds into the crème fraîche. Refrigerate until ready to serve. (Can be made up to 1 week in advance.)

MAPLE-BRINED PORK TENDERLOIN Combine maple syrup, salt, brown sugar, and 3 cups water in a large saucepan over medium-high heat and stir just until salt and sugar are dissolved. Set aside to cool to room temperature (you can add a few ice cubes to speed it up).

Pour mixture into a ziptop bag and add pork tenderloins. Set in a bowl (in case there's a leak) and refrigerate for 4 to 24 hours.

Remove the pork from the brine and pat dry. Discard the brine.

Heat 1 tablespoon butter in a cast-iron skillet over medium heat. Add tenderloins and cook for 4 minutes, untouched, until golden brown on the bottom. Repeat on the other three sides, until cooked through and the internal temperature is 135°F to 140°F. Transfer to a cutting board and tent with aluminum foil.

Meanwhile, heat remaining tablespoon butter in another cast-iron skillet over medium heat. Add fennel and cook for 3 minutes on each side, until golden brown. Transfer to a bowl.

ASSEMBLY Wipe both skillets clean and return to medium-high heat. Melt 1 tablespoon butter in each pan. Add a layer of gnocchi to each pan, taking care not to overcrowd them. Sear for about 2 minutes, until browned, and repeat on the other side. They should be crunchy on the outside but fluffy on the inside. Transfer to a bowl. Repeat with the remaining gnocchi, adding more butter if needed.

Combine the warm lentils with the seared fennel. Cut pork into ¾-inch-thick medallions.

Place a few spoonfuls of pickled mustard seed crème fraîche on each plate and swipe using the back of the spoon. Scoop a large spoonful of lentils and fennel onto one side of the plate. Set gnocchi on the other. Fan a few tenderloin pieces in between. Garnish with chives.

ARGYLE WINERY

NATE KLOSTERMANN
WINEMAKER

REGION
WILLAMETTE VALLEY

It's not uncommon for winemakers to dabble in brewing, but for Nate Klostermann it worked the other way around. As a homebrewer studying food science at a Midwest college ("They didn't have any beer degrees," he says), he had a chance encounter with a winemaker that altered the course of his life.

"I had a little taste of winemaking and was intrigued by it. I knew I had to move west to do it properly on a bigger scale," he says.

So, in 2005, Nate put out feelers to work as an intern at harvest. Where did he land? Argyle—and he's been there ever since. "I had no idea what I was doing, but I fell in love with it and kept working and learning. I landed in a good spot."

In fact, he couldn't have landed in a better spot. The Willamette Valley's pioneering sparkling wine producer satisfied his innate need to tinker. "Sparkling wine is a year-round process," he says. "There's always something to taste or wrap my head around. It's a longer process, but I gravitate to its slowness—small, fine-tuned decision-making is what fits my personality best."

He became head winemaker in 2013, overseeing all of Argyle's wine production, including Pinot Noir, Chardonnay, Riesling, and various styles of sparkling wine. "They all inform each other in a way, which keeps it dynamic and exciting. We farm all of our fruit from the same four vineyards, and that consistency lets us make small tweaks and allows for experimentation."

Ever the sparkling wine advocate, Nate says one of the best parts about making bubbly at Argyle is that they have the longevity and scale to keep the price within reach. "We can make a high-end sparkling wine that is relatively accessible and affordable for most people," he says. "I'm all about getting people to treat it more as an everyday wine rather than saving it for celebrations. The food friendliness is amazing."

Roasted Garlic and Chèvre Timbales (p. 64)

ROASTED GARLIC AND CHÈVRE TIMBALES

CHEF: GREG HIGGINS, HIGGINS RESTAURANT

WINE PAIRING: Argyle Nuthouse Pinot Noir

Serves 6

Timbales are savory baked custards that can be adapted to any seasonal vegetables and garnishes. In this pillowy, chèvre-enriched version, chef Greg Higgins adds a layer of peppery caramel to perfectly offset the bitter notes from the accompanying balsamic-dressed chicories. Argyle's Nuthouse Pinot Noir, with its bright berry fruit and silky finish, is an ideal partner to these rich custards.

Preheat oven to 375°F.

Combine garlic and olive oil in a small baking dish (the oil should cover the cloves). Roast for 30 to 40 minutes, stirring occasionally, until cloves are a rich golden brown and softened. Remove from the oven and reduce the oven temperature to 350°F. (Roasted garlic can be made 2 days ahead and refrigerated.)

Meanwhile, combine sugar and ½ cup water in a small, heavy-bottomed saucepan. Cover with a loose-fitting lid and bring to a boil over medium heat. Simmer for 8 minutes, checking frequently and swirling occasionally, until the color changes to a rich gold. Remove the lid and, watching closely, boil for another 2 minutes, until syrup reaches an amber hue. Remove the pan from the heat and place it in the sink. Very carefully add ¼ cup water and quickly cover the pan with the lid to avoid being splashed by the vigorously boiling syrup. Add the pepper and let the residual heat bloom the pepper flavor. Keep warm. (Syrup can be made 3 days ahead and refrigerated; rewarm before using.)

In a medium saucepan, combine potatoes and enough cold water to cover. Season generously with salt. Bring to a boil over high heat, reduce to a simmer, and cook for about 8 minutes, until tender. Drain, then set aside.

Ingredients

15 cloves garlic
½ cup extra-virgin olive oil
1 cup granulated sugar
1 Tbsp black pepper, plus extra to taste
1 lb waxy potatoes, such as Yukon Gold, diced into ¾-inch cubes
¼ cup balsamic vinegar
1 Tbsp Dijon mustard
8 oz chèvre, plus extra for garnish
3 eggs
1 cup half-and-half
8 cups chopped chicories or sturdy greens such as kale or Swiss chard
Salt, to taste

Pour 1 tablespoon of warm pepper-caramel syrup into six (6-oz) ramekins, just enough to cover the bottom.

Strain the roasted garlic oil and reserve the cloves. In a small bowl, whisk together garlic oil, vinegar, mustard, and 2 tablespoons of pepper-caramel syrup. Season vinaigrette to taste with salt and pepper.

In a food processor, combine roasted garlic cloves, potatoes, and chèvre and process until smooth. Add eggs and half-and-half and mix again. Season with salt and pepper. Fill the syrup-lined ramekins with the custard mixture.

Arrange the ramekins in a roasting pan. Bring a saucepan of water to a boil. Pour the hot water into the roasting pan until it comes halfway up the sides of the ramekins. Cover the pan tightly with aluminum foil and carefully place it in the oven. Cook for 60 to 90 minutes, until centers are set and their surfaces just barely puff like a souffle.

Remove the foil and allow the timbales to cool in their warm water bath for 20 minutes.

Combine chicories (or greens) and a splash of vinaigrette in a large skillet and cook for 3 minutes over medium-high heat, until slightly wilted.

ASSEMBLY Run the tip of a small knife around the edge of each timbale and invert ramekin onto a salad plate. Portion salad onto plates and remove the ramekins to reveal the timbales. Garnish with a drizzle of vinaigrette and top with crumbled chèvre. Finish with a grind of black pepper.

CHILLED CHARENTAIS MELON GAZPACHO with Albacore Ceviche

CHEF: GREG HIGGINS, HIGGINS RESTAURANT

Serves 4 to 6

6 cups diced Charentais melon,
   or cantaloupe, galia,
   or honeydew (1-inch cubes)
¾ cup lime juice (divided)
Salt and black pepper, to taste
2 Tbsp honey
2 shallots, thinly sliced
1 to 2 serrano chiles, stemmed,
   seeded, and thinly sliced
1 tsp toasted cumin seeds
   (see Note)
1 lb sashimi-grade albacore tuna
   loin, cut into ½-inch dice
¾ cup cilantro leaves (divided)
½ cup sliced almonds, toasted
   (see Note)
Extra-virgin olive oil

NOTE To toast cumin seeds, heat a small dry skillet over medium heat. Add seeds and toast for 3 minutes, stirring frequently, until they smell fragrant and darken slightly in color. Transfer to a plate to cool immediately.

To toast almonds, preheat oven to 350°F. Spread nuts in an even layer on a baking sheet and bake, stirring occasionally, for 5 minutes or until golden.

WINE PAIRING: Argyle Vintage Brut

When chef Greg Higgins opened his eponymous Portland restaurant in 1994, he sparked a farm-to-table movement that has since become synonymous with the Portland food scene. This light and refreshing chilled soup is his ode to summer, when both pristine albacore tuna caught off the Oregon coast and sweet, juicy, fragrant melons are in season. The addition of Pinot Meunier in Argyle's Vintage Brut gives the sparkler floral, poached apricot, and creamy almond notes that pair gorgeously with the honeyed melon flavor of the soup.

In a blender or food processor, combine melon and ¼ cup lime juice and purée until smooth. Season with salt and pepper to taste. Refrigerate until cold.

In a nonreactive mixing bowl, mix the remaining ½ cup lime juice and the honey. Add shallots, chiles, and cumin seeds. Season with a couple pinches of salt and pepper. Add tuna and stir gently to coat. Cover and refrigerate for 2 to 3 hours.

Fold half of the cilantro leaves into the tuna ceviche. Taste, and season with more salt, pepper, lime juice, or honey if desired.

Divide the chilled melon soup into shallow bowls. Place a spoon of ceviche in the center. Garnish with the remaining cilantro leaves, toasted almonds, and a drizzle of oil.

BLACK WALNUT INN & VINEYARD/ THE FOUR GRACES WINERY

TIM JONES
WINEMAKER

CHASE WILLIAMS
EXECUTIVE CHEF

REGION
WILLAMETTE VALLEY

After a particularly riveting class on fermentation in high school, Tim Jones (shown here) was captivated.

That was when his deep curiosity to observe, examine, and analyze took root. Those attributes still drive Tim for each and every vintage. "Every year is different and has unique challenges that arise," he says. Especially in Oregon. The forecasting and unpredictability is part of what he enjoys most about winemaking. "It requires you to be very present. Always on your feet, tasting, checking, making changes."

Tim first immersed himself in the culture of food and wine while studying abroad in Chile and Argentina. When he returned to the States, he worked harvest in Sonoma County and was hooked. After graduating from the viticulture and enology program at

UC Davis, he landed in Walla Walla at Ste. Michelle Wine Estates.

In 2018, he moved to Oregon and joined the Four Graces, eager for the opportunity to work with Pinot Noir and smaller-lot winemaking. One of the four estate vineyards he works with is at the Black Walnut Inn, a stunning property that includes a vineyard villa with a fine-dining culinary program run by chef Chase Williams. "We have very similar philosophies on food and wine pairing," says Chase. Both the winemaker and chef pursue elegance and balance and aspire to evoke a taste of place.

Taking full advantage of the surrounding meadows, Chase forages for wild ingredients to feature on the menu, from wild carrots and chicory to sorrel. "We'll walk around the estate while menu planning and get ideas based on what's growing," he says. Once, the chef hosted John Kallas, Oregon's most famous forager, who "identified fourteen different wild ingredients within minutes."

Together, their shared goal is to create taste memories that are not only delicious, but that bring people together. "You open a bottle of wine with people you enjoy and inevitably end up talking about family and life," says Chase. "That's what I love about wine."

Dungeness Crab–Stuffed Latkes with Gremolata and Crème Fraîche (p. 70)

DUNGENESS CRAB–STUFFED LATKES
with Gremolata and Crème Fraîche

CHEF: CHASE WILLIAMS, BLACK WALNUT INN & VINEYARD

WINE PAIRING: The Four Graces Reserve Pinot Blanc

Serves 4

Crispy potato latkes are a beloved comfort food all on their own, but stuff them with herbed Dungeness crab and they become positively posh. Chef Chase Williams tops these with crème fraîche and a piquant gremolata to cut the richness. Serve them as an appetizer or as an entrée for brunch or dinner with a peppery arugula salad on the side. Add in the bright citrus notes and creamy texture of the Four Graces Reserve Pinot Blanc and you've got a classic white wine and crab pairing.

GREMOLATA In a food processor, pulse garlic, parsley, and lemon zest until finely chopped. With the machine running, add lemon juice and olive oil. Season with salt to taste. (Can be made several days ahead and refrigerated.)

LATKE BATTER Grate potatoes and onions using the large holes of a box grater or the grating disk of a food processor. Scrape mixture into a colander and toss with 1 teaspoon salt. Set aside for 10 minutes in the sink or over a bowl. Squeeze the mixture to remove as much moisture as possible, then place in a salad spinner and spin dry. (Alternatively, place in cheesecloth, gather up ends, and wring out until mixture is completely dry.) For crispy latkes, all liquid must be removed.

Beat the egg in a large mixing bowl. Add the grated mixture, panko, flour, pepper, and the remaining ¼ teaspoon salt. Gently mix until well combined.

GREMOLATA
2 cloves garlic
1 cup Italian parsley
Grated zest and juice of 1½ lemons
½ cup extra-virgin olive oil
Salt, to taste

LATKE BATTER
2 large russet potatoes (1½ lbs), peeled
1 small onion
1¼ tsp salt (divided)
1 egg
¼ cup panko breadcrumbs, finely ground in a blender or food processor
2 Tbsp all-purpose flour
¼ tsp black pepper

CRAB FILLING

8 oz Dungeness crabmeat, picked
through
1 Tbsp finely chopped chives
1 Tbsp finely chopped parsley
Grated zest of ½ lemon
Salt and black pepper, to taste

ASSEMBLY

Vegetable oil, for frying
1 cup crème fraîche

NOTE Feel free to make smaller, appetizer-size versions by using half the amount of potato mixture and crab filling.

CRAB FILLING In a medium bowl, mix the ingredients together. Season with salt and pepper.

ASSEMBLY Fold a couple sheets of parchment paper into quarters and then cut along the lines to make eight 6-inch squares. Place two squares side by side. Scoop ¼ cup of latke batter onto each parchment piece and press into thin 4-inch circles (see Note).

Scoop 2 tablespoons of crab mixture on top of a latke round. Spread crab out, leaving space along the edges. Invert the other latke round on top. Remove parchment and press, sealing the edges together. Lightly flatten the stuffed latke into a ¼-inch-thick circle. Repeat with the remaining latke batter and crab filling until you have 4 stuffed latkes.

Preheat oven to 200°F. Set a wire rack on a baking sheet and preheat in the oven.

Heat a large heavy-bottomed skillet with ⅛ inch of oil over high heat until it reaches a temperature of 375°F. Reduce heat to medium-high and place 2 latkes in the oil. Fry for 2 to 4 minutes per side, until golden brown. Transfer the cooked latkes to the wire rack in the oven. Repeat with the remaining latkes.

To serve, divide latkes among plates or bowls. Top with crème fraîche, gremolata, and any remaining crab filling.

CONFIT CHICKEN
with Pommes Aligot and Chanterelles

CHEF: CHASE WILLIAMS, BLACK WALNUT INN & VINEYARD

WINE PAIRING: The Four Graces Pinot Noir

At the Black Walnut Inn in Dundee, chef Chase Williams has made an art of elevating humble, locally grown ingredients into exceptionally elegant meals. This dish of pasture-raised chicken thighs is a prime example. Think meltingly tender meat, crispy golden skin, and a blanket of silky cheese and potatoes gilded with pickled pearl onions, tender herbs, and sautéed chanterelles. Paired with the Four Graces Pinot Noir, it's a date-night dream and if you make the chicken and pickled onions in advance, you can have it on the table in under an hour.

PICKLED PEARL ONIONS In a medium saucepan, combine vinegar, sugar, mustard seeds, coriander seeds, peppercorns, and ½ cup water. Bring to a boil over medium heat.

Meanwhile, if using fresh pearl onions, cut off the root and the stem ends and peel off the outer skin. Place onions in a heatproof container and carefully pour the boiling pickling liquid over them. Refrigerate overnight. (Can be made 1 week ahead.)

CHICKEN CONFIT In a food processor, combine half the thyme with the garlic, shallots, salt, sugar, and black pepper. Process for 1 minute, until fully mixed. Liberally coat all sides of the chicken thighs with the mixture and place in a shallow container. Cover and refrigerate for at least 12 hours.

Preheat oven to 250°F. Rinse chicken well under cold water, removing all excess seasoning. Pat dry. Place chicken in a Dutch oven and add rosemary, bay leaves, and the remaining thyme. Pour oil over chicken until fully submerged. Cover and cook for 4 to 6 hours, until meat pulls away from the bone. Set aside to cool.

When it is cool enough to handle, transfer the chicken to a chopping board. Carefully pull out the bone and cartilage, keeping the meat intact in one piece. Refrigerate until ready to use. (Can be made 3 days ahead.)

Serves 4

PICKLED PEARL ONIONS
½ cup champagne vinegar
¼ cup granulated sugar
1 Tbsp mustard seeds
1 tsp coriander seeds
1 tsp black peppercorns
1 cup fresh red and white pearl onions or frozen and thawed pearl onions

CHICKEN CONFIT
6 sprigs thyme (divided)
6 cloves garlic
2 shallots, peeled and halved
3 Tbsp salt, plus extra to taste
1 Tbsp granulated sugar
1 tsp black pepper, plus extra to taste
4 skin-on, bone-in chicken thighs
2 sprigs rosemary
2 bay leaves
4 to 6 cups vegetable oil

POMMES ALIGOT

1 cup (2 sticks) butter

2 lbs Yukon Gold potatoes, peeled and sliced ⅛-inch thick

Vegetable oil, to cover

1 cup heavy cream

¾ lb raclette or Gruyère cheese, shredded

¾ lb mozzarella cheese, shredded

Salt and white pepper, to taste

CHANTERELLES

2 Tbsp butter

1 lb chanterelles, cleaned

3 cloves garlic, thinly sliced

1 shallot, thinly sliced

1 tsp thyme leaves

Salt and black pepper, to taste

1 tsp roughly chopped Italian parsley

ASSEMBLY

2 Tbsp vegetable oil

16 small sprigs tarragon

16 small sprigs chervil

16 small sprigs parsley

16 small sprigs chives, thinly sliced

16 edible flowers, such as chive blossom, marigold, or calendula

POMMES ALIGOT Melt butter in a medium saucepan over medium heat. Add potatoes and top up with vegetable oil to ensure potatoes are mostly submerged. Cover and cook on medium-low heat for 15 minutes, stirring occasionally, until potatoes are fully cooked and tender.

Meanwhile, gently heat cream in a large saucepan over medium heat. (The pan should be large enough to fit the potatoes later.)

Drain potatoes, reserving ½ cup of the poaching butter. Place potatoes in a food processor and, working in batches if needed, pulse on low while slowly drizzling in the warmed cream. Pulse in both cheeses and the reserved butter. Process until smooth.

Season potatoes with salt and pepper. Pour into the saucepan used to heat the cream. Keep warm.

CHANTERELLES Melt butter in a skillet over medium heat. Add chanterelles and sauté for 4 to 5 minutes, until slightly browned. Add garlic, shallot, and thyme. Cook for another minute, until softened. Season with salt and pepper. Stir in parsley. Keep warm.

ASSEMBLY Slice pickled pearl onions into rings and set aside.

Heat oil in a large skillet set over medium-high heat. Add confit chicken skin side down and cook for 10 minutes until golden brown. Flip and cook for another 2 to 3 minutes, until chicken is heated through.

To serve, place chicken in the center of each dish. Spoon pommes aligot over chicken until fully covered. Place 4 to 5 sautéed chanterelles around the edge of the potatoes, spaced evenly apart, then fill in the perimeter with the herbs, edible flowers, and pickled pearl onion rings.

BROOKS
WINE

JANIE BROOKS HEUCK

MANAGING DIRECTOR

REGION
WILLAMETTE VALLEY

Many stories about Brooks Winery start by bringing up the past. But as important as that is to the winery's unique history, it makes it all too easy to overlook the myriad ways Janie Brooks Heuck and her team are leading Brooks into the future. "My mindset is: 'How can I use this winery as a platform for a broader message on how to take care of your people and your environment?'" she says.

Janie has been the managing director since 2004, when her brother and original owner Jimi Brooks unexpectedly passed away and left the winery to his then eight-year-old son, Pascal. Ever since, Janie has made it her mission to do right by her nephew, as well as her employees, customers, and the world at large. "We're very focused on continuing to do our part on a local and global scale," she says.

She has built on her brother's legacy of sustainable, biodynamic farming by earning Demeter certification in 2012, joining 1% for the Planet, and partnering with Ecologi, which allows her to buy carbon offsets for employees and invest in the future. "When someone spends $50 at Brooks, we plant a mangrove tree in the rainforest."

Though forward-thinking in business (under her leadership Brooks became the eighth winery in the country to earn a B Corp certification), Janie and head winemaker Chris Williams stay true to Jimi's vision when it comes to winemaking. "Jimi was making 2,500 cases with a two-ton fermenter as his largest vessel and we do the same but are making ten times more wine."

That's because the Brooks philosophy is built on individually fermenting small lots sourced from a wide variety of vineyards, then blending them into magic. "Because we don't manipulate the wines at all, blending is such an important part of the process."

Janie says she's looking forward to when Pascal, now in his twenties and learning the wine-growing ropes in France, returns to the winery and she can focus more on her business activism. "There's more we can do as a business in a broader community and in getting the wine industry involved in some of this stuff," she says. "That's what I absolutely love."

BUTTER-POACHED SHRIMP
with Wild Mushrooms and Lemon Cream Sauce

CHEF: NORMA BUCHHOLZ-GREEN, BROOKS WINE

Serves 2 to 4

SHRIMP
1 cup (2 sticks) butter
¼ cup Brooks Riesling
4 cloves garlic, smashed
Grated zest and juice of 1 lemon
10 colossal shrimp (U/15), peeled and deveined (see Note)
Salt and black pepper

MUSHROOMS AND CREAM SAUCE
2 Tbsp olive oil
8 oz maitake or other wild mushrooms, roughly chopped (3 cups)
Salt
2 Tbsp finely chopped garlic
1 cup heavy cream
2 Tbsp lemon juice
4 cups baby spinach

ASSEMBLY
3 Tbsp microgreens
1 tsp lemon-infused olive oil, for garnish (optional)

NOTE Although Brooks Winery's resident chef Norma Buchholz-Green uses colossal shrimp for this recipe, extra jumbo or even jumbo shrimp will do, though you may need to reduce the cooking time.

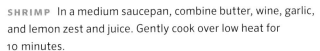

WINE PAIRING: Brooks Ara Riesling

Gently poaching shrimp in lemon-and-Riesling-spiked butter is a foolproof way to keep them from overcooking and infuses them with luscious flavor at the same time. A lemony cream sauce swimming with wild mushrooms provides an ideal accompaniment. Here the dish is served on its own but consider adding warm focaccia to soak up every last drop. Although a silky Chardonnay would play well with the butteriness in this dish, Brooks Ara Riesling offers a drier and sprightlier partner, with layers of apples, citrus, and baking spice.

SHRIMP In a medium saucepan, combine butter, wine, garlic, and lemon zest and juice. Gently cook over low heat for 10 minutes.

Season shrimp with salt and pepper. Add to the pan and cook for 4 minutes over low heat until light pink in color. Remove from heat.

MUSHROOMS AND CREAM SAUCE Heat oil in a large skillet set over high heat. Add mushrooms and a pinch of salt and sauté for 5 minutes, until soft. Add garlic and sauté for another 1 minute.

Add cream and bring to a boil. Add lemon juice and cook for about 2 minutes, until cream is slightly reduced and thickened. Add spinach and let it wilt in the pan.

ASSEMBLY Divide the mushroom mixture among bowls and top with poached shrimp (discard the poaching liquid). Garnish with microgreens and a drizzle of lemon-infused oil, if using.

Fry Bread Beef Tacos with Cilantro Crema (p. 78)

FRY BREAD BEEF TACOS
with Cilantro Crema

CHEF: NORMA BUCHHOLZ-GREEN, BROOKS WINE

WINE PAIRING: Brooks Rastaban Pinot Noir

These open-faced tacos are made with wonderfully puffy rounds of chewy fry bread instead of the traditional corn tortillas. The dough is simple to make and fries up in mere minutes. Topped with spiced ground beef and cilantro crema, they're a fun departure from the usual Taco Tuesday suspects. Chef Norma Buchholz-Green often tops these tacos with edible flowers, lending them a fresh and summery vibe. Brooks Rastaban Pinot Noir is a gorgeously savory partner, with brambly fruit and peppercorns to complement the spiced beef.

CILANTRO CREMA In a blender or food processor, combine jalapeños, cilantro, sour cream, garlic, lime juice, olive oil, and vinegar. Purée until smooth. Season to taste with salt and pepper. (Can be made several days ahead and refrigerated.)

FRY BREAD In a medium mixing bowl, combine flour, baking powder, and salt. Add ¾ cup warm water and mix until fully incorporated. Turn dough out onto a lightly floured surface and knead for 5 minutes. Form into a ball, place in a clean bowl, and cover with plastic wrap. Set aside to rest for 10 to 15 minutes.

Divide the ball into 6 equal portions. Roll out each on a lightly floured surface until 6 to 8 inches in diameter.

Heat 1 inch of oil in a deep cast-iron skillet set over medium-high heat until it reaches a temperature of 350°F. Add a bread round to the pan and fry for 45 seconds on each side, until golden brown. Drain on a wire rack set over a baking sheet and sprinkle with salt. Repeat with remaining fry bread. Keep warm.

Serves 6

CILANTRO CREMA
3 jalapeños, seeded
2 cups cilantro leaves
½ cup sour cream
1 clove garlic
Juice of 1 lime
⅓ cup extra-virgin olive oil
1 tsp apple cider vinegar
Salt and black pepper, to taste

FRY BREAD
2 cups all-purpose flour, plus extra for dusting
2½ tsp baking powder
1 tsp salt, plus extra for sprinkling
Vegetable oil, for frying

SPICED BEEF

1 lb lean (80/20) ground beef
1 Tbsp chili powder
1½ tsp ground cumin
¼ tsp garlic powder
¼ tsp onion powder
¼ tsp cayenne pepper
Salt and black pepper, to taste

ASSEMBLY

1 (16-oz) can refried beans, heated
½ cup shredded sharp cheddar
    or cotija cheese
1 cup thinly shredded cabbage
⅓ cup diced white onion or
    pico de gallo
1 avocado, thinly sliced
Edible flowers, for garnish
    (optional)

SPICED BEEF Heat a large skillet over medium-high heat. Add beef and cook for 5 minutes, or until no longer pink. Add remaining ingredients and cook for another 5 minutes. Keep warm.

ASSEMBLY Spread a layer of refried beans over each fry bread, then top with a spoonful of beef, a sprinkle of cheese, cabbage, diced onion (or pico de gallo), and a few slices of avocado. Top with cilantro crema and garnish with edible flowers, if using.

CHEHALEM WINERY

KATIE SANTORA
WINEMAKER

REGION
WILLAMETTE VALLEY

Katie Santora loves science. "But I didn't want to be a scientist," she says. She couldn't imagine donning a lab coat and spending her days indoors, so she had trouble imagining her future at all—until a family friend suggested winemaking school.

"I'm thinking, 'Nobody gets their degree in winemaking, that's silly.' But when I looked into it, I realized it was really science-based and centered around things I enjoyed learning about but didn't know how to fit into my life."

Four years later, Katie had a degree in enology and viticulture from UC Davis in hand and was traveling the world, working as an intern and cellar hand in Australia, New Zealand, and South America. When it was time to put down roots, "Oregon drew me back," she says. "In Oregon, every vintage is extremely different. It can be super-hot or have too much rain. You're always on your toes for what to expect and how to pivot."

She landed in the Northwest in 2012 as assistant winemaker at storied Chehalem Winery, known for its single-vineyard Pinots and Chardonnays with bracing acidity. "I thought I could only commit to four years in one place, but Chehalem is amazing."

In 2018, she earned the role of winemaker, giving her the opportunity to build her team and spend more time in the vineyard. "I love the two women I work with. They're smart and ambitious and I want to empower them—that allows me to put my energy and vision into the vineyard."

That's because, for Katie, the vineyard is where the magic happens. "Even though we use winemaking tools, the goal is to try not to tweak or alter the fruit much at all," she says. "You have to trust in what is coming to you and guide it. That comes with knowing where it's coming from, knowing the weather through the year, and knowing the land."

SALMON RILLETTES
with Crème Fraîche

CHEF: BECCA RICHARDS, STOLLER WINE GROUP CULINARY DIRECTOR

Serves 8

2 cups Chehalem Reserve
    Chardonnay
2 shallots, roughly chopped
1 Tbsp salt, plus extra as needed
2 lbs salmon fillets, fat trimmed,
    cut into 1-inch cubes
6 oz cold-smoked salmon,
    finely chopped
½ cup crème fraîche
½ cup mayonnaise
¼ cup lemon juice
2 Tbsp thinly sliced chives
Black pepper, to taste
Warm baguette, cut into ½-inch
    slices, to serve

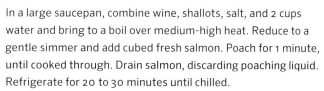

WINE PAIRING: Chehalem Reserve Chardonnay

Perhaps the best thing about this rich salmon spread is how it pairs so perfectly with both Chardonnay and Pinot Noir. "It's a dream pairing with either one," says chef Becca Richards. She uses a combination of fresh king salmon and cold-smoked salmon for the silkiest texture and serves it simply on slices of warm baguette. It's a tasting-room favorite and Becca says it's ideal for brunch. "Invite eight of your friends over, then add a cheese and charcuterie board, fruit, and a salad. It'll be the best and easiest component of your menu." You can easily halve the recipe to serve four.

In a large saucepan, combine wine, shallots, salt, and 2 cups water and bring to a boil over medium-high heat. Reduce to a gentle simmer and add cubed fresh salmon. Poach for 1 minute, until cooked through. Drain salmon, discarding poaching liquid. Refrigerate for 20 to 30 minutes until chilled.

In a large mixing bowl, combine smoked salmon and chilled poached salmon, gently breaking the cubes into pieces. Stir in crème fraîche, mayonnaise, and lemon juice. Add chives, then season with salt and pepper. Cover and refrigerate until chilled.

Spread rillettes on baguette slices and serve.

GRILLED PORK CHOPS
with Stone Fruit Pico and Balsamic Glaze

CHEF: BECCA RICHARDS, STOLLER WINE GROUP CULINARY DIRECTOR

WINE PAIRING: Chehalem Ridgecrest Vineyards Pinot Noir

Chef Becca Richards is responsible for producing everything from picnic sandwiches to 1,000-person events for both Chehalem Winery and Stoller Family Estate, and that means she's always collaborating with the winemakers to find the perfect pairings. To balance the tight tannins and "underripe plum" acidity of Chehalem's Ridgecrest Pinot Noir, she created a riff on pico de gallo with a parade of stone fruits. Rich pork chops tinged with smoke from the grill provide the perfect backdrop to round out the flavors.

PORK CHOPS Pat the pork chops dry. In a small bowl, combine cilantro, rosemary, lemon and lime zests, brown sugar, salt, pepper, and paprika. Rub mixture all over chops and refrigerate for at least 2 hours or overnight.

STONE FRUIT PICO In a large mixing bowl, combine plums, peach, nectarine, tomatoes, vinegar, and sugar. Toss to coat, then drain off excess liquid so the mixture isn't runny. Add remaining ingredients and set aside.

ASSEMBLY Let the chops come to room temperature for an hour before grilling.

Preheat a grill over medium-high heat, to 350°F to 400°F. Clean and oil the cooking grates. (Alternatively, heat a grill pan over medium-high heat.) Add chops and cook for 4 minutes, or until they easily release from the grates or pan. Give the chop a quarter turn on the same side to create diamond grill marks. Cook for another 4 minutes. Flip chops and repeat on the other side, until the internal temperature reaches 130°F to 135°F. Transfer chops to a plate. Set aside to rest for 3 minutes.

Toss stone fruit pico with olive oil. Divide chops among plates and generously top with pico. Drizzle with aged balsamic vinegar.

Serves 4 to 6

PORK CHOPS
4 to 6 bone-in pork loin chops, 1½ to 2 inches thick
1 Tbsp finely chopped cilantro stems
1 Tbsp finely chopped rosemary
Grated zest of 1 lemon
Grated zest of 1 lime
1 Tbsp packed brown sugar
1 Tbsp salt
2 tsp black pepper
1 tsp smoked paprika

STONE FRUIT PICO
2 plums, cut into ¼-inch cubes
1 peach, cut into ¼-inch cubes
1 nectarine, cut into ¼-inch cubes
1 pint yellow, orange, and red cherry tomatoes, quartered
2 Tbsp white balsamic vinegar
1 tsp granulated sugar
1 small red bell pepper, seeded, deveined, and cut into ¼-inch pieces
1 jalapeño pepper, seeded and cut into ¼-inch pieces
1 red onion, diced small
1 clove garlic, finely chopped
1 Tbsp finely chopped cilantro leaves
1 Tbsp finely chopped basil
½ tsp salt
½ tsp black pepper
Pinch of red pepper flakes
Grated zest and juice of 1 lemon
Grated zest and juice of 1 lime

ASSEMBLY
2 Tbsp extra-virgin olive oil
High-quality aged balsamic vinegar, for drizzling

COOPER MOUNTAIN VINEYARDS

BARBARA GROSS
CO-OWNER

REGION
WILLAMETTE VALLEY

When asked how she and her father have complemented each other over the years, Barbara Gross responds: "I'm a firecracker. He's grounded." Together, they've used those traits to push the needle in regenerative agriculture on over 200 acres of vineyards in the Willamette Valley.

Barbara grew up in the vineyards when the industry was just beginning and her wine country roots run deep. One of the early trailblazers in sustainable farming, her father, Dr. Robert Gross, first planted wine grapes with his wife Corrine in 1978. Born in New York City, he and his wife made the move west to raise their three children surrounded by nature.

Like other pioneers, his love of Pinot Noir landed them in the Willamette Valley. A homeopathic doctor by day, Robert was at the forefront of holistic viticulture, pursuing organic and biodynamic

farming practices and certifications in the early 1990s. "He was always ahead of his time," says Barbara.

"Every practitioner has a different pillar of why they move in that direction. And for us, homeopathy for viticulture is the foundation of everything." As more vineyards and farms across the state embrace organic agriculture, Barbara reflects and adds, "We are having an incredible moment right now."

Since producing their first estate Pinot Noir in 1987, Cooper Mountain Vineyards has expanded and now bottles seven varietals under three different labels, including Chardonnay, Pinot Gris, Gamay Noir, and a tiny amount of Tocai Friulano.

In the tasting room, they sell another rarity in the States: true balsamic vinegar, inspired by Robert's trips to Modena, Italy. The most recent batch was made in 2000—the estate Chardonnay and Pinot vines provided the juice for the vinegar, followed by twenty years of aging in five different barrels by historic producer F. Renzi of Modena.

"It requires a lot of patience," says Barbara. A virtue her father has in spades. "At the end of the day, I feel very honored to work with my father," she says. For them, wine not only brings people together, it's a beacon for change.

Hazelnut Crostata with Roasted Cabbage, Apple, and Goat Cheese (p. 86)

HAZELNUT CROSTATA
with Roasted Cabbage, Apple, and Goat Cheese

CHEF: KIR JENSEN

WINE PAIRING: Cooper Mountain Old Vines Chardonnay

Serves 6 to 8

This gorgeous crostata takes full advantage of some of the most delicious Oregon-grown ingredients found at the farmers' market every fall and winter. Hazelnuts in the buttery crust offer a nutty richness to round out the acidity of Cooper Mountain's crisp and lively Chardonnay, while the tart apples play off the wine's ripe fruit flavors. Slice this beauty into thin wedges to serve as an appetizer or go bigger and make it the centerpiece of brunch or dinner with a fresh green salad on the side.

TOASTED HAZELNUT DOUGH Preheat oven to 350°F. Arrange hazelnuts in an even layer on a baking sheet and toast for 8 to 10 minutes, until golden. If they have brown papery skins, fold nuts into a clean dish towel while still hot and vigorously rub. Some skins will remain on, which is fine.

Pulse hazelnuts in a food processor, until finely chopped with a coarse meal texture. Add flour, sugar, salt, and pepper and pulse several times. Add butter and pulse until the butter pieces are roughly the size of chickpeas. Pour in the ice-cold water and pulse until dough forms a ball.

Turn dough out onto a lightly floured surface and knead several times to form a flat patty. Wrap with plastic wrap and chill for at least 30 minutes.

FILLING Preheat oven to 375°F. Lightly oil a baking sheet.

In a large mixing bowl, combine cabbage, garlic, parsley, dill, salt, pepper, oil, vinegar, and anchovy paste (or anchovies). Add half of the apple. Mix thoroughly. Spread in an even layer on the prepared baking sheet.

Roast for 10 minutes. Rotate the pan and stir the mixture, then cook for another 10 to 15 minutes, until the cabbage begins to caramelize. Cool completely.

Transfer the cooled cabbage mixture back to the mixing bowl and add the remaining apple and half of the goat (or sheep's milk) cheese.

TOASTED HAZELNUT DOUGH
¼ cup hazelnuts
1¾ cups all-purpose flour, plus extra for dusting
1 tsp granulated sugar
1 tsp salt
⅛ tsp black pepper
1 cup (2 sticks) cold butter, cut into 1-inch cubes
⅓ cup ice-cold water

FILLING
1 lb green cabbage, cut into ¾-inch-wide ribbons
3 large cloves garlic, finely chopped
1 Tbsp finely chopped parsley
1 Tbsp finely chopped dill
1 tsp salt
¼ tsp black pepper
¼ cup extra-virgin olive oil, plus extra for greasing
1 Tbsp sherry vinegar
1 tsp anchovy paste or finely chopped anchovies
1 large tart apple, such as Honeycrisp or Granny Smith, skin on, cored, and cut into 1-inch pieces (divided)
3 to 4 oz fresh goat or sheep's milk cheese (divided)

All-purpose flour, for dusting
Cold heavy cream, for brushing
Flaky sea salt

ASSEMBLY Preheat oven to 375°F. Remove dough from the refrigerator and set aside at room temperature for 5 to 10 minutes.

Roll out the dough on a lightly floured surface, making quarter turns between each roll. Dust with flour as needed, until dough is approximately 16 inches in diameter and ¼ inch thick. Brush off any excess flour with a pastry brush.

Trim dough to a 13-inch-diameter circle. Gather the excess dough, wrap in plastic wrap, and save for another use, such as mini jam tarts. (The leftover dough can be refrigerated for 3 days or frozen for 1 month.)

Center the pastry over a deep, 10-inch cast-iron skillet. The dough should come up and drape slightly over the edges of the pan. If there is more, trim excess pastry. Gently press dough into the bottom and corners of the pan. Sprinkle the remaining goat (or sheep's milk) cheese on the bottom. Spoon filling on top. Fold the border of the dough over the filling, pleating the pastry as you go. Brush the dough evenly with cold cream and sprinkle with sea salt.

Bake on the center rack for 25 minutes. Rotate the pan and bake for another 20 to 25 minutes, until crust is deep golden brown.

Cool crostata for 10 minutes, then serve.

DARK CHOCOLATE PUDDINGS
with Coffee-Cardamom Cream

CHEF: KIR JENSEN

Serves 6 to 8

DARK CHOCOLATE PUDDING
- ½ cup sifted extra brute or dark cocoa powder, such as Green & Black's or Valrhona (see Note)
- 1 cup granulated sugar
- 3 Tbsp cornstarch
- 1 tsp salt
- 2½ cups whole milk
- ¾ cup heavy cream
- 2 egg yolks, room temperature
- 3 Tbsp butter, room temperature
- 2 tsp vanilla extract
- 3 oz bittersweet chocolate, such as Green & Black's or Valrhona, finely chopped

COFFEE-CARDAMOM CREAM
- 1½ cups cold heavy cream
- 1½ Tbsp granulated sugar
- 1¼ tsp instant espresso powder, such as Medaglia d'Oro
- ¼ tsp ground cardamom
- ½ tsp vanilla extract

ASSEMBLY
- Grated bittersweet chocolate
- Fresh Bing cherries with stem or preserved Amarena cherries

> **NOTE** Extra brute cocoa powder is a dark, rich Dutch-process cocoa powder. It's commonly found online through gourmet retailers.

WINE PAIRING: Cooper Mountain Vineyards Life Pinot Noir

Pastry chef Kir Jensen made her name in Portland—and beyond—with her pioneering food truck (and later, café) called The Sugar Cube, where she put inventive spins on comforting desserts. These rich puddings fit squarely in that tradition, offering an easy-breezy childhood favorite with grown-up flavors. The dark cocoa, espresso, and cardamom beautifully complement the cola and mocha notes in Cooper Mountain's supple and fruit-forward Life Pinot Noir.

DARK CHOCOLATE PUDDING In a large saucepan, combine cocoa powder, sugar, cornstarch, and salt. Whisk in milk, cream, and egg yolks. Cook over medium-high heat, stirring constantly, until the mixture starts to bubble vigorously. Immediately remove from the heat and whisk in butter, vanilla, and chocolate. Stir until smooth and glossy.

Divide the pudding into six to eight (8-oz) mason jars, highball glasses, or ramekins. Set aside for 10 minutes. Or, to serve cold, refrigerate for at least 1 hour or overnight. (Puddings can be tightly covered with plastic wrap and refrigerated for several days.)

COFFEE-CARDAMOM CREAM In a deep mixing bowl or the bowl of a stand mixer fitted with the whisk attachment, combine all ingredients. Whip on medium-high speed until soft peaks form.

ASSEMBLY Generously spoon coffee-cardamom cream over puddings. Sprinkle with grated chocolate and top with a cherry.

COROLLARY WINES

DAN DIEPHOUSE
CO-FOUNDER

JEANNE FELDKAMP
CO-FOUNDER

REGION
WILLAMETTE VALLEY

It all started over ten years ago in Dogpatch, a creative hub in San Francisco's Central Waterfront district. Jeanne Feldkamp and Dan Diephouse met, fell head over heels for each other, and promptly launched a supper club.

"When you put a bunch of strangers around the table together, it's magical," says Jeanne. At least one couple got married after meeting at a dinner, and the conversations were always riveting. "We saw it as a way to make connections with people we otherwise wouldn't cross paths with," she adds. "That was the best part about it."

At the time, they both had ties to the corporate world but they began dreaming about their future. "We were talking about what we could do for the rest of our lives— what would be worthy of spending decades on," she says. "We always came back to wine."

Originally from Oregon, Jeanne was familiar with the state's esteemed wine regions. She and Dan share a mutual love for sparkling wine, especially from Champagne, where they often traveled together. In 2017, they took a leap of faith and moved to Portland with the intent to make *méthode champenoise* (traditional method) sparkling wines.

"We made a list of all the vineyards we'd want to source fruit from, focusing on high-elevation sites in the Eola-Amity Hills and Van Duzer Corridor," says Dan. "We were looking for really delicate flavors with a lot of acidity," he adds. For their first vintage, they released five different wines, most under a hundred cases.

In addition to a rare sparkling Pinot Blanc made with fruit from Winter's Hill Estate Vineyard (page 236), the couple is excited to produce a portfolio of traditional method sparklings in a range of styles from single-vineyard bottlings that highlight the character of specific sites to classic blends that explore unusual winemaking approaches, like their carbonic rosé. Tastings are intimate and hosted around a large and welcoming table that harkens back to the couple's supper club days. "Food and wine, more than anything else, are the ultimate connectors," says Jeanne.

Sea Urchin on Toasted Brioche with Cauliflower Purée, Fava Beans, and Preserved Lemon (p. 92)

SEA URCHIN ON TOASTED BRIOCHE
with Cauliflower Purée, Fava Beans, and Preserved Lemon

CHEF: IAN MUNTZERT

WINE PAIRING: Corollary Cuvée One

Sea urchin roe (aka uni) is becoming increasingly easy to find in the States as people fall in love with its salty-sweet, umami-rich, oceanic flavor. Here, chef Ian Muntzert feathers the briny, bright orange uni on a creamy backdrop of cauliflower purée and buttery brioche with pops of preserved lemon for brightness.

For the ultimate food-friendly sparkler, pop open Corollary Cuvée One for fresh, crisp flavors to play off the buttery brioche and the sea salt kiss from the uni.

CAULIFLOWER PURÉE Melt butter in a medium saucepan over medium-high heat. Reduce heat to medium and simmer for 5 to 8 minutes, until the milk solids settle at the bottom of the pan and turn golden brown. Remove from heat and scrape the melted butter and browned solids into a bowl to stop the cooking.

In the same pan, combine cauliflower, leek, and just enough water to almost cover the vegetables. Bring to a simmer over medium heat and cook for 10 to 15 minutes, until most of the water has evaporated. Add cream and simmer for 5 minutes, until reduced by half and cauliflower is tender.

Reserve 6 tablespoons of the melted butter for later (spoon up just the liquid, which is essentially clarified butter, not the solids). Combine the cauliflower mixture and remaining butter and solids in a blender or food processor and process until smooth. Press through a fine-mesh strainer set over a bowl. Season to taste with salt and pepper.

ASSEMBLY Set a large skillet over medium heat. Brush one side of the brioche slices with the reserved clarified butter. Toast, buttered side down, until golden. Spread a thin layer of cauliflower purée onto the toasted sides.

In a small bowl, combine fava beans, lemon juice, and olive oil and toss to coat. Scatter across the surface of the toasts. Top with preserved lemon. Arrange "leaves" of sea urchin on the toast. Finish with a sprinkle of sea salt, a few sprigs of dill, and red chili threads.

Serves 4

CAULIFLOWER PURÉE
½ cup (1 stick) butter
2 cups cauliflower florets
¼ cup thinly sliced leek,
    white parts only
½ cup heavy cream
Salt and black pepper, to taste

ASSEMBLY
4 (1-inch) slices brioche, cut into
    rounds or planks
Reserved clarified butter
1 to 2 lbs fava beans (see Note)
Squeeze of lemon juice
Drizzle of extra-virgin olive oil
1 Tbsp finely diced preserved lemon
4 oz fresh sea urchin roe
Flaky sea salt
12 small sprigs dill
Red chili threads (see Note)

NOTE To prepare fava beans, remove the fuzzy outer pods and cook the beans in a saucepan of salted, boiling water for 30 seconds. Plunge beans into cold water to stop the cooking. Squeeze to slip off the waxy skin and pop out the tender bean inside. Shelled fava beans will keep refrigerated for several days.

Red chili threads are thin strips of mildly spicy dried chili with an earthy smoky flavor. This common Asian garnish can be found in most Asian markets or online. If you can't find them, feel free to substitute Espelette or Aleppo pepper.

GRILLED BLACK COD

with Oyster Pil Pil, Cherry Tomatoes, and Kale

CHEF: IAN MUNTZERT

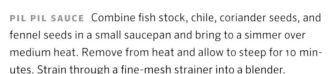

WINE PAIRING: Corollary Cuvée One Rosé

Known for his Northwest takes on Spanish cuisine, chef Ian Muntzert swaps in luscious Oregon black cod (sablefish) for the dried salt cod used in the traditional Basque dish *bacalao al pil-pil*. To layer in more sea-inspired notes, he emulsifies the flavorful sauce with oysters and drizzles the dish with bright green and briny plankton-infused olive oil. It's easy to find online and phenomenal on fish, but any grassy finishing olive oil will do. The lively bubbles with baked apple and stone fruit flavors in the Cuvée One Rosé make a perfect counterpoint.

PIL PIL SAUCE Combine fish stock, chile, coriander seeds, and fennel seeds in a small saucepan and bring to a simmer over medium heat. Remove from heat and allow to steep for 10 minutes. Strain through a fine-mesh strainer into a blender.

Leave the blender lid slightly ajar and drape a clean dish towel on top (this will allow steam to escape and protect you from hot splatters). Turn on the blender, lift the dish towel, and carefully add the oyster and its liquor. Gradually pour in oil in a steady stream to emulsify. Season to taste with salt and a few squeezes of lemon juice.

ASSEMBLY Preheat a grill over high heat, to 400°F to 500°F. Clean and oil the grates. (Alternatively, preheat a large sauté pan over high heat and sear fish and vegetables separately.) Brush cod with vegetable oil and season with salt and pepper.

Toss tomatoes and kale with just enough vegetable oil to coat. Season with salt and pepper. Transfer to a grill pan and cook for 2 to 3 minutes, until kale is charred. Transfer to a plate. Place cod on the grill and cook for 2 to 3 minutes per side, until charred and just cooked.

Divide the pil pil sauce among four shallow bowls. Place a piece of cod on top and garnish with the grilled vegetables. Finish with a drizzle of olive oil.

Serves 4

PIL PIL SAUCE
1 cup fish stock
1 Thai bird's eye chile
1 tsp coriander seeds, toasted (see Note)
½ tsp fennel seeds, toasted (see Note)
1 small oyster, shucked, with its liquor
¾ cup neutral oil, such as grapeseed
Salt, to taste
Lemon juice, to taste

ASSEMBLY
1 (1-lb) skin-on black cod fillet, cut into four equal pieces
Vegetable oil, for coating
Salt and black pepper, to taste
1 pint cherry tomatoes
Bunch of lacinato kale, stems removed, torn into bite-sized pieces
Grassy extra-virgin olive oil or Castillo de Canena Plancton Olive Oil (see Note)

NOTE To toast fennel and coriander seeds, set a small dry skillet over medium heat. When hot, add seeds and toast for 3 minutes, stirring frequently, until fragrant and darker in color. Transfer to a plate to cool immediately.

Castillo de Canena is a centuries-old Spanish olive oil producer that makes olive oil infused with sea phytoplankton. It's available online.

COWHORN VINEYARD & GARDEN

MINI BYERS
OWNER AND GENERAL MANAGER

REGION
APPLEGATE VALLEY

One of the state's youngest winery owners, Mini Byers agrees that her path to Oregon's Applegate Valley was serendipitous. Originally from California, she moved to New York City for college, then rose up the ranks working in communications for fashion and lifestyle brands including Goop, where the ethos for pushing boundaries stuck with her.

When a potential wine project came her way, "the gears started turning and I felt like I could create something really wonderful," she says. Mini, who grew up steeped in both the wine and hospitality industries, was ready to return to those roots and build something of her own.

She was originally scouting property in upstate New York, then a friend connected her with the founders of Cowhorn, an estate that had garnered numerous accolades for producing exceptional Rhône grape varieties, including Syrah, Viognier, Marsanne, and Roussanne.

When Mini first walked the property—a majestic 117-acre patchwork of vineyards, gardens, and Douglas fir groves—she knew. "The stars were aligning and this was exactly where I was supposed to be," she says.

She was especially drawn to the history of the land: Cowhorn was among the first certified biodynamic estate wineries and commercial farms in the United States. "Our goal is to build on that foundation and create our own polyculture farm, eventually growing everything we need here," Mini says.

Most often found in the vineyard, Mini works closely with her winemaker throughout the year. "Our goal is to get everything as happy as it can possibly be out there so that minimal work is done in the cellar," she says. "We want the wines to express what happened in a given year," she adds. "What makes wine special is that it's history in a bottle."

Asparagus Three Ways (p. 96)

ASPARAGUS THREE WAYS

CHEF: TIM PAYNE, COWHORN VINEYARD & GARDEN

WINE PAIRING: Cowhorn Viognier

Serves 6

The purple asparagus bed in Cowhorn's garden is so prolific, it produces over a ton annually. So when asparagus season finally arrives, chef Tim Payne takes pride in showing off its culinary versatility in dishes like this one, where the grassy stalks get a trifecta of treatments: grilled, pickled, and raw.

Cowhorn's Viognier, a richly textured white wine, is perfect for this dish. Asparagus can be a bit difficult to pair, but the wine's generous floral and tropical notes complement the earthy, grassy crunch from the fresh asparagus—making it a radiant celebration of spring flavors.

In a large bowl, combine 24 asparagus stalks, the scallions, and just enough olive oil to coat. Toss, then season to taste with sea salt.

Thinly slice half of the remaining asparagus diagonally and place in a heatproof container.

Shave the remaining asparagus with a vegetable peeler, creating long, thin ribbons.

In a small saucepan, combine vinegar, sugar, and salt and cook over medium-high heat until sugar has dissolved and liquid is about to boil. Pour into the container of sliced asparagus. Set aside to pickle for at least 20 to 30 minutes. (Can be made a day ahead and refrigerated.)

Place eggs in a saucepan and cover with 2 inches water. Bring to a simmer over high heat, then reduce heat to medium-high and cook for exactly 6 minutes. Carefully drain eggs and rinse in cold water to stop the cooking. When cool enough to handle, gently crack and peel eggs. Set aside until ready to serve.

2 to 3 bunches medium-thick asparagus, woody ends removed (divided)

Bunch of scallions, ends trimmed

1 Tbsp extra-virgin olive oil, plus extra for coating

Flaky sea salt, to taste

1 cup apple cider vinegar

½ cup granulated sugar

1 Tbsp salt

6 eggs

3 lemons, halved and seeded

1 cup mixed herb leaves, such as parsley, mint, tarragon, and chives

2 radishes, thinly sliced

Preheat a grill over medium-high heat, to 350°F to 400°F. (Alternatively, use a cast-iron grill pan over medium-high heat.) Arrange the oiled asparagus and scallions and the lemons, cut side down, on the grill. Grill lemons, untouched, for 3 minutes, until nicely browned. Grill asparagus and scallions for 4 to 6 minutes, turning frequently, until cooked and slightly charred but not burned. Transfer to a plate.

To serve, place 4 pieces of grilled asparagus in a crisscross design on each plate. In a medium bowl, combine shaved asparagus, herbs, the 1 Tbsp olive oil, and a pinch of flaky salt and mix well. Mound a small nest of the mixture in the center of the grilled asparagus. Top with a soft-boiled egg and lean 1 or 2 grilled scallions on the nest. Arrange radishes and a few pickled asparagus slices around the edges. Place a charred lemon half on each plate for guests to squeeze over their entire dish.

SPRING PEA FARINATA
with Goat Cheese

CHEF: TIM PAYNE, COWHORN VINEYARD & GARDEN

Serves 3 to 6

½ cup fresh or frozen English peas

⅓ lb mild Italian sausage

¾ cup extra-virgin olive oil (divided)

1 cup chickpea flour

1 tsp salt, plus extra to taste

⅓ cup thinly sliced leeks, white and light green parts only

1 cup crumbled goat cheese (divided)

2 cups pea shoots or baby arugula (divided)

¼ cup mint leaves

1 small clove garlic, finely chopped

1 lemon, cut into wedges, to serve

Flaky sea salt, to serve

WINE PAIRING: Cowhorn Grenache

A favorite snack in the Italian and French Rivieras, farinata (also called *socca*) is akin to pizza or flatbread, but crispy outside, custardy inside, and made with chickpea flour and water. It goes great with almost any kind of toppings—in this case, goat cheese, sausage, and springy pea pesto.

Cowhorn's light-bodied Grenache, with its playful, bright red fruit balanced with nice acidity, counteracts the richness of the dish.

Preheat oven to 500°F.

Bring a small saucepan of water to a boil. Add peas and cook for 2 minutes. Drain, then rinse under cold water to stop the cooking. Set aside.

Sauté the sausage in a 12-inch cast-iron skillet over medium heat, breaking it up, for 5 minutes or until cooked through. Transfer to a paper-towel-lined plate to drain.

In a medium mixing bowl, combine chickpea flour, 1 tablespoon olive oil, salt, and 1 cup water. Whisk until smooth.

Wipe out the skillet and set over medium-high heat until hot. Turn off heat, add ¼ cup olive oil and swirl to thoroughly coat the bottom of the pan. Pour in chickpea batter, letting it spread to cover the bottom of the pan. Scatter sausage, leeks, and ½ cup goat cheese on top. Place in the oven and cook for 10 to 15 minutes, until set and browned at the edges. (If the middle still seems wet, place under the broiler for a minute or two.)

In a food processor, combine peas, 1 cup pea shoots (or baby arugula), mint, the remaining ½ cup goat cheese, and garlic. With the machine running, add ⅓ cup olive oil. Season to taste with salt.

In a small bowl, toss the remaining 1 cup greens with just enough olive oil to lightly coat.

Remove farinata from the skillet and cut into 6 slices. Place a spoon of the pea purée on each slice. Pile the dressed greens in the center. Serve with lemon wedges and flaky sea salt on the side.

DANCIN VINEYARDS

DAN AND CINDY MARCA

OWNERS

REGION
ROGUE VALLEY

In Hollywood, meet-cute stories rule in many films. Dan and Cindy Marca share their own movie-worthy tale that started in Monterey. In town for business, Dan asked a friend for restaurant recommendations. After scanning the hundreds of good options in her mind, his friend named two: Fandango and Peppers.

"It was March 1995 on a Sunday," says Dan, who remembers the day and each moment to a tee. He enjoyed an alfresco lunch at Fandango and on his way out, he noticed a beautiful server who wished him a good day. After a few more work meetings, he began his drive home to Sacramento but was diverted back to Monterey due to flooding that closed multiple highways. He checked back in to his hotel and decided to try the other restaurant his friend suggested.

After walking into Peppers, he glanced over at the bar and noticed the same young woman from Fandango was working as the bartender. They talked for an hour and scheduled a first date. It was kismet. "We were married three months later in June," says Dan.

Soon after, the newlyweds began taking wine and viticulture classes at UC Davis, eager to explore their shared love for food and wine. Because life is too short for should-haves, Dan and Cindy decided to take the leap into wine, and their search for vineyards in 1999 brought them to Oregon. "We scoured the entire state on multiple occasions and then discovered the majestic Rogue Valley," says Dan.

The region is prime for growing not only Pinot Noir and Chardonnay but also a smattering of Italian varieties like Barbera, Sangiovese, and Nebbiolo, which Dan pursues as an ode to his Italian roots.

Everything at DANCIN has a level of intention and detail that is delightful when revealed. All the wines are related to dance or music by name. The Pas de Chat Pinot Noir, for example, gets its name from a classical ballet term meaning "cat's step." And it's also named "in honor of the winery cat who loves to hunt in the block where those grapes grow," says Dan.

CACIO E PEPE BRUSSELS SPROUTS
with Toasted Hazelnuts

CHEF: DESIREE BAIRD, DANCIN VINEYARDS

Serves 6

½ cup hazelnuts

1 lb Brussels sprouts, halved

¼ cup extra-virgin olive oil (divided)

2 tsp salt (divided)

1 tsp black pepper, plus extra to taste (divided)

1 cup ricotta

¼ cup grated pecorino or Parmesan

Lemon juice or balsamic vinegar, to taste (optional)

WINE PAIRING: DANCIN Capriccio Chardonnay

Brussels sprout recipes so often include bacon, they can seem like a one-trick pony. But they're far more versatile than that. This version marries the nuttiness of the roasted sprouts with saltier cheeses, toasted Oregon hazelnuts, and black pepper. The Capriccio Chardonnay pairs well because its herbal notes play off the Brussels sprouts while crisp pear flavors complement the earthiness of the hazelnuts.

Preheat oven to 350°F.

Arrange hazelnuts in an even layer on a baking sheet and toast for 8 to 10 minutes, until golden. If they have brown papery skins, fold nuts into a clean dish towel while still hot and vigorously rub. Some skins will remain on, which is fine. Gently crush hazelnuts with a heavy bowl or pan until they split in half.

Increase heat to 400°F. Wipe the baking sheet clean. Spread Brussels sprouts on the baking sheet. Drizzle with 2 tablespoons oil, then add 1 teaspoon salt and ½ teaspoon pepper. Toss to coat. Arrange the sprouts in an even layer, cut side down. Roast for 30 to 40 minutes, until browned and tender when pierced with a fork.

In a small bowl, whisk together ricotta and the remaining 2 tablespoons oil, 1 teaspoon salt, and ½ teaspoon black pepper until smooth. Chill until ready to use.

Spread a generous spoonful of the ricotta on a large platter or individual plates. Arrange Brussels sprouts on top and sprinkle with hazelnuts. Top with pecorino (or Parmesan) and a pinch of black pepper. Drizzle with a little lemon juice (or balsamic vinegar), if using.

PLUM COBBLERS

CHEF: DESIREE BAIRD, DANCIN VINEYARDS

WINE PAIRING: Luna Notte Oregon Port Style Barbera

While there are many fruits that make their way into cobblers and crisps, plums offer the perfect balance of sweet and tart. Still, if you don't have plums, you can substitute 4 cups of any other fruit. Cherries, blackberries, or even a trio of blueberries, blackberries, and raspberries would all be delicious with the brambly fruit flavors of the Luna Notte Oregon Port Style Barbera.

Preheat oven to 350°F. Lightly butter six (6-oz) ramekins and place on a baking sheet.

In a bowl, combine plums, ¼ cup sugar, cinnamon, and vanilla. Divide mixture among the prepared ramekins.

In another bowl, whisk together flour, baking powder, salt, and the remaining ¾ cup sugar. Add egg and melted butter and mix until combined. Divide topping over the plums.

Bake for 30 to 40 minutes, until topping is evenly and lightly browned and plums begin to bubble. Let cool slightly.

Top each with a small scoop of ice cream and serve.

Serves 6

½ cup (1 stick) butter, melted, plus extra for greasing
12 plums, pitted and chopped (about 4 cups)
1 cup granulated sugar (divided)
1½ tsp ground cinnamon
1¼ tsp vanilla extract
1 cup all-purpose flour
1½ tsp baking powder
1 tsp salt
1 egg, beaten
Vanilla bean ice cream, to serve

DAY WINES

BRIANNE DAY
OWNER AND WINEMAKER

REGION
WILLAMETTE VALLEY

If there's one thing Brianne Day is known for, it's her adventurous spirit in wine. After all, during her most recent harvest, she worked with twenty-five grape varieties and over thirty vineyards. "I love experimentation, it's one of the best parts of the job," she says. "I get a big kick out of making something new."

Her gutsy journey into wine took flight in 2006, when she sold everything she owned and traveled to over eighty wine regions in the course of two years. Confident that wine was her destiny, she tacked on harvest stints in Burgundy, Argentina, and New Zealand. Back on her home turf in Oregon, she gained invaluable experience at wineries including the Eyrie Vineyards, GC Wines (page 136), and Brooks (page 74).

In 2012, Brianne made her inaugural wine, a Pinot Noir sourced from the Eola-Amity Hills. Since then, she's expanded her portfolio: in addition to pursuing expressive vineyard-designated Pinot Noir and Chardonnay, she pushes boundaries by making tiny batches of unexpected varietals such as Vermentino and Tannat.

One of her most popular bottlings is Tears of Vulcan, an orange wine blend of Viognier, Pinot Gris, and Muscat. "It's something I love making because there's no precedent for those varieties to be blended together," she says.

Since Brianne sources all of her grapes instead of growing her own, she has creative rein and considerable flexibility in terms of what she makes. She's currently co-fermenting Gamay and Dolcetto. "I'm going for a bright, juicy style. It's delicious," she says. A grape grower in Southern Oregon just planted Zibibbo, a Muscat from Sicily, and Nero d'Avola for her.

"As long as I can get a grower on board for these ideas, there's a huge amount of freedom and possibility that doesn't exist in more traditional wine-growing areas," Brianne says.

The offbeat grape varieties don't just capture her imagination. The wines sell out. "People get very jazzed up," she says. Perhaps *they* are tasting the sense of possibility, too.

CRISPY POTATO SALAD
with Peas and Smoked Mussels

CHEF: SARA HAUMAN, TINY FISH CO.

Serves 4 to 6

CHIMICHURRI VINAIGRETTE

Grated zest and juice of 1 navel
    orange
1 shallot, finely chopped
2 cloves garlic
Bunch of parsley, stems trimmed
⅓ cup oregano leaves, lightly
    packed
½ tsp salt
⅔ cup extra-virgin olive oil

CRISPY POTATO SALAD

1½ lbs new potatoes
    (baby potatoes), red potatoes,
    or fingerlings
Salt
2 Tbsp vegetable oil
1 cup fresh or frozen peas
1 can smoked mussels en
    escabeche
Oregano leaves, for garnish

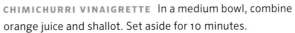

WINE PAIRING: Day Wines Tears of Vulcan

Chef Sara Hauman has worked in some of the most exhilarating wine-focused restaurants on the West Coast, but the bounty of the Pacific is what has really stolen her heart. In 2022, she launched Tiny Fish Co., her own line of sustainable, Northwest seafood packed with flavorful sauces in fetching cans, and she now spends her days dreaming up new ways to use them. The citrusy, floral, and mild fennel notes in Day Wines's Tears of Vulcan inspired this easy and herby potato salad topped with smoked mussels plumped in a tangy and spiced escabeche sauce. The chimichurri vinaigrette makes more than you need for one serving but it's versatile and can easily zest up a simple grilled fish the next day.

CHIMICHURRI VINAIGRETTE In a medium bowl, combine orange juice and shallot. Set aside for 10 minutes.

Using a food processor, mix the remaining ingredients together and pulse until smooth, scraping down the sides of the bowl as needed. Transfer mixture to the bowl of orange juice and shallot and stir together.

CRISPY POTATO SALAD Place whole potatoes in a medium saucepan, cover with water, and salt generously. Bring to a boil over high heat, then reduce heat to medium. Simmer for 20 to 45 minutes (depending on the size of your potatoes), until fork tender but not falling apart. Drain, then set aside to cool to room temperature. Slice in half.

Preheat oven to 475°F. Place a baking sheet on the center rack. When the oven is hot, remove baking sheet and coat with oil. Arrange potatoes cut side down on the baking sheet. Roast for 15 minutes, or until cut sides of potatoes are golden brown and crispy. Add peas to the baking sheet and return to the oven for 3 to 5 minutes, until the peas have warmed through.

Transfer potatoes and peas to a large bowl. Add chimichurri vinaigrette and toss to coat. Season with salt and arrange on a serving platter. Scatter smoked mussels on top and finish with oregano.

Crispy Potato Salad with Peas and Smoked Mussels (p.105)

DUCK BREASTS
with Umbrian Lentil Salad and Balsamic-Brown Butter Vinaigrette

CHEF: ERIK VAN KLEY, ARDEN

WINE PAIRING: Day Wines TNT Tannat

Earthy lentils and rich duck are a classic combination, and here acclaimed chef Erik Van Kley of Arden Wine Bar in Portland elevates the duo with a nutty-tangy brown butter vinaigrette and whipped goat cheese.

One of the first winemakers to scout out blocks of Tannat, Brianne Day uses this up-and-coming varietal in blends and this standalone wine. A robust red with gusto, the dark fruit and spices meld with this earthy and soulful duck dish.

BRINED DUCK BREASTS In a large container, stir salt and sugar into 4 cups water until dissolved. Add duck breasts and refrigerate overnight (18 to 24 hours).

BALSAMIC-BROWN BUTTER VINAIGRETTE Melt butter in a medium saucepan over medium heat. Heat for 5 to 10 minutes, stirring occasionally, until milk solids sink to the bottom, turn golden brown, and smell nutty. Remove from heat.

Whisk in vinegars, soy sauce, and stock. Season with salt to taste. Keep warm. (Or refrigerate for up to 1 week and reheat over low heat when ready to serve.)

WHIPPED GOAT CHEESE In a food processor, or with a hand mixer, beat cheese and salt together until gently whipped.

LENTILS Preheat oven to 375°F.

Combine stock and bay leaf in a medium saucepan and bring to a boil. Season with salt to taste.

Place lentils in a large baking dish. Pour hot stock over lentils, cover with aluminum foil, and bake for 20 minutes, until liquid is absorbed and lentils are tender but not overcooked. If needed, cook for another 5 to 10 minutes. Remove bay leaf. Keep warm.

Serves 4

BRINED DUCK BREASTS
¼ cup salt
¼ cup granulated sugar
4 duck breasts

BALSAMIC-BROWN BUTTER VINAIGRETTE
½ cup (1 stick) butter
1 Tbsp balsamic vinegar
1 Tbsp sherry vinegar
1 Tbsp soy sauce
¼ cup duck or chicken stock
Salt, to taste

WHIPPED GOAT CHEESE
8 oz chèvre
½ tsp salt

LENTILS
5 cups duck or chicken stock
1 bay leaf
Salt, to taste
1 lb Umbrian lentils or French
green lentils, rinsed

4 Brined Duck Breasts (see here)

Lentils (see here)

6 figs, quartered

1 lb red grapes, halved (about 2¾ cups)

2 scallions, sliced (about ¼ cup)

¼ cup chopped Italian parsley

¼ cup chopped pistachios

¼ cup pomegranate seeds

½ cup lemon juice, or to taste

½ cup extra-virgin olive oil, or to taste

Salt, to taste

Whipped Goat Cheese (see here)

Balsamic–Brown Butter Vinaigrette (see here)

ASSEMBLY Remove breasts from brine and pat dry. Using a sharp knife, carefully score skin by making diagonal cuts about ¼-inch apart (avoid cutting meat).

Place duck breasts skin side down in a large skillet. Gently cook over medium-low heat for 15 minutes, or until the skin is crisp and brown. Turn the breasts over, cover, and cook for another 3 to 5 minutes, until the internal temperature reaches 135°F to 140°F for medium-rare (it should still be pink in the middle). Transfer duck to a cutting board and tent with aluminum foil. (The rendered fat can be saved, refrigerated, for another use.)

In a salad bowl, combine warm lentils with figs, grapes, scallions, parsley, pistachios, and pomegranate seeds. Gently toss to combine. Drizzle with lemon juice and olive oil, toss again, and season to taste with salt.

With the back of a large spoon, smear the whipped goat cheese on a serving platter. Spoon lentil salad on top.

Slice each duck breast into 6 to 8 slices and arrange on top of the lentil salad. Drizzle with balsamic–brown butter vinaigrette and serve.

DIVISION WINEMAKING COMPANY

KATE NORRIS AND THOMAS MONROE
CO-OWNERS AND WINEMAKERS

REGION: PORTLAND

Inspired by deep memories of wine-centric dinner parties growing up and post-college jaunts to Napa and Sonoma, Thomas Monroe and Kate Norris dove into the world of winemaking together. They learned their trade working with wineries tucked in villages in France's Loire Valley and Beaujolais regions, gaining an education glass by glass and developing their winemaking style in the process. "I wasn't sucker-punched by wine until I had certain ones in France," says Tom.

But the two creatives balked at France's strict regional regulations, so when they were finally ready to strike out on their own, they headed to the place where Old World varieties merged with New World sensibilities. "Oregon has the right climate in terms of both humans and what Mother Earth is doing to grow the wines I want

to drink," says Kate. In her view, this region has "the weather, the culture, the focus on food and wine, and quality and appreciation."

Tom adds, "It was about bringing what I thought were the best wines that I've had, meshing that with the American spirit of choice, and being able to make whatever I want."

But instead of settling in the country, they launched Division Wine Company right in the middle of Portland in 2010, setting up an urban winemaking facility called Southeast Wine Collective that also served as an incubator for dozens of other winemakers. "The words 'urban winery' weren't in our

lexicon," Kate says. "The idea was to open a winery in the area we live in and be a part of the community."

In the years since, they've earned a reputation for embracing less understood French grapes, the varieties they fell for the hardest in France, and giving them a deliciously lively, playful, and often world-class presentation. "Tom and I make almost thirty wines. We're not scared of trying new things and pushing ourselves. Our focus is delicious variety and immense enjoyability. Sometimes just finding those varieties is the hardest part."

ÉPOISSES JUICY LUCY BURGERS

CHEF: ANDREA SLONECKER

Serves 4

WINE PAIRING: Division Lutte Gamay Noir

Versatile Gamay really shines in summer—light, bright, and bursting with fresh berry notes. It's fabulous at cutting through the richness of beefy burgers and decadent soft-ripened cheeses like savory Époisses. This recipe brings both together into a match made in Gamay heaven. Inspired by Minneapolis's famed cheese-stuffed burgers, chef and cookbook author Andrea Slonecker (who is also winemaker Tom Monroe's wife and the talented stylist behind the gorgeous food in this book) layers on even more decadence with bright tomato jam, pickled onions, and cornichon-flecked burger sauce.

PICKLED RED ONIONS

1 small red onion, thinly sliced into rings

1 tsp granulated sugar

½ tsp salt

⅓ cup champagne vinegar or white wine vinegar

ÉPOISSES JUICY LUCY BURGERS

1½ lbs lean (80/20) ground beef

Salt and black pepper

4 oz Époisses cheese, cold (see Note)

¼ cup mayonnaise

2 Tbsp Dijon mustard

1 Tbsp finely chopped cornichons

4 brioche burger buns

2 Tbsp butter, softened

4 leaves butter lettuce

4 thick slices heirloom tomato

¼ cup Pickled Red Onions (see here)

¼ cup store-bought tomato jam (such as Girl Meets Dirt)

NOTE Époisses is a soft, pungent, washed-rind cheese. If you can't find it (or it's too odiferous for you), taleggio is a good substitute.

PICKLED RED ONIONS Combine all ingredients in a medium bowl. Set aside for 1 hour, stirring occasionally, until onions are pickled. (Can be made 1 week in advance and refrigerated.)

ÉPOISSES JUICY LUCY BURGERS Preheat a grill over medium-high heat.

Divide beef into 8 equal portions. On a baking sheet, pat each portion into 4-inch patties about ¼-inch thick. Sprinkle both sides generously with salt and pepper. Keeping the rind on, cut cheese into 4 equal portions and mold each into a 1½-inch disk. Place one disk in the center of 4 patties. Top with the other 4 beef patties, using a spatula to lift them off the baking sheet. Pinch the seams together to fully enclose the cheese.

In a small bowl, combine mayonnaise, mustard, and cornichons. Set aside.

Brush cut sides of burger buns with butter. Set aside.

Grill burgers for 2½ minutes on each side, until both sides are nicely charred. Avoid pressing on the burgers too firmly and squeezing out the cheese. About 1 minute before the burgers are done, place buttered buns on the grill, cut sides down, to toast.

To assemble, generously spread cornichon sauce on the bottom buns. Layer with lettuce, tomato, burger patty, and a pile of pickled onions. Spread a thick layer of tomato jam on the top buns and set on top.

KALE SALAD
with Wine-Poached Currants and Candied Pepitas

CHEF: ALTHEA GREY POTTER, CULINARY PARTNER OF DIVISION WINEMAKING COMPANY

WINE PAIRING: Division Sauvignon Blanc

Serves 4

At Division Winemaking Company's beloved (though dearly departed) Oui Wine Bar, chef Althea Grey Potter became renowned for her highly flavorful, highly textural, and supremely delicious salads. Sweet, bright, nutty, and creamy, this salad quickly became the house favorite and it pairs wonderfully with Division's fruity-flinty Sauvignon Blanc. The lemon vinaigrette makes more than you need for one salad, but it's so versatile you'll be happy to have extra.

PICKLED RED ONIONS Place onion in a heatproof lidded container.

In a small saucepan, combine the remaining ingredients with ½ cup water. Bring to a boil over medium-high heat. Pour the hot liquid over the onions and set aside to cool, occasionally pressing onions to submerge. Cover and refrigerate overnight.

LEMON VINAIGRETTE Blend all ingredients except the oil in a food processor until well combined. With the machine running, slowly add oil in a thin steady stream until emulsified.

WINE-POACHED CURRANTS Combine all the ingredients in a small saucepan and bring to a simmer over medium heat. Simmer for 5 minutes, stirring occasionally, until the currants are plumped and the liquid is syrupy. Set aside to cool, then remove cinnamon stick and bay leaf.

PICKLED RED ONIONS
1 large red onion, halved and thinly sliced
2 bay leaves
2 sprigs thyme
¼ cup granulated sugar
1½ Tbsp salt
1½ tsp black peppercorns
1½ tsp whole allspice
½ cup red wine vinegar

LEMON VINAIGRETTE
Grated zest and juice of 1½ lemons
1½ tsp pure maple syrup
2 Tbsp apple cider vinegar
2 Tbsp Dijon mustard
1 clove garlic
1 small shallot
Pinch of red pepper flakes
1 cup extra-virgin olive oil

WINE-POACHED CURRANTS
¼ lb dried currants
1 bay leaf
1 cinnamon stick
1 Tbsp granulated sugar
½ cup red wine

CANDIED PEPITAS

Olive oil, for greasing
½ lb raw pepitas
2 Tbsp salt
1½ tsp smoked paprika
2 Tbsp pure maple syrup
½ cup packed brown sugar

SALAD

8 cups lacinato kale,
    stemmed and very thinly sliced
½ cup Lemon Vinaigrette
    (see here)
Salt and black pepper, to taste
2 beets, cut into matchsticks
    (1 cup)
¾ cup roughly crumbled sheep's
    milk feta
½ cup Candied Pepitas (see here)
½ cup Pickled Red Onions,
    drained (see here)
¼ cup Wine-Poached Currants
    (see here)

CANDIED PEPITAS Preheat oven to 325°F. Lightly oil a mixing bowl and a baking sheet.

In a small bowl, combine pepitas, salt, and smoked paprika. Add maple syrup and mix until seeds are coated. Spread onto the prepared baking sheet. Bake for 30 minutes, stirring every 10 minutes, until lightly toasted.

Scrape seeds into the prepared mixing bowl, then set aside to cool for just 3 minutes, so the seeds are still warm. Stir in brown sugar. Using your hands, massage sugar into the seed mixture and break apart any clusters. Set aside to cool completely. Using a colander, shake off excess sugar.

SALAD In a large bowl, combine kale, lemon vinaigrette, salt, and pepper. Gently massage dressing into kale to tenderize it. Add the remaining ingredients and toss gently to combine.

Note: All components can be refrigerated in airtight containers for 1 week.

DURANT VINEYARDS

PAUL DURANT
WINEMAKER

REGION
WILLAMETTE VALLEY

For a lucky few, destiny is close to home. Paul Durant grew up riding tractors and picking grapes on his family farm in the Dundee Hills. He left for over fifteen years, building a career as a mechanical engineer. "But I always wanted to farm and knew I'd return at some point," he says.

Back in 1973, his parents, Ken and Penny Durant, planted some of the first grape vines in the state. Today, the family manages over sixty acres of vineyards, selling most of their fruit to neighboring winemakers, while also producing a small amount of Pinot Noir, Chardonnay, and a beautiful rosé bottled under the Durant label.

But this family of agricultural explorers has a rich legacy that extends well beyond wine. In the 1980s, Penny Durant, the matriarch of the family, created a destination nursery. Cascading wisteria enchants in the spring, and come summer you'll find heirloom herbs and over forty varieties of lavender.

"Land is a great passion of hers," says Paul. And when his mother became fascinated by olive trees, he and his father planted a few thousand for her in 2004. Today, the grove totals around 13,000 olive trees and is the largest in the state. Durant Vineyards is the first place in Oregon where you can see the old Italian proverb "Grow grapes for your children and olives for your grandchildren" come to life.

Always in motion, the family founded the only olioteca in the Pacific Northwest in 2008. After purchasing a small Italian olive mill, Paul trained with master miller Duccio Morozzo della Rocca for two seasons.

"What I loved most was learning the cultural history of olives and olive oil," he says. "Both wine and olive oil are such ancient crafts." One of the rituals the family adopted from Italy is the Olio Nuovo Festival, where millers invite the community to taste the freshly pressed olive oils. "We look forward to this event every year," says Paul. "It's the perfect way to celebrate the harvest season with family and friends."

PASTA AGLIO E OLIO

CHEF: PAUL DURANT, DURANT VINEYARDS

Serves 4

1 lb spaghetti or linguine
½ cup garlic-infused olive oil
   (preferably Durant Olive Mill
   Garlic-Fused Olive Oil), plus
   extra for finishing
3 cloves garlic, finely chopped
1½ tsp red pepper flakes,
   or to taste
¾ cup finely chopped Italian
   parsley
Salt and black pepper, to taste
1 cup grated Parmesan

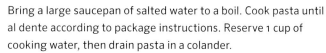

WINE PAIRING: Durant Vineyards Southside Chardonnay

With a recipe this simple, success is determined by the quality of the ingredients. Paul Durant uses his family's garlic-infused olive oil, milled from their estate-grown trees. Of course, a different garlicky olive oil will do, or you can increase the amount of fresh garlic and use regular extra-virgin olive oil. Either way, these classic noodles are a comfort dish in any season. Elevate the pasta with Durant's full-bodied Southside Chardonnay. The white wine brims with citrus, stone fruit, and toasted almonds, bringing a medley of flavors that marry perfectly on the palate.

Bring a large saucepan of salted water to a boil. Cook pasta until al dente according to package instructions. Reserve 1 cup of cooking water, then drain pasta in a colander.

Meanwhile, heat a large skillet over medium-low heat. Add olive oil and garlic and sauté for 3 minutes, until garlic softens and starts to turn golden. (Be careful not to let it brown.) Add red pepper flakes and parsley and cook for another minute. Add the reserved pasta water and simmer for 5 minutes, until slightly thickened.

Add cooked pasta to the pan and toss to coat. Simmer for 2 minutes. Season to taste with salt and pepper. Divide among bowls or plates and top with Parmesan. Drizzle with more garlic-infused oil if desired.

HERB-CRUSTED ROAST LEG OF LAMB

CHEF: PENNY DURANT, DURANT VINEYARDS

WINE PAIRING: Durant Vineyards Bishop Pinot Noir

Serves 6 to 8

For the juiciest and most flavorful leg of lamb, roasting on the bone is the way to go. But that makes carving not so fun. Penny Durant offers this savvy solution: just ask the butcher to cut the bone out and put it back in. Inspired by herbs that thrive around the Durant property, Penny gives the roast a generous shower of rosemary and dried thyme and, of course, ample olive oil from the family's trees. Pinot Noir is always an ideal pairing for lamb, as it won't overwhelm the meat's quintessential flavor. Durant's Bishop Pinot Noir, with its warm spices on the nose and cranberry notes on the palate, is an ideal match.

1 (7- to 8-lb) leg of lamb (ask butcher to debone it, put the bone back inside, and tie the roast)

5 large cloves garlic, thinly sliced

½ cup plus 1 Tbsp extra-virgin olive oil (preferably Durant Olive Mill Frantoio) (divided)

2 Tbsp plus 2 tsp dried thyme leaves (divided)

2 Tbsp plus 1 tsp rosemary leaves, plus extra sprigs for garnish (divided)

2 Tbsp plus 1 tsp black pepper (divided)

2 tsp ground coriander

30 red new potatoes, quartered

1 tsp coarse salt

Preheat oven to 425°F. With the tip of a sharp knife, cut slits all over the lamb. Insert the garlic into the slits, then brush lamb with ¼ cup of olive oil.

In a small bowl, combine 2 tablespoons each of thyme, rosemary, pepper, and all of the coriander. Pat the herb mixture all over the lamb to form a crust. Place the lamb in a shallow roasting pan.

In a large mixing bowl, combine potatoes, the remaining 5 tablespoons of olive oil, 2 teaspoons thyme, 1 teaspoon rosemary, 1 teaspoon pepper, and salt. Arrange around the lamb.

Roast on the center rack in the oven for 45 minutes. Gently stir potatoes occasionally to prevent them from sticking to the pan. Reduce heat to 375°F and roast for another 30 minutes, until a meat thermometer inserted in the thickest part of the lamb registers 120°F for rare.

Loosely tent lamb with aluminum foil and set aside for 15 minutes to rest. (The meat will continue to cook a bit more, and the temperature will rise to 135°F to 140°F.) Carve roast and arrange on a serving platter, surrounded by potatoes. Garnish with rosemary sprigs.

ERATH WINERY

LEAH ADINT
WINEMAKER

REGION
WILLAMETTE VALLEY

She grew up in a place better known for its wolves than its wines, and yet by the time she graduated high school, Anchorage native Leah Adint knew she wanted to be a winemaker.

As a young woman with unquenchable wanderlust, she saw winemaking as her ticket to travel, a career that would allow her to explore the people, places, and foods of the world—things she watched her dad, who worked in wine sales, enjoy. But the clincher was the science. "My favorite part is the microbiology," she says, "the yeast and bacteria that make the fermentation happen."

After earning her bachelor's degree in viticulture and enology from Washington State University, Leah immediately made good on her goal to globe-trot, first working harvests in Napa and Sonoma, then relocating to Australia, where

she earned her master's in enology at the University of Adelaide in 2012. A few years later, with harvests around Australia and even Burgundy, England, and Switzerland under her belt, she returned to the U.S. to join the team at Ste. Michelle Wine Estates as a traveling winemaker.

It was the perfect position for the incessant explorer, but when the company offered her the opportunity to put down roots in Oregon as a winemaker at Erath in early 2021, she didn't hesitate. The chance to carry on the legacy of one of Oregon's pioneering wineries was impossible to resist. "The history at Erath is part of the history of the Willamette Valley.

It all started with this small group of winemakers who were like, 'I'm going to do something different because I believe in it,' and one of them was Dick Erath."

That independent spirit drives Leah too, earning her the head winemaker role in 2022. "My approach is: what stands out about the vineyard and how do I accentuate it?" she says. "It's exciting to discover what we can do to make one wine stand out from another. I want to pull the different winemaking levers, and they don't have to be big levers, to get something really different."

WILD MUSHROOM RISOTTO
with White Truffle Oil

COURTESY OF: STE. MICHELLE WINE ESTATES

Serves 4 to 6

6 cups chicken or vegetable stock

3 Tbsp olive oil (divided), plus extra if needed

¼ cup chopped pancetta (about 1½ oz)

1 lb mixed button and wild mushrooms, cleaned and chopped

Salt and black pepper, to taste

½ onion, diced

½ fennel bulb, diced

3 cloves garlic, finely chopped

1 tsp porcini powder (see Note)

2 cups arborio rice

½ cup Pinot Noir

½ cup grated Parmesan

2 Tbsp chopped Italian parsley

2 tsp grated lemon zest

1 tsp chopped thyme

1 tsp white truffle oil

NOTE Porcini powder is available at well-stocked spice shops and gourmet markets. You can make your own by grinding dried porcini in a spice grinder or using a mortar and pestle.

WINE PAIRING: Erath Knight's Gambit Pinot Noir

Pinot Noir and mushrooms make a classic pairing, as the earthiness of each complements the other. Here, mushrooms take center stage in a simple, creamy risotto just begging for the dark berry notes and zesty brightness of Erath's Knight's Gambit Pinot. It features wild and cultivated mushrooms, porcini powder, and truffle oil for a triple hit of fungi flavor. Although the pancetta adds porky depth, you can skip it to make this dish vegetarian—just go a little harder on the porcini powder to fill that savory niche.

Bring stock to a simmer in a large saucepan over medium-high heat. Reduce to low, cover, and keep warm.

Heat 1 tablespoon olive oil in a wide, deep skillet or Dutch oven over medium-high heat. Add pancetta and sauté for 4 to 5 minutes until crisp. Using a slotted spoon, transfer pancetta to a paper-towel-lined plate.

To the same skillet, add about half the mushrooms in an even layer, season with salt and pepper, and sauté for 5 minutes, or until well browned. Transfer to the plate of pancetta. Repeat with the remaining mushrooms, adding more oil if necessary.

Add 1 tablespoon olive oil, onion, and fennel to the skillet. Sauté over medium-high heat for 7 minutes, or until vegetables are translucent. Add garlic and porcini powder and cook for another 1 minute. Reduce heat to medium.

Add the remaining 1 tablespoon oil and the rice and sauté for 1 minute. Pour in Pinot Noir and 1 cup stock. Cook, stirring, until the liquid is absorbed. Add ½ cup of stock and stir for 3 to 5 minutes, until stock is absorbed. Repeat until all of the stock is used and rice is tender, or al dente, about 18 minutes. Stir in pancetta and mushrooms.

Turn off heat. Stir in Parmesan, parsley, lemon zest, thyme, and truffle oil. Season with salt and pepper to taste.

BUTTERMILK CHICKEN PICCATA
with Caper–Brown Butter Sauce

CHEF: TRAVIS WESTROPE, STAG'S LEAP WINE CELLARS

WINE PAIRING: Erath Willakia Vineyard Chardonnay

Serves 4

A bath in buttermilk keeps these breaded chicken cutlets incredibly juicy, while the pan sauce of nutty browned butter, briny capers, and tart lemon makes them downright irresistible. Erath's Willakia Vineyard Chardonnay offers enough bright, citrusy acidity to cut through the richness and echo the dish's lemony vibe, with notes of hazelnut tying in those browned butter flavors.

CHICKEN MARINADE Cut each chicken breast in half horizontally to make two thinner fillets.

In a nonreactive bowl, combine buttermilk, garlic, half the shallots, tarragon (or Italian parsley), and half the lemon slices. Add chicken and toss to coat. Cover and refrigerate for 2 hours or overnight.

BREADING Preheat oven to 400°F. Set a rack on a baking sheet and place nearby.

Drain chicken, discarding the marinade.

Combine all the breading ingredients in a medium bowl. Toss chicken, one piece at a time, in the flour mixture to thoroughly coat. Shake off excess, then place on rack.

Heat ½ inch of oil in a large skillet over medium-high heat to a temperature of 350°F. Working in batches, carefully add chicken in a single layer. Fry for 3 minutes, or until golden brown at the edges. Turn over and cook about 1½ minutes more. Transfer to a baking sheet. Repeat with the remaining chicken. Place chicken in the oven and bake for 10 to 12 minutes.

CAPER–BROWN BUTTER SAUCE Meanwhile, drain all but 1 tablespoon oil from the skillet. Add remaining sliced shallots and sauté over medium heat for 2 minutes, or until beginning to brown. Add Chardonnay, stirring to scrape up the browned bits, and cook until nearly evaporated.

Add butter and increase heat to high. Allow white milk solids of butter to settle to the bottom of the pan and cook for 3 to 5 minutes, until golden brown. Add capers, lemon slices, and heavy cream, if using. Remove from heat.

Divide chicken among plates and spoon sauce on top. Garnish with herbs, Parmesan, and/or more lemon slices, if desired. Season with salt to taste and serve with salad.

CHICKEN MARINADE
4 (6- to 8-oz) boneless skinless chicken breasts
2 cups buttermilk
5 cloves garlic, thinly sliced
3 shallots, thinly sliced (divided)
2 sprigs tarragon or Italian parsley, roughly chopped
1 lemon, thinly sliced (divided)

BREADING
2 cups white rice flour
1 cup almond flour
½ cup all-purpose flour
2 tsp salt
2 tsp cornstarch
1 tsp baking powder
Black pepper, to taste
Vegetable oil, for frying

CAPER–BROWN BUTTER SAUCE
Reserved shallots
¼ cup Chardonnay
½ cup (1 stick) butter
1 (2-oz) jar capers, drained
Reserved lemon slices
2 Tbsp heavy cream (optional)
Herbs, grated Parmesan, and lemon slices, for garnish (optional)
Salt, to taste
Arugula salad, to serve

FULLERTON WINES

ERIC, SUSANNE, AND ALEX FULLERTON

REGION: PORTLAND

In college, Alex Fullerton studied economics, but his passion was to geek out over the science of fermentation—or, as he admits now, to brew his own beer. All that changed on an epic father-son trip to Burgundy following his graduation. Tracing the route his father took decades earlier, they arrived at Domaine Mouton in Givry late one afternoon.

The gates were closed and as they were turning to leave, the winemaker came bounding down the stone pathway. He was in the middle of a family dinner but persuaded them to stay. "We tasted wine in the cellar with him for hours," says Alex. "That was the moment I caught the wine bug."

While those French wines were exquisite, what Alex remembers most is the vintner's generous spirit and hospitality—attributes he thinks define the wine industry overall. A few weeks later, when Alex and his father Eric, a long-time wine collector, returned to Oregon, they found themselves in the Willamette Valley. Tasting wines.

Alex was musing to his father, how do you even get started in the wine business? Minutes later, a fortuitous encounter with winemaker Lynn Penner-Ash revealed a last-minute harvest internship. And Alex returned to the winery the very next day to jumpstart his wine career.

In 2011, he and Eric made a few barrels of Pinot Noir in the family garage and the family-run Fullerton Wines was born. Today, their focus is on crafting single-vineyard Pinot Noirs, one from each of the eleven sub-appellations in the Willamette Valley. In 2017, they opened a wine bar and tasting room in Northwest Portland. "Our model was to bring wine country to the city," says Eric. "A place where you can taste the diversity of the Willamette Valley in one spot."

GRAVLAX
with Mustard-Dill Sauce

CHEF: SUSANNE FULLERTON, FULLERTON WINES

Serves 8 to 10

GRAVLAX
1 (2-lb) salmon fillet, skin on and bones removed (see Note)
½ cup salt
½ cup granulated sugar
2 Tbsp crushed white peppercorns
Large bunch of dill

MUSTARD-DILL SAUCE
¼ cup Dijon mustard
1 Tbsp granulated sugar, or to taste
2 tsp white wine vinegar
1 cup vegetable oil
1 tsp white pepper
½ tsp salt
¼ cup chopped dill

ASSEMBLY
Rye bread, to serve
Salted butter, to serve
Butter lettuce, to serve
Dill sprigs, for garnish
Lemon slices, for garnish

NOTE To be safe, use commercially frozen salmon and thaw before using. If using fresh salmon and your freezer has a setting below -4°F, you can freeze it yourself for 7 days to kill any parasites.

WINE PAIRING: Fullerton Bjornsen Vineyard Pinot Noir

It takes no skill or special equipment to make your own gravlax, and not even much effort. All you need is time—about three or four days in the refrigerator—and the result is silky and delicately dilly fish that's ideal for serving atop slices of rye bread with a traditional Swedish mustard sauce. While crisp white wines are often matched with gravlax, Fullerton's elegant Bjornson Vineyard Pinot Noir, with its mixed berry flavors and supple tannins, plays off the richness of the salmon.

GRAVLAX Trim away the thin tail portion of the salmon fillet to create a mostly even fillet of mostly even thickness. (Refrigerate the trim for another use, if you like.) Cut the fillet in half.

In a small bowl, combine the salt, sugar, and crushed peppercorns.

Put one piece of the salmon skin side down in a wide glass dish. Cover with half the salt mixture and all of the dill. Cover the second piece of salmon with the remaining salt mixture. Place face down on top of the salmon in the dish, so the seasoned sides are touching. Cover just the salmon with plastic wrap, then set a plate on top and weight with heavy cans. Refrigerate for 12 hours.

Turn the fillets over. Replace the weights and refrigerate for another 12 hours. Repeat 1 to 2 more times. The salmon will be cured in 36 hours.

Scrape off all the salt mixture and dill and pat the salmon dry. Wrap the salmon in plastic wrap and refrigerate for 1 to 2 days.

Using a very sharp knife, remove the salmon skin and cut the fillets into thin slices. The traditional cutting technique starts diagonally at one corner of the salmon working towards the center and the opposite corner.

MUSTARD-DILL SAUCE Combine mustard, sugar, and vinegar in a small bowl. Whisk in the oil in a slow, steady stream until emulsified. If necessary, add a teaspoon of cold water to thin out. Season with pepper and salt and more sugar, if desired. Stir in dill. (Can be made 3 days ahead and refrigerated.)

ASSEMBLY To serve, spread slices of rye bread with butter. Add a piece of lettuce, top with a slice of gravlax, and drizzle with mustard-dill sauce. Garnish with a dill sprig and a slice of lemon.

SWEDISH SHRIMP SALAD
on Rye Toast

CHEF: SUSANNE FULLERTON, FULLERTON WINES

WINE PAIRING: Fullerton Lux Chardonnay

Swedish-born Susanne Fullerton has prepared this classic dish for decades. It's a recipe that her mother would make and has been served as the first course at many dinners with family and friends. "In Sweden, they are served at every festive occasion and as often as possible," she says. In this version, she cuts the bread into rounds for easy serving at wine events, but notes that the traditional way is to leave the toast larger in size. It's a lovely nibble, particularly in spring and summer, paired with the bright citrus and ripe orchard fruit flavors found in Fullerton's Lux Chardonnay.

Combine shrimp, onion, chives, and dill in a medium bowl. Stir in mayonnaise, adding more if needed, until the mixture holds together. Add lemon zest and juice.

Cut bread into rounds, using a 2-inch cookie cutter.

Melt 1 tablespoon butter in a large skillet over medium-high heat. Add a single layer of bread and toast on both sides until golden. Repeat with the remaining butter and bread.

To serve, spoon a mound of shrimp salad onto each toast. Top each with about ½ teaspoon whitefish roe. Garnish with the small slices of lime (or lemon) and dill sprigs.

Serves 6 to 8

2½ cups bay shrimp, peeled and cooked

2 Tbsp finely chopped red onion

12 chives, finely chopped (about 1 Tbsp)

10 sprigs dill, chopped (about 2 Tbsp), plus extra sprigs for garnish

3 Tbsp mayonnaise, plus extra if needed

Grated zest of ½ lemon

1 Tbsp lemon juice

8 to 12 slices rye sandwich bread

2 Tbsp butter (divided)

2 oz whitefish roe

3 thin slices lime or lemon, for garnish

FURIOSO VINEYARDS

GIORGIO FURIOSO
OWNER

REGION
WILLAMETTE VALLEY

"No detail is too small to consider." That phrase peppers the conversation when Giorgio Furioso talks about wine, art, and architecture. Which is why it's no surprise that he's a virtuoso in all three. Giorgio started his art career as a ceramicist after graduating from the School of the Museum of Fine Arts at Tufts University. He continued his education, receiving an MFA at the School for American Crafts at Rochester Institute of Technology, eventually expanding into painting and sculpture.

After a decade of art and teaching at the university level, a growing family led him to parlay his artistic sensibilities into residential and commercial real estate, which is where he's spent the majority of his career, designing elegant buildings that fuse high style and function in the Washington, DC, area.

Born in Tagliacozzo in central Italy, Giorgio grew up steeped in the culture of food and wine. His most vivid memories from that time are of watching his father and grandfather, both named Vincenzo, make wine in the cellar for friends and family.

In 2013, when his long-ago dreams of winemaking were rekindled, a friend encouraged him to visit the Willamette Valley. "I was struck by how much the geography reminded me of Umbria," he says. "And every wine we tasted was amazing." The timing was right, and he bought an established vineyard and winery in the storied Dundee Hills.

It was the perfect opportunity to obsess over art and design as he set to transform the space. "I wanted it to be really contemporary but also to maintain the Northwest vocabulary," he says. Winemaker Dominique Mahé, originally from Brittany, France, heads the wine program, where the emphasis is on Pinot Noir and Chardonnay. "One thing that sets us apart is our focus on art and how it intersects with food and wine," says Giorgio. An artist at heart, when recently asked what art and wine offer humanity, Giorgio was quick to respond: "That's easy," he says. "One feeds the soul, one feeds the spirit."

Mamma Anna's Lasagna (p. 132)

MAMMA ANNA'S LASAGNA

CHEF: ANNA FURIOSO

WINE PAIRING: Furioso Anna Pinot Noir

This meatball-studded lasagna is adapted from that made by Giorgio Furioso's mother, Anna. The original recipe was handed down for five generations and now Anna's grandchildren carry on the tradition of making it. It uses hard-boiled eggs to add richness to the cheese filling without resorting to heavy béchamel, which makes the lasagna lighter and perfect for pairing with a light-bodied red like Pinot Noir. It's a comforting crowd-pleaser worthy of special occasion status when served with a bottle of Furioso's Anna Pinot Noir, an elegant and silky small-lot wine with dark fruit and earthy notes.

TOMATO SAUCE Purée tomatoes and basil in a blender or food processor.

Heat oil in a large saucepan or Dutch oven over medium heat. Add onion, carrot, and celery and sauté for 5 to 7 minutes, until tender. Add garlic and sauté for another minute. Add puréed tomatoes and bring to a simmer. Reduce heat to medium-low and simmer gently, occasionally stirring, for about 30 minutes while you make the meatballs.

MEATBALLS Combine all the ingredients in a large bowl. Mix thoroughly by hand until well combined. Shape mixture into small, marble-sized meatballs (about ½ inch in diameter), adding them to the simmering sauce as you go. Simmer for 10 minutes after adding the last meatball, stirring occasionally. (Meatballs and sauce can be made 3 days ahead and refrigerated.)

Serves 8 to 10

TOMATO SAUCE

1 (28-oz) can whole peeled Italian plum tomatoes with purée
1 (14½-oz) can whole or diced Italian plum tomatoes with purée
1 cup packed basil leaves, roughly chopped
2 Tbsp extra-virgin olive oil
1 onion, chopped
1 large carrot, chopped
1 stalk celery, chopped
4 cloves garlic, finely chopped
Salt and black pepper, to taste

MEATBALLS

½ lb ground beef
½ lb Italian sausage, casings removed
½ cup dry breadcrumbs
½ cup freshly grated Parmesan
½ cup finely chopped Italian parsley
3 cloves garlic, finely chopped
1 egg
Salt, to taste
½ tsp black pepper

FILLING

8 hard-boiled eggs, roughly grated
16 oz fresh mozzarella, shredded
    (divided)
¾ cup freshly grated Parmesan
¾ cup freshly grated pecorino
1 tsp salt
½ tsp black pepper

ASSEMBLY

Butter, for greasing
Salt
1 lb fresh pasta sheets
1 cup reserved mozzarella
¼ cup freshly grated Parmesan
¼ cup freshly grated pecorino

FILLING Combine eggs, all but 1 cup of the mozzarella, Parmesan, pecorino, salt, and pepper in a medium bowl. Save the remaining mozzarella for topping. (Can be made 3 days ahead and refrigerated.)

ASSEMBLY Preheat oven to 375°F. Butter a 9- by 13-inch baking dish.

Bring a large saucepan of water to a boil and salt generously. Set a bowl of ice water nearby. Cook 2 to 3 sheets of pasta at a time for 1 to 1½ minutes. Remove from the hot water and place in the ice water to stop the cooking.

Lay the pasta on a clean towel and pat dry. Lay 2 sheets in the bottom of the pan, cutting to fit as necessary to create an even layer with some overlap.

Spoon about 1½ cups of sauce with the meatballs over the pasta, followed by 1½ cups of egg filling. Repeat with another layer of pasta, sauce, and filling. Repeat layering one or two more times until the pan is filled to the top, ending with a layer of pasta. Ladle the last of the sauce on the top.

Cover loosely with aluminum foil and bake for 45 to 60 minutes, until bubbling. Remove the foil, sprinkle with the cheeses, and bake 10 to 15 minutes, until cheese has melted and browned. Allow to cool for 10 to 20 minutes, then cut into squares and serve.

ROASTED RABBIT
with Mustard Sauce

CHEF: VITALY PALEY

WINE PAIRING: Furioso Chardonnay

Serves 4

Rabbit in a white wine mustard sauce is a Parisian classic, but acclaimed chef Vitaly Paley's version is smartly streamlined to make this entrée accessible for any weeknight meal. Look for rabbit hindquarters at good butcher shops, though you may have to order it in advance. The piquant mustard sauce enriched with crème fraîche pairs seamlessly with the bright and robust layers of tropical fruit and lemon zest in Furioso's lively Chardonnay.

4 rabbit hindquarters
Salt and black pepper
2 Tbsp extra-virgin olive oil
1 Tbsp butter
1 large onion, halved and
   thinly sliced
1 large carrot, sliced into
   ¼-inch-thick discs
4 sprigs thyme
1 bay leaf
¾ cup white wine
¾ cup chicken stock
3 Tbsp Dijon mustard
3 Tbsp crème fraîche
1 lb cooked egg noodles,
   for serving

Preheat oven to 375°F.

Season rabbit with salt and pepper. Heat oil and butter in a large cast-iron skillet over medium heat. Place rabbit in the skillet and turn it a few times, coating it in the butter and oil.

Scatter onion and carrot over and around the rabbit. Add thyme and bay leaf. Cover tightly with an ovenproof lid or aluminum foil and roast for 30 minutes. Uncover and roast for another 15 to 20 minutes to give the rabbit a bit of color.

Transfer the rabbit and vegetables onto a serving platter. Cover with foil to keep warm while finishing the sauce.

Pour wine and stock into the same skillet and simmer over medium heat for 10 minutes, or until reduced by half. Whisk in mustard and crème fraîche and bring to a boil. Pour sauce over rabbit and serve with cooked egg noodles.

GC WINES

JOHN GROCHAU
OWNER
AND WINEMAKER

REGION
WILLAMETTE VALLEY

While some winemakers are lured to the craft by the science, the farming, or the wine itself, for John Grochau the journey began with a love of food.

"My mother has always been a great cook," he says. "My parents taught me there's so much more flavor out there than I thought."

His early appreciation paved the way for an even broader culinary awakening while racing bikes in France as a young adult. When he returned to Oregon and was searching for a new career path, he gravitated to the restaurant industry and landed a job as a server and bartender at Portland's famed farm-to-table restaurant Higgins.

"Things with palate, flavor, and connections to farmers intrigued me," says John. "Higgins had a somm who was also a good teacher, so I started exploring wine more.

And when you're working in fine-dining adjacent to a good wine-producing region, you see a lot of winemakers come into the restaurant. I began to ask questions."

Soon he was learning the ropes as a volunteer, then a harvest intern, then landed year-round positions. In 2002, he was ready to start his own label, informed by the Old World varietals he enjoyed during his years in France.

"Pinot Noir is such an amazing varietal and transparent grape. It shows where it's from and the season. I want the nuances of the growing season reflected in the wine."

But John was too curious about flavor to focus on one grape. At GC Wines, he explores a wide range of varieties—Gamay, Pinot Blanc, Tempranillo, Syrah, Albariño, Melon de Bourgogne, and the list goes on.

No matter the grape, though, the goal is always the same: "It's always about food for me," he says. "That's why we make wines that are lighter bodied, wines with texture and structure both in acidity and tannin, because they are important to balancing foods. I'm always looking to bring out that energy in the wine, the effusiveness."

Grilled Octopus with Bloody Mary Vinaigrette (p. 138)

GRILLED OCTOPUS
with Bloody Mary Vinaigrette

CHEF: GREGORY SMITH

WINE PAIRING: GC Wines Melon de Bourgogne

Serves 4

Chef Gregory Smith's Bloody Mary–inspired dressing offers a zesty partner to charred and meaty octopus served on a piquant slaw of cabbage and pickled peppers. A common bycatch of the cod fishing industry, octopus can usually be found at well-stocked fishmongers and Asian markets. This recipe employs a sous-vide machine to slowly cook the tentacles until tender before grilling. (Or you can speed things up and opt for squid or shrimp instead.) GC Wines's Melon de Bourgogne provides a bright minerality that's perfect with seafood dishes like this.

PICKLED PEPPERS Place all the ingredients except the peppers in a medium saucepan. Add ¼ cup water and bring to a boil over high heat. Add the peppers, then remove from heat. Set aside to cool, then transfer to an airtight container and refrigerate until cold. (Can be made 1 week in advance.)

BLOODY MARY VINAIGRETTE Combine all the ingredients except the oils, salt, and pepper in a blender or food processor and purée. With the machine running, add the oils in a thin stream until emulsified. Season to taste with salt and pepper.

PICKLED PEPPERS
¾ cup white vinegar
¼ cup granulated sugar
3 cloves garlic, thinly sliced
1 tsp whole allspice
1 bay leaf
2 sprigs thyme
Salt, to taste
1 red bell pepper, deveined, seeded, and sliced
1 yellow bell pepper, deveined, seeded, and sliced
1 jalapeño pepper, sliced into rings

BLOODY MARY VINAIGRETTE
1 shallot
1 clove garlic
1½ tsp prepared horseradish
1¼ tsp granulated sugar
1 tsp dried dill
1 tsp celery seeds
1 tsp smoked paprika
¼ tsp red pepper flakes
⅓ cup tomato paste
¼ cup red wine vinegar
2 tsp Worcestershire sauce
Grated zest and juice of 1 lemon
½ cup extra-virgin olive oil
½ cup vegetable oil
Salt and black pepper, to taste

OCTOPUS

4 large octopus tentacles or
　3 lbs small octopuses,
　heads removed (see Note)
2 Tbsp extra-virgin olive oil,
　plus extra for greasing
6 cloves garlic, smashed
1 bay leaf
1½ tsp smoked paprika
2 tsp salt

CABBAGE SALAD

4 scallions, thinly sliced
¼ head red cabbage, finely
　shredded (5 cups)
Bunch of cilantro, leaves only
1 cup drained Pickled Peppers
　(see here)
½ cup Bloody Mary Vinaigrette
　(see here)
Salt and black pepper, to taste

NOTE The octopus can be replaced with 2 lbs jumbo shrimp, peeled and deveined, or 2 lbs squid bodies and tentacles (or a combination). In a large bowl, toss with ¼ cup Bloody Mary vinaigrette, 2 tablespoons lemon juice and 1 tablespoon salt. Allow to marinate in the refrigerator for 2 hours. Thread onto metal or pre-soaked wood skewers and grill for 1 to 2 minutes on each side, until just opaque.

OCTOPUS Bring a medium saucepan of salted water to a boil over high heat. Add octopus and simmer for 8 minutes. Place a large bowl of ice water near the stove. Using a slotted spoon or tongs, transfer octopus to the bowl of ice water to stop the cooking.

Pack the octopus into a large vacuum bag along with olive oil, garlic, bay leaf, paprika, and salt. Tightly seal using a vacuum sealer. (Alternatively, use a food-safe silicone ziptop bag and squeeze as much air out as possible.) Using a sous-vide machine, prepare a 175°F water bath. Add the bag of octopus and cook for 4 hours. (Can be made 1 day ahead and refrigerated.)

Preheat a charcoal grill over high heat. Brush the grates clean and lightly oil. Remove octopus from the bag and arrange on the grates. Cook 1 to 2 minutes per side, until charred.

CABBAGE SALAD Toss all ingredients together in a large bowl. Adjust salt, pepper, and vinaigrette to taste.

Divide among plates and top with grilled octopus. Drizzle with a little more vinaigrette and serve.

Caramelized Onion–Smothered
ROAST CHICKEN

CHEF: GREGORY SMITH

Serves 4 to 6

1 (4½-lb) whole chicken
3 Tbsp salt (divided)
1 head garlic
10 sprigs thyme
2 large yellow onions, halved and
    cut into ½-inch-thick slices
¼ cup chicken stock, plus extra
    if needed

WINE PAIRING: GC Wines Convivial Gamay–Pinot Noir

Be forewarned: Once you try this recipe, you won't want to roast chicken any other way. With this genius technique from private chef Gregory Smith, formerly a fixture behind the stoves of Portland's venerable Noble Rot restaurant, the oven does all the work, resulting in a juicy bird and a generous supply of caramelized onions to go with it. It's a heavenly, deeply comforting combo perfectly suited to GC Wines's lively Gamay–Pinot Noir blend.

Preheat oven to 425°F.

Salt the chicken, inside and out, with 2 tablespoons salt. (This can be done right before cooking or up to a day prior.) Cut the top third off the head of garlic to expose the cloves. Tuck it inside the cavity of the chicken, along with the thyme sprigs.

In a roasting pan, combine onions and the remaining 1 tablespoon salt and toss to mix. Set the chicken breast side down on the onions. Roast for 40 to 45 minutes or until the back is golden in color.

Remove chicken from the oven and reduce heat to 350°F. Turn chicken over and transfer to a plate. Pour stock into the pan and stir with the onions, scraping up any browned bits. Push the onions to one side and return the chicken to the pan, breast side up. Spoon the onions over the top of the chicken, covering the breast and legs. Roast for 30 to 45 minutes, basting the chicken every 15 minutes with juices from the pan, until a meat thermometer reads 165°F in the thickest part of the thigh. If the pan seems dry, add more stock.

Remove from the oven and tent with aluminum foil. Rest for 10 minutes, then carve and serve alongside the caramelized onions.

GRAN MORAINE

SHANE MOORE
WINEMAKER

REGION
WILLAMETTE VALLEY

Even though he's worked in wineries around the globe, Shane Moore says the best surprise he's ever had in the industry was discovering the wonders of Willamette Valley Chardonnay.

In 2016, when he joined the team at Gran Moraine, he remembers tasting through a series of Chardonnays from the area and being struck by how much the wines reminded him of white Burgundy. "It's a magical wine," he says. "More people need to know about it."

Today, Chardonnay is his favorite grape to work with. "You bring in beautiful fruit, you put it in a press, and it becomes something otherworldly," he says.

Born and raised in Idaho, Shane worked as a cellar rat throughout his college years in Coeur d'Alene, where his early mentors encouraged him to pursue a career in wine. He furthered his wine education while feeding his wanderlust, working at wineries around the world, including in Canada, Australia, and Israel's Golan Heights.

He found his way to California after he met his future wife during harvest in Margaret River, Australia, and the two returned to her Sonoma County roots, where Shane joined the Jackson Family Wines team in 2011. He jumped at the opportunity to work at their Oregon properties, including Gran Moraine.

"I love the Northwest because we can head out to the coast and go crabbing for the day on a whim," he says. In the fall, he and his wife forage for chanterelles. "Then we've got the best pairing for Chardonnay," he says: a simple brioche bun, piled with Oregon Dungeness crab, cheese, and chanterelles. "And lots of butter," he adds.

In addition to Chardonnay, Shane runs a focused sparkling and Pinot Noir program. The winery celebrated the inaugural release of their estate-grown 2014 Blanc de Blancs in 2021. Shane's overall goal with wine is to make something fun to enjoy with friends, but also a memorable experience.

"The best wines stop time," he says. "A great bottle of wine gives me that same feeling I get whenever I'm on a powder run, skiing, totally in the moment. And that's incredible."

SAFFRON RISOTTO
with Dungeness Crab and Scallops

CHEF: THOMAS GHINAZZI, EARTH & SEA

Serves 4

RISOTTO

5 cups fish, chicken, or veggie
    stock
2 Tbsp extra-virgin olive oil
1 yellow onion, finely chopped
2 cloves garlic, finely chopped
Pinch of saffron
1½ cups arborio or carnaroli rice
¾ cup dry white wine
Salt and black pepper, to taste

SCALLOPS

½ lb dry-packed sea scallops,
    side muscle removed
    (10 to 20; see Note)
Canola oil
Salt and black pepper, to taste

ASSEMBLY

2 Tbsp butter, cut into pieces
1 lemon, cut into wedges
Chopped tarragon, for garnish
2 oz lump Dungeness crabmeat

NOTE Scallops are often "wet-packed," which means they're treated with chemical additives such as phosphates that keep them fresher longer but also cause them to absorb more water. The water releases during cooking, causing the scallops to steam instead of sear. To avoid this, look for scallops labeled "dry-packed."

WINE PAIRING: Gran Moraine Yamhill-Carlton Chardonnay

The luxe earthiness of golden saffron risotto provides a grounding backdrop for some of the sweetest, most succulent seafood on the Oregon coast. It's one of chef Thomas Ghinazzi's all-time favorite dishes, and one that makes frequent appearances on his menu at Earth & Sea in Carlton. Gran Moraine's Yamhill-Carlton Chardonnay, with its medley of crisp kumquat, pear, and tangelo flavors, makes a beautiful match for this celebration of the sea.

RISOTTO Bring stock to a simmer in a saucepan over medium heat. Reduce heat to low, cover, and keep warm.

Heat oil in a wide, deep skillet or Dutch oven over medium-low heat. Add onion and gently sauté for 10 minutes, until translucent. Add garlic and sauté for 1 minute. Add saffron and cook for 1 minute. Increase heat to medium, add rice, and sauté for another minute.

Stir in wine and cook until liquid is absorbed. Add 1 cup of stock and stir until absorbed. Add ½ cup of stock and stir for 3 to 5 minutes, until stock is absorbed. Repeat until 1 cup of stock is left and rice is al dente. Turn off the heat. Season to taste with salt and pepper. Reserve the remaining stock to add before serving.

SCALLOPS Pat scallops dry. Heat a large, wide skillet over high heat until almost smoking. Add enough oil to cover the bottom of the pan. Add scallops and sear for 3 minutes, or until golden brown. Turn over and cook for another 3 minutes, or until cooked through.

ASSEMBLY Return risotto to medium heat. Add the remaining 1 cup stock and the butter. Stir until rice is tender and stock is absorbed. Divide among plates. Squeeze a lemon wedge over the risotto and sprinkle with tarragon. Top with crabmeat and scallops and serve.

143

DUNGENESS CRAB ROLLS
with Smoked Trout Roe and Hazelnut Dust

CHEF: JODY KROPF, RED HILLS MARKET

WINE PAIRING: Gran Moraine Brut Rosé

Lobster rolls reign on the East Coast, but we take a Dungeness crab approach here in Oregon. The sweet meat is more tender than lobster, and certainly more plentiful. Even farmers' markets offer fresh Dungeness crabmeat nearly year-round. Here, chef Jody Kropf, of Dundee's beloved Red Hills Market, brushes the rolls with butter infused with crab shells to layer on the flavor and mixes the crabmeat with the warm heat of Calabrian chili aioli. Gran Moraine's Brut Rosé, with its notes of wild strawberries, stone fruit, and a whisper of brioche, makes for a decadent pairing.

GARLIC–CALABRIAN CHILI AIOLI In a food processor, pulse garlic until finely chopped. Add egg yolks and pulse to combine. With the machine running, very slowly drizzle in oil to emulsify the mixture.

Add lemon juice, mustard, and chiles (or chili flakes). Season to taste with salt and pepper. If the aioli seems too thick, thin it out with cold water. (Aioli will keep for 7 days refrigerated.)

DUNGENESS CRAB ROLLS Combine crab shells (if using), butter, and saffron in a medium saucepan over medium heat. Cook for 10 minutes. If using shells, strain melted butter through a strainer into a bowl. Discard shells.

Preheat a large skillet over medium heat. Brush buns with the butter and toast cut side down until lightly browned. Set aside.

Place crabmeat in a medium bowl and pick through carefully to remove any shell fragments. Add celery, aioli, lemon juice, Worcestershire sauce, chives, and Old Bay seasoning. Gently mix, preserving big lumps of crab for texture. Season to taste with salt and pepper.

Fill toasted buns with crab mixture. If desired, warm briefly under a broiler or on a grill. Garnish with shiso leaves, trout roe, and a sprinkle of hazelnut dust. Serve with charred lemons.

Serves 4

GARLIC–CALABRIAN CHILI AIOLI
3 cloves garlic
2 egg yolks
2 cups canola oil
1 Tbsp lemon juice
½ tsp Dijon mustard
1 tsp chopped Calabrian chiles or chili flakes
Salt and black pepper, to taste

DUNGENESS CRAB ROLLS
8 oz crab shells, crushed (optional)
½ cup (1 stick) butter
Pinch of saffron, crushed
4 quality hot dog buns
1 lb lump Dungeness crabmeat (from about two 2-lb crabs)
½ cup roughly chopped celery hearts and leaves
½ cup Garlic–Calabrian Chili Aioli (see here)
1 Tbsp lemon juice
1½ tsp Worcestershire sauce
1½ tsp finely chopped chives
¾ tsp Old Bay seasoning
Salt and black pepper, to taste
½ cup thinly sliced shiso leaves (available at Asian markets)
2 Tbsp smoked trout roe
1 Tbsp finely crushed toasted hazelnuts
Charred lemon, sliced or cut into wedges, to serve

IDIOT'S GRACE WINERY

BRIAN MCCORMICK
WINEMAKER

REGION
COLUMBIA GORGE

"Food is a source of pleasure, three times a day at least," says Brian McCormick. It's a fitting philosophy from a man who grew up with a chef for a mom and never had the same dinner twice. But when Barbara McCormick gifted her son a book on wine in college he was "weirdly, suddenly captivated." Here was a whole world of craftsmanship to explore that could make one of his favorite forms of pleasure even *better*.

"The book pushed me to discover what wine does to food," he says. "Having it at the table, it brings food to another power."

That sense of curiosity drives Brian every day and every vintage. After completing his master's in horticulture at UC Davis and working as a vineyard manager in California's wine country for several years, he and his young

family, along with his parents, decided to venture north into new territory together, putting down roots in the Columbia River Gorge to see what would grow.

They started with Memaloose Winery and its vineyard on the Washington side in 2002, then established Idiot's Grace in Mosier a year later. Since then, Brian has planted nearly two dozen varieties, mostly Old World, with the goal of determining the handful that truly thrive in his family's particular patch of ground.

"It doesn't matter what you grow as long as you find something that connects with the ground," he says. "That's the magic—to have that site-specific harmony that's yours. Europe has taken centuries to figure it out and that's our long-term assignment here."

Brian dry farms organically, doing "as little as possible to produce grapes as interesting as they can be," he says. In the cellar, the discovery continues. "I'm aiming for a more impressionistic version of what's happening in the field. It's a record of an entire year's events and circumstances."

WINE-POACHED HALIBUT
with Beurre Rouge

CHEF: ANNE RIEDL, IDIOT'S GRACE WINERY

Serves 4

WINE-POACHED HALIBUT

1 (750-ml) Idiot's Grace Syrah Grenache

2 cups chicken, fish, or vegetable stock

2 cloves garlic, crushed

1 small onion, roughly chopped

1 stalk celery, roughly chopped

3 whole cloves

2 sprigs thyme

1 star anise

1 bay leaf

1 tsp black peppercorns

4 (6-oz) halibut fillets, skin and pin bones removed

Salt and black pepper

BEURRE ROUGE

½ cup (1 stick) butter (divided)

3 shallots, thinly sliced (about 1 cup)

½ tsp thyme leaves

½ tsp granulated sugar

1½ Tbsp raspberry vinegar or red wine vinegar

3 cups reserved poaching liquid

Salt and black pepper, to taste

ASSEMBLY

Mashed potatoes, to serve

Steamed green vegetables, such as broccoli rabe or asparagus, to serve

WINE PAIRING: Idiot's Grace Syrah Grenache

This elegant dish, served with creamy mashed potatoes and tender-crisp asparagus or broccoli rabe on the side, is perfect for a celebratory dinner. The robust poaching liquid uses the same silky Idiot's Grace Syrah Grenache the dish is paired with and forms the base for the buttery sauce so you don't waste a drop. Halibut is the ideal choice, but thick-cut, line-caught cod is more affordable and works well, too.

WINE-POACHED HALIBUT In a large saucepan or Dutch oven, combine all ingredients except the halibut, salt, and pepper and bring to a simmer over medium heat. Reduce heat to medium-low and gently simmer for 30 minutes. (Can be made a day in advance.)

Preheat oven to 170°F.

Strain poaching liquid and discard solids. Return the liquid back to the pan and gently simmer over medium-low heat.

Season the halibut fillets generously with salt and pepper on both sides. Add fillets to the pan, cover, then turn off the heat and set aside for 3 to 7 minutes to gently poach. (You want it slightly undercooked as it will be kept warm in the oven while you make the sauce and you don't want to overcook it.)

Transfer halibut to a baking sheet and baste with some poaching liquid. Keep warm in the oven. Reserve poaching liquid.

BEURRE ROUGE Melt ¼ cup (½ stick) of butter in a medium skillet over medium-high heat. Add shallots and sauté for 3 minutes, until they just start to take on color. Add thyme and sugar and cook for another minute. Add vinegar and simmer until reduced and syrupy. Add reserved poaching liquid, increase heat to high, and boil for 10 minutes, or until liquid is reduced to 1½ cups.

Remove from heat. Whisk in the remaining ¼ cup (½ stick) butter, a tablespoon at a time. The sauce will become thick and glossy. Season to taste with salt and pepper.

ASSEMBLY Place a scoop of mashed potatoes on each plate, nestle a poached halibut fillet on it, and spoon sauce on top. Position vegetables alongside.

MUSHROOM BOURGUIGNON

CHEF: ANNE RIEDL, IDIOT'S GRACE WINERY, ADAPTED FROM DEB PERELMAN

WINE PAIRING: Idiot's Grace Cabernet Franc

Serves 4

¼ cup extra-virgin olive oil (divided)

¼ cup (½ stick) softened butter (divided)

1 lb cremini mushrooms, sliced

1 lb wild mushrooms, roughly chopped

1 cup pearl onions, thawed if frozen and patted dry

Salt and black pepper, to taste

2 large shallots, finely diced (1 cup)

1 small carrot, finely diced

1 tsp chopped thyme leaves

2 cloves garlic, finely chopped

2 Tbsp tomato paste

1 cup full-bodied red wine such as Idiot's Grace Cabernet Franc

1½ Tbsp red wine vinegar

3 cups vegetable stock

1½ Tbsp all-purpose flour

Cooked egg noodles or polenta, to serve

Sour cream and chopped Italian parsley, for garnish

If you think a rich and savory bourguignon stew must have beef, think again. Anne Riedl, longtime tasting room manager at Idiot's Grace, adapted this dish from cookbook author Deb Perelman's incredibly popular recipe in *Smitten Kitchen* (2012), which has spawned innumerable variations over the years. This one adds a few twists, including a mix of wild mushrooms, a heap of shallots, and a splash of vinegar to wake up the flavors. The Cab Franc from Idiot's Grace, with its medium-high acidity, offers another perky enhancement to this earthy dish.

Heat 1 tablespoon olive oil and 1 tablespoon butter in a large, deep skillet over medium-high heat. Working in three batches so as not to crowd the pan, add mushrooms and pearl onions in a single layer and sauté for 5 minutes, until caramelized. Season with salt and pepper, then transfer to a plate. Repeat two more times with more butter and oil and the remaining mushrooms and pearl onions.

Heat the remaining 1 tablespoon olive oil in the same pan. Add shallots, carrot, and thyme, then season with salt and pepper to taste. Sauté for 10 minutes, until the onions are light brown. Add garlic and cook for 1 minute.

Add tomato paste and cook for 1 to 2 minutes, until it starts to caramelize on the bottom of the pan. Add wine and vinegar, scraping up the brown bits from the bottom of the pan. Increase heat to high and boil for 3 minutes, until reduced by half.

Stir in stock, then add mushrooms, pearl onions, and any juices. Bring to a boil, reduce heat to medium-low, and partially cover. Simmer for 40 minutes, until mushrooms are very tender.

In a small bowl, combine remaining 1 tablespoon butter and flour. Stir paste into the stew until dissolved. Simmer gently for another 10 minutes, stirring occasionally to prevent it sticking, until thickened. Season to taste with salt and pepper.

To serve, spoon stew over egg noodles (or polenta). Dollop with sour cream and sprinkle with parsley.

KING ESTATE WINERY

BRENT STONE
WINEMAKER

REGION
WILLAMETTE VALLEY

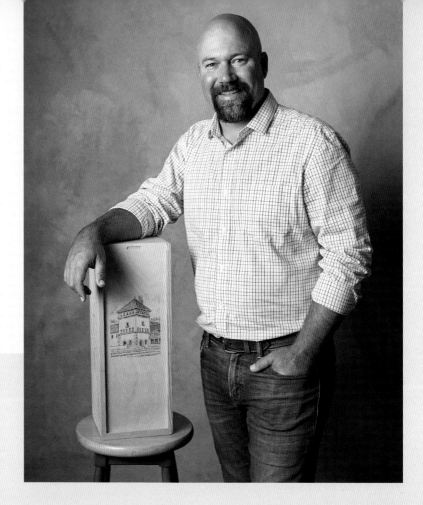

It's not that Brent Stone didn't enjoy applying his food science background to ice cream, but when given the opportunity to put his chemistry skills to use in wine, he jumped at the chance.

"I always had a passion for wine," he says. "And the allure of wine, for me, is a move away from the recipe-driven approach that you see in the food industry. With food, you want to make it the same every time. But with wine, particularly in Oregon, you're embracing the vintage and what the year gave you."

Brent joined King Estate in 2011, first as a lab manager and director of quality assurance. By 2016, his affinity for the grape quickly launched him into the role of winemaker for the state's third-largest winery. In 2018, he added chief operating officer to his role.

Although he has the entire day-to-day operations in his hands, he takes a hands-off approach in the cellar. "We do very little to manipulate the wine once the grapes arrive," Brent says. "The idea is to embrace vintage and embrace place. You want them to come across in the wine."

King Estate works with more than twenty-five varieties and half of its 1,033-acre estate is planted with vines. Another twenty-six acres grow produce and flowers for its destination restaurant. Even more impressive? Everything is biodynamically grown. "We're the largest certified biodynamic vineyard in North America. It's different from organic in that the whole property has to be certified, so it's a huge commitment to sustainability."

Brent says now that he's immersed in the art of winemaking in Oregon he can't imagine doing it anywhere else. "Every year is so exciting and terrifying at the same time, and that's the draw for us in Oregon—you see that vintage variation here more than in Washington or California. You have to take what comes and make it great every year, and there are new challenges every time. You never really master it, but you can continue to get better."

Beet and Burnt Honey Salad (p. 152)

BEET AND BURNT HONEY SALAD

COURTESY OF: THE RESTAURANT AT KING ESTATE

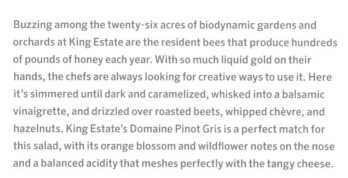

WINE PAIRING: King Estate Domaine Pinot Gris

Buzzing among the twenty-six acres of biodynamic gardens and orchards at King Estate are the resident bees that produce hundreds of pounds of honey each year. With so much liquid gold on their hands, the chefs are always looking for creative ways to use it. Here it's simmered until dark and caramelized, whisked into a balsamic vinaigrette, and drizzled over roasted beets, whipped chèvre, and hazelnuts. King Estate's Domaine Pinot Gris is a perfect match for this salad, with its orange blossom and wildflower notes on the nose and a balanced acidity that meshes perfectly with the tangy cheese.

Preheat oven to 350°F. Arrange hazelnuts in an even layer on a baking sheet and toast for 8 to 10 minutes, until golden. If they have brown papery skins, fold nuts into a clean dish towel while still hot and vigorously rub. Some skins will remain on, which is fine. Set aside.

Increase oven heat to 375°F. In a baking dish, combine unpeeled beets and enough oil to lightly coat. Season with salt and pepper. Add water to a ¼-inch depth and cover tightly with aluminum foil. Roast for 1 hour, or until beets are tender and easily pierced with a fork. Set aside to cool.

When cool enough to handle, peel beets and cut into ½-inch pieces. Transfer to a bowl and refrigerate until cold. (Can be prepared 2 days ahead and refrigerated.)

In a small saucepan, heat honey over medium-high heat for 5 minutes, or until dark amber but not black. While hot, carefully whisk in vinegar. Set aside to cool, then refrigerate for 1 hour, or until chilled. Whisk in olive oil and season to taste with salt. (Can be made 3 days ahead and stored in an airtight container.)

Serves 4

1 cup hazelnuts
1 lb beets, tops removed
Olive oil, for coating
Salt and black pepper, to taste
⅓ cup honey
⅔ cup balsamic vinegar
1 cup extra-virgin olive oil
6 oz chèvre, room temperature
¼ cup heavy cream
1 Tbsp thinly sliced chives
1 Tbsp finely chopped chervil
 or tarragon
1 Tbsp finely chopped Italian
 parsley
6 oz arugula (about 4 cups)

In a medium mixing bowl, combine chilled beets with enough dressing to coat.

In a small bowl, combine chives, chervil (or tarragon), and parsley.

Crush hazelnuts by pressing on them with the bottom of a heavy pan until most are in half, with some smaller pieces.

In a small mixing bowl, dress arugula with just enough dressing to lightly coat.

In another small mixing bowl, whisk chèvre and cream until spreadable. Using the back of a spoon, spread whipped chèvre in a circle along the bottom of the wall of four shallow bowls. Evenly sprinkle mixed herbs on the goat cheese.

Place dressed beets in a circle slightly overlapping the cheese, leaving the center of the bowls open. Top beets with ¼ cup hazelnuts per bowl. Place a small handful of arugula in a neat pile in the center and serve.

KING ESTATE CRAB CAKES
with Apple-Radish Slaw

COURTESY OF: THE RESTAURANT AT KING ESTATE

Makes 10

APPLE-RADISH SLAW

½ cup apple cider vinegar

¾ cup extra-virgin olive oil

1 Tbsp apple butter

½ tsp whole grain mustard

¼ tsp salt, plus extra to taste

½ Granny Smith apple, peeled, cored, and cut into matchsticks (1 cup)

1 bunch radishes, cut into matchsticks (1 cup)

1 small kohlrabi, peeled, cut into matchsticks (1 cup)

CRAB CAKES

1⅔ cups panko breadcrumbs

1 egg, beaten

3 Tbsp mayonnaise

2 Tbsp lemon juice

1½ Tbsp Dijon mustard

1½ Tbsp finely chopped herbs, such as chives, tarragon, and parsley

1 Tbsp grated lemon zest

1 lb lump Dungeness crabmeat (from about two 2-lb crabs)

¼ cup (½ stick) butter

Microgreens, for garnish

WINE PAIRING: King Estate Brut Cuvée

Crab cakes rarely leave the menu at the King Estate's restaurant. And they're a must whenever the winery hosts its annual crab fest for wine club members. Some crab cake recipes feature a long list of ingredients, but this one keeps it simple with the spotlight on the crab. Try pairing these crispy bites with a glass of bubbly, especially King Estate's biodynamically grown Brut Cuvée, which offers apple, hazelnut, and brioche notes that go wonderfully with the autumnal flavors of the slaw.

APPLE-RADISH SLAW In a small saucepan, simmer vinegar over high heat for several minutes, or until reduced to ¼ cup. Transfer to a jar with a lid. Allow to cool. Add oil, apple butter, mustard, and salt. Shake until emulsified.

In a mixing bowl, combine apple, radishes, and kohlrabi. Drizzle with just enough dressing to coat. Season to taste with salt. Leftover dressing will keep in the fridge for 1 week.

CRAB CAKES In a food processor, pulse panko a few times until finely ground. Transfer to a shallow bowl.

In a medium mixing bowl, combine egg, mayonnaise, lemon juice, mustard, herbs, and lemon zest and mix well. Fold in crab and ⅔ cup of the panko, taking care to keep some crab lumps intact.

Using a ¼-cup measure, scoop crab mixture and form into patties. Press each patty into the remaining panko crumbs to coat.

Melt butter in a large skillet over medium heat. Add crab cakes and cook for 3 minutes per side, until firm and browned. Transfer to a paper-towel-lined plate.

Garnish with microgreens and serve with apple-radish slaw on the side.

KNUDSEN VINEYARDS

PAGE KNUDSEN COWLES
OWNER AND
MANAGING PARTNER

REGION
WILLAMETTE VALLEY

When Page Knudsen Cowles remembers her father, C. Calvert "Cal" Knudsen, his love for cooking and wine are top of mind. "He was a longtime member of the Seattle Gourmet Society," she says. The society was an informal supper club that took cooking and wine very seriously: each elaborate multi-course dinner included equally lavish wine pairings.

Page has a few of the archived menus, circa 1985, and they are a wonderful time capsule to revisit. Some of the recipes became favorite traditions at family gatherings and on special occasions with friends.

Early visionaries in Oregon's wine industry, Cal and his wife Julia Lee bought a 200-acre former walnut orchard in 1971, and promptly planted grape vines. "He and my mom went to France in the late 1960s and they both came back very smitten with the regions of Champagne and Burgundy," says Page.

An attorney by trade, Cal grew this early investment in the Willamette Valley into one of the premiere vineyards in the area and, in 1975, formed the first commercial wine-making facility in the Dundee Hills along with partner Dick Erath (page 122).

"It was always very clear growing up what the vineyard meant to him," says Page. "It was his passion project." In 1987, Cal established a long-term grape supply partnership with Argyle Winery (page 62) and its founding winemaker, Rollin Soles, that shaped the future of sparkling wine in Oregon.

Today, the second generation builds on that family legacy. Page and her three brothers returned to the land their parents loved and took the reins. In 2014, they released the first Knudsen Vineyards wine label in twenty-five years. Since then, they have created a series of wines honoring their parents. "Our goal is to be good stewards of the vineyards they loved," says Page, "and to grow their dream with the next generation."

ROASTED SHRIMP, AVOCADO, AND BLOOD ORANGE SALAD

CHEF: DANIELLE CENTONI

WINE PAIRING: Knudsen Vineyards Family Series Chardonnay

Inspired by memories of a composed salad Page Knudsen's father, Cal, enjoyed as a member of the Seattle Gourmet Society, this pink-hued beauty is both earthy and refreshing. Roasting the shrimp in their shells results in moist and tender flesh, and the oven does double duty crisping up a bed of wild mushrooms. With crisp citrus aromas and hints of lemon brioche, the Knudsen Family Series Chardonnay enlivens the layers of flavor in this dinner party salad.

SALAD   Preheat oven to 425°F.

Devein the shrimp by using a paring knife or small scissors to cut through the shell along the back of the shrimp and pulling out the vein. Or, if you can see it, pull the vein out through the opening where the head was. Arrange the shrimp on one half of a rimmed baking sheet.

In a medium bowl, combine the mushrooms and oil and toss until evenly coated. Season with salt and pepper. Arrange mushrooms in a single layer on the other half of the baking sheet. Roast for 6 to 8 minutes, until shrimp are opaque. Transfer shrimp to a bowl and return the pan to the oven. Roast mushrooms for another 5 minutes until golden brown.

Peel the shrimp, then put into a medium bowl. Add pesto and lemon juice and toss. Season to taste with salt and pepper.

Cut the top and bottom off the blood oranges to expose the flesh. Cut along the curvature of the fruit to remove the peel and white pith. Working over a bowl, cut between the membranes of the fruit to release the segments, letting them drop into the bowl along with any juice. Squeeze the membranes to extract all the blood orange juice to use in the vinaigrette.

BLOOD ORANGE VINAIGRETTE   In a small bowl, combine all ingredients except the hazelnut oil. Drizzle in the oil, whisking until emulsified.

ASSEMBLY   Divide the roasted mushrooms among four plates. Arrange a few blood orange segments and avocado slices on top of each serving, alternating them. Divide shrimp among the plates and drizzle with blood orange vinaigrette.

Serves 4

SALAD
¾ lb large shrimp (16/20), shells on, heads removed
¾ lb wild mushrooms, roughly chopped
2 Tbsp extra-virgin olive oil
Salt and black pepper, to taste
2 Tbsp pesto
1 Tbsp lemon juice
2 blood oranges

BLOOD ORANGE VINAIGRETTE
1 shallot, finely chopped (¼ cup)
2 Tbsp champagne vinegar
2 Tbsp reserved blood orange juice
1 tsp Dijon mustard
½ tsp salt
¼ tsp black pepper
¼ cup hazelnut oil

ASSEMBLY
1 avocado, sliced

BEEF BOURGUIGNON

COURTESY OF: THE KNUDSEN FAMILY, KNUDSEN VINEYARDS

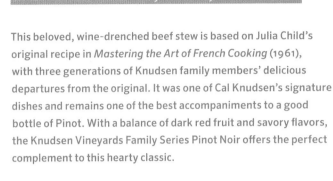

WINE PAIRING: Knudsen Vineyards Family Series Pinot Noir

Serves 4

This beloved, wine-drenched beef stew is based on Julia Child's original recipe in *Mastering the Art of French Cooking* (1961), with three generations of Knudsen family members' delicious departures from the original. It was one of Cal Knudsen's signature dishes and remains one of the best accompaniments to a good bottle of Pinot. With a balance of dark red fruit and savory flavors, the Knudsen Vineyards Family Series Pinot Noir offers the perfect complement to this hearty classic.

Preheat oven to 350°F.

Set a large Dutch oven over medium heat. Add pancetta (or bacon) and cook for 10 minutes, until fat is rendered and pieces are browned and crisp. Using a slotted spoon, transfer to a paper-towel-lined plate. Reserve the fat in the pot.

Increase heat to medium-high. Pat beef cubes dry, then season all sides with salt and pepper. Working in batches to avoid overcrowding, add enough beef to cover the bottom of the pot in a single layer. Sauté beef cubes until lightly seared on all sides and transfer to a large bowl. Repeat with the remaining beef. Sprinkle flour over the cubed beef and toss.

Drain all but 1 tablespoon fat from the pot. Add carrots and onion to the pot and sauté for 7 minutes, or until beginning to brown. Add garlic and sauté another 1 minute. Stir in tomato paste and cook for 2 minutes, until darkened. Add a splash of wine, stirring to scrape up the browned bits, then add the rest. Add 2½ cups stock, 1 bay leaf, and thyme. Add pancetta, beef, and any juices. Season with ½ teaspoon salt and ¼ teaspoon pepper. Bring liquid to a simmer, then cover and place in the oven. Cook for 3 hours, until meat is easily pierced.

6 oz diced pancetta or 6 slices
    bacon, cut into ¼-inch pieces
3 lbs beef chuck, cut into 2-inch
    cubes
Salt and black pepper
2 Tbsp all-purpose flour
2 large carrots, sliced
1 white onion, halved and sliced
2 large cloves garlic, finely chopped
1 Tbsp tomato paste
1 (750-ml) bottle red wine,
    such as Pinot Noir
3¼ cups beef stock (divided)
2 bay leaves (divided)
1 tsp chopped thyme
2 Tbsp extra-virgin olive oil
    (divided)
12 oz pearl onions, peeled,
    thawed if frozen
3 Tbsp bourbon
1 herb bouquet (4 sprigs parsley,
    2 sprigs thyme, and 1 sprig
    rosemary tied together with
    cooking twine)
3 Tbsp butter
1 lb button mushrooms, quartered
Chopped Italian parsley, for garnish

An hour before the stew is done, heat 1 tablespoon of olive oil in a 10-inch skillet with a lid over medium-high heat. Add pearl onions and sauté for 5 minutes, until they begin to brown. Add bourbon, light a match, and carefully hold near liquid to ignite. If the flames don't die out after 30 seconds, put a lid on the pan to extinguish.

Stir in ½ cup stock, the herb bouquet, and the remaining bay leaf, and season with salt and pepper. Reduce heat to low, partially cover, and simmer for 40 minutes, until liquid has reduced to a glaze and onions are tender. Transfer onions to a bowl and discard the herb bouquet and bay leaf.

Heat butter and the remaining 1 tablespoon oil in a skillet over medium-high heat. Add mushrooms and sauté for 5 minutes, or until browned. Add the remaining ¼ cup stock and stir to scrape up the brown bits.

When the stew is ready, add the mushrooms and pearl onions and simmer on medium-high for 3 to 5 minutes to heat through. Divide among bowls, top with parsley, and serve.

MARTIN WOODS WINERY

EVAN MARTIN
WINEMAKER

REGION
WILLAMETTE VALLEY

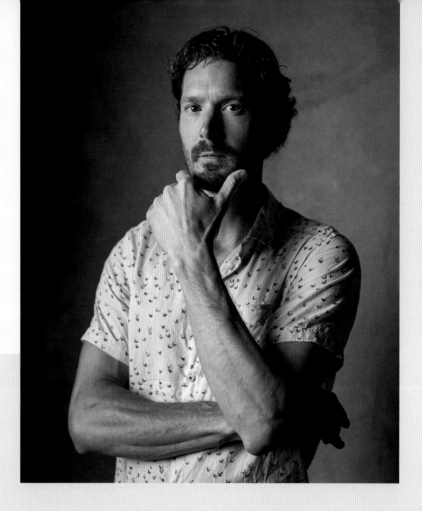

Growing up in Indiana, wine was commonplace on Evan Martin's family table, although it was never the object of conversation. The focus instead was his mother's food—always delicious and often Mediterranean driven. It made a lasting impact, so Evan started cooking while finishing college in Seattle. He also began studying the world of wine appreciation in earnest. "I was romanced by the idea of terroir and this ability to transport myself around the world through a glass of wine," he says. In 2004 he followed up on this interest with an internship at Seven Hills Winery in Walla Walla.

Not yet ready to put down roots, Evan spent the next few years traveling and working in restaurants. He landed in Santa Fe, where he eventually studied with the Court of Master Sommeliers. The sommelier's role provided an opportunity to taste widely.

He developed a deep love for the wines of France and noticed the wines of Oregon seemed capable of bearing a welcome resemblance.

In 2009 Evan returned to wine production, securing a harvest gig at Belle Pente. There he patiently gleaned lessons from a careful winegrowing and winemaking process, while tasting wines from all around the Willamette Valley to gain a greater appreciation of the diverse terroir.

In 2017, Evan acquired a wooded property (subsequently named Martin Woods) in the beautiful and secluded McMinnville AVA, and he established his own winery on site. Evan's diverse portfolio explores the cool-climate neighborhoods

of the Willamette Valley and the unique terroir of the Rocks District, producing wines of classic balance, elegance, and structure. The wines are inspired by the Old World yet clearly display the distinctive terroir of Oregon, and they are prized by the sommelier community.

In 2021, Evan opened HiFi Wine Bar in downtown McMinnville, where vinyl DJs work the turntables and an extensive international bottle list offers the opportunity to explore the great wines of the world. "It's our way to showcase the art of wine, music, and hospitality together in one place. We want to offer the wine community the chance to refresh their passion for the craft," he says.

Parmesan and Chive Gougères with Oregon Shrimp and Citrus Aioli (p. 164)

PARMESAN AND CHIVE GOUGÈRES
with Oregon Shrimp and Citrus Aioli

CHEF: RAUL SALINAS, HIFI WINE BAR

WINE PAIRING: Martin Woods Koosah Vineyard Chardonnay

The only thing better than a puffy, cheesy gougère is one (or four) filled with tiny, tender Oregon bay shrimp. In this dish, chef Raul Salinas goes all in on the citrus, using lemons, limes, and oranges for a triple-threat of flavor. It's a great appetizer and the signature plate at winemaker Evan Martin's HiFi Wine Bar. It's no wonder it's a hit, especially when paired with Martin Woods's Koosah Vineyard Chardonnay, with its flinty citrus and fresh herb notes that carry through a long and satisfying finish.

GOUGÈRES Preheat oven to 450°F. Line two baking sheets with parchment paper.

In a medium saucepan, combine butter, salt, sugar, and 1 cup water and bring to a boil over medium heat. Add flour and stir constantly with a wooden spoon for 2 minutes, until flour is thoroughly incorporated and the dough starts to pull away from the sides of the pan to form a ball. Remove pan from the heat.

Transfer dough to the bowl of a stand mixer fitted with a paddle attachment. Beat on low speed for 5 minutes, until slightly cooled. Beat in 4 eggs, one at a time, until fully incorporated. Stir in Parmesan, chives, and pepper.

Using a small scoop (about ¾ tablespoon), scoop dough onto the prepared baking sheets, evenly spaced 1 inch apart. You should have about 32 mounds.

In a small bowl, whisk the remaining egg with 1 tablespoon water. Brush the tops of the dough mounds with egg wash. Bake for 10 minutes. Reduce heat to 350°F and bake for another 25 minutes, until golden brown.

CITRUS AIOLI In the bowl of a food processor, combine egg yolk, lemon juice, and a pinch each of cayenne and salt. With the machine running, slowly add olive oil in a thin steady stream until emulsified. Transfer to a container and whisk in citrus zests. Season to taste with more salt and cayenne. (Can be refrigerated for up to 1 week.)

Serves 8

GOUGÈRES
5 Tbsp butter
1 tsp salt
1 tsp granulated sugar
1 cup all-purpose flour
5 eggs (divided)
½ cup grated Parmesan
¼ cup finely chopped chives
¼ tsp black pepper

CITRUS AIOLI
1 egg yolk
2 tsp lemon juice
Pinch of cayenne pepper, plus extra to taste
Pinch of salt, plus extra to taste
½ cup extra-virgin olive oil
Grated zest of ½ lemon
Grated zest of ½ lime
Grated zest of ½ orange

SHRIMP SALAD

18 oz cooked Oregon bay shrimp,
   chilled

2 Tbsp finely chopped shallots
   (1 small shallot)

⅓ cup finely diced celery

⅓ cup julienned radish

¼ cup finely chopped herbs, such
   as tarragon, parsley, and chervil

1 tsp grated orange zest

1 tsp grated lime zest

1 tsp grated lemon zest

3 Tbsp Citrus Aioli (see here)

1 Tbsp extra-virgin olive oil, plus
   extra for drizzling

Juice of 1 lemon (3 Tbsp)

Salt and black pepper, to taste

ASSEMBLY

Flaky salt, for sprinkling

Extra-virgin olive oil, for drizzling

4 to 6 edible flowers, such as
   pansies, for garnish

NOTE Gougères can be made several hours ahead and re-crisped in a 350°F oven for 2 to 3 minutes before filling.

SHRIMP SALAD Combine all ingredients in a large bowl. Refrigerate until ready to use. Adjust to taste with more herbs, citrus aioli, salt, pepper, and olive oil, if desired. (Can be made several hours ahead and refrigerated.)

ASSEMBLY Using a serrated knife, cut gougères in half.

When gougères are cooled to the touch, fill each half with 1 tablespoon shrimp salad. Place filled gougères on a serving platter or individual plates and sprinkle with salt. Drizzle a little oil on top and garnish with edible flowers.

OREGON WILD RICE BOWL

CHEF: RAUL SALINAS, HIFI WINE BAR

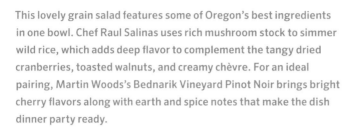

WINE PAIRING: Martin Woods Bednarik Vineyard Pinot Noir

Serves 6

This lovely grain salad features some of Oregon's best ingredients in one bowl. Chef Raul Salinas uses rich mushroom stock to simmer wild rice, which adds deep flavor to complement the tangy dried cranberries, toasted walnuts, and creamy chèvre. For an ideal pairing, Martin Woods's Bednarik Vineyard Pinot Noir brings bright cherry flavors along with earth and spice notes that make the dish dinner party ready.

MUSHROOM STOCK Heat oil in a stockpot over medium-high heat. Add mushrooms and salt and sauté for 5 to 6 minutes, until mushrooms begin to brown. Add celery, garlic, and onion and sauté for 2 minutes. Add bay leaves, thyme, parsley, peppercorns, dried mushrooms, and 3 quarts of cold water.

Bring to a boil over high heat, reduce heat to low, and simmer for 45 minutes. Turn off the heat and allow to steep for 30 minutes. Strain stock into a bowl through a fine-mesh strainer. Discard solids. Allow any remaining sediment from the dried mushrooms to settle and strain again, leaving the sediment behind. Makes about 2 quarts. (Can be made 5 days ahead and refrigerated or frozen for 3 months.)

CHAMPAGNE VINAIGRETTE Combine all ingredients in a jar and shake until blended. Adjust to taste with more salt, vinegar, or honey. (Can be made up to 5 days ahead and stored in an airtight container.)

MUSHROOM STOCK
2 Tbsp neutral oil
1 lb button or cremini mushrooms, roughly chopped
1 Tbsp salt
4 stalks celery, roughly chopped
3 cloves garlic, chopped
1 onion, roughly chopped
3 bay leaves
3 sprigs thyme
3 sprigs Italian parsley
1 Tbsp black peppercorns
½ cup (½ oz) dried mushrooms (preferably porcini)

CHAMPAGNE VINAIGRETTE
½ cup mild-flavored oil, such as canola or avocado
¼ cup champagne vinegar
2 Tbsp honey
1 Tbsp Dijon mustard
1 tsp salt
½ tsp black pepper

2¼ cups Mushroom Stock
   (see here)

1½ cups wild rice or wild rice blend,
   rinsed

1 tsp salt

1 cup walnut halves

3 carrots, peeled and shaved into
   4-inch-long ribbons

2 stalks celery, finely diced

1 cup dried cranberries

1 cup crumbled chèvre

5 cups arugula or sliced lacinato
   kale

2 Tbsp finely chopped shallots

Champagne Vinaigrette (see here)

Extra-virgin olive oil, for drizzling

Flaky salt and black pepper,
   to taste

RICE BOWL Combine the mushroom stock, rice, and salt in a large saucepan and bring to a boil over medium-high heat. Reduce heat to low, cover, and simmer for 40 minutes, or until rice is tender. Spread cooked rice on a parchment-lined baking sheet to cool.

Meanwhile, preheat oven to 350°F. Spread walnuts in an even layer on a baking sheet and bake for 8 minutes, stirring occasionally, until golden. Set aside to cool.

In a large bowl, combine rice, walnuts, carrots, celery, cranberries, chèvre, arugula (or kale), and shallots. Drizzle with champagne vinaigrette and olive oil and toss to coat. Season to taste with salt and pepper.

MAYSARA WINERY

MOE MOMTAZI
OWNER AND GROWER

TAHMIENE MOMTAZI
WINEMAKER

REGION
WILLAMETTE VALLEY

It's hard not to draw parallels between the Momtazi family and their 500-plus-acre certified biodynamic estate in the hills southwest of McMinnville. There's a thread of harmony and synergy that runs through both, as Iranian immigrants Moe and Flora Momtazi and their three adult daughters all work together and support each other in the business in a way that's not unlike their holistic approach in the vineyard.

Winemaker and eldest daughter Tahmiene grew up seeing firsthand the transformational power of ecological farming. Her father, Moe, an engineer by trade, farmer at heart, and a pioneer of biodynamic agriculture in Oregon, transformed the abandoned wheat field he purchased in 1997 into a lush vineyard of Pinot Noir, Pinot Blanc, Pinot Gris, and Riesling, the fruit of which is sought after among winemakers all over the valley.

After earning her degree in food science and technology as well as fermentation science from Oregon State University, Tahmiene worked at several wineries around the state and at Kim Crawford in New Zealand before joining the family business as the inaugural wine-maker in 2007.

"Working with our grapes is truly a blessing because I can always count on knowing I'm working with the best fruit, and it shows in the wine," she says. "By creating healthy soil and in return healthy grapes, we produce high-quality fruit without having to harm or take away from the local environment."

While many Willamette Valley winemakers point to Pinot Noir as their true love, Tahmiene says her heart belongs to white wine. "At Kim Crawford, I found my love of working with white wines. They had me step out of tradition and explore other ways to make it, and it set my white wines to be different from many of the other producers here in Oregon. Our Pinot Blanc is bright in acidity, full-flavored with mineral, lychee, lemon zest, and tropical fruits."

No matter what variety she works with, the goal is always the same: let the fruit speak for itself. "I make sure that I'm not taking away from the fruit, but rather showcasing it in its truest nature."

Persian Herbed Rice with Fish (Sabzi Polo ba Mahi) (p. 170)

PERSIAN HERBED RICE WITH FISH
(Sabzi Polo ba Mahi)

COURTESY OF: THE MOMTAZI FAMILY, MAYSARA WINERY

WINE PAIRING: Arsheen Pinot Gris

The Momtazi family follows tradition and always makes this dish on Nowruz, the first day of the Persian New Year that begins on the spring equinox. It requires a little planning to do it right, but it's worth the effort for the crispy crust (*tahdig*) that forms at the bottom of the pot during cooking. Paired with fresh fish simply seared until golden and flaky, it's a lovely spring dish to pair with Maysara's bright and lightly grassy Arsheen Pinot Gris.

HERBED RICE Place rice in a bowl, cover with water, and stir in 1 tablespoon salt. Allow to soak in a cool location for 1 to 2 hours. Rinse the rice under cold water.

In a food processor, combine the garlic, scallions, dill, cilantro, parsley, and 1 teaspoon salt and pulse until finely chopped.

Bring 5 cups water to a boil in a large nonstick saucepan over medium-high heat. Add the rice and the remaining 2 tablespoons salt. Bring back to a boil and cook, uncovered, for 3 minutes, until rice is al dente. (Break a grain in half; it should be hard in the center and soft on the outside.) Drain, then rinse rice with cold water to stop the cooking.

In a large bowl, mix a scoop of rice and a scoop of the herb mixture, taking care so the rice does not break. Repeat until all the rice and herbs are mixed in the bowl.

Grind or crush the saffron and mix with ¼ cup hot water in a small bowl.

Heat oil in the saucepan over medium-low heat for several minutes until hot. Spread 2 cups of herbed rice evenly across the bottom of the pot. Drizzle with half of the saffron water and season with a pinch of salt. Press down on the rice to create a packed layer. (This creates the crispy tahdig.) Mound the remaining rice on top. Insert the handle of a wooden spoon into the rice to make a few holes for steam to escape.

Arrange 2 cubes of butter on top of the rice. Cover, increase heat to medium-high, and cook for 10 minutes. Reduce heat to very low and wrap the lid in a clean dish towel to absorb condensation (see Note). Cook for 45 minutes.

Serves 4 to 6

HERBED RICE
2 cups basmati rice
3 Tbsp plus 1 tsp salt (divided), plus extra to taste
3 cloves garlic
2 scallions, roughly chopped
1 cup dill
1 cup cilantro
1 cup Italian parsley
½ tsp saffron
3 Tbsp extra-virgin olive oil
¼ cup (½ stick) butter, cut into 4 cubes (divided)

NOTE If your burners can't go very low, place a metal heat diffuser or upside-down metal pie tin on the burner to avoid hotspots. Iranians use a cloth lid cover called a *damkesh* when making rice, but you can also wrap the lid like a bundle in a large flour-sack-style dish towel, tying the ends up near the knob. Just be sure the fabric is secure and won't hang over the sides near the burner.

4 to 6 salmon or steelhead fillets
Salt and black pepper, to taste
2 Tbsp vegetable oil
3 lemons or 2 sour oranges (or a
    combination), cut into wedges
Dill, for garnish

Remove from heat. Arrange remaining 2 cubes of butter on top of the cooked rice. Drizzle with the remaining saffron water. Lightly fluff the top layer of the rice. Cover the pan and set aside for 5 minutes.

Uncover pan. Place a large serving dish over the pan and, holding both tightly against each other, carefully invert the pan over the dish. The rice should have a golden, crunchy crust on top.

FISH Season the fillets with salt and pepper.

Heat the oil in a large skillet over high heat. Reduce heat to medium, then place fillets in the pan. Cover with a splatter screen, if necessary. Cook for 4 minutes, or until fillets are golden on bottom and opaque halfway up the sides. Turn and repeat on the other side until the fish is cooked through and flakes easily.

Serve fillets alongside the herbed rice and lemon (and/or sour orange) wedges and garnish with dill.

SLOW-COOKED VENISON
in Red Wine with Tomato and Mushroom Orzo

COURTESY OF: THE MOMTAZI FAMILY, MAYSARA WINERY

WINE PAIRING: Maysara Cyrus Pinot Noir

Serves 4

You don't need a lot of meat to have a satisfying meal, especially when cooking with venison, which has a richer, earthier flavor than beef. You can find it (usually frozen) at good butcher shops, but elk or good ol' chuck roast works great, too. Maysara's Cyrus Pinot Noir offers plentiful earthy ripe plum and spice notes to complement the meat and its creamy orzo accompaniment.

VENISON IN RED WINE Preheat oven to 350°F.

Season venison with salt and pepper on all sides. Heat 1 tablespoon oil in a Dutch oven over medium-high heat. Arrange venison in an even layer and sear until deep brown and meat easily releases from the pan. Repeat on all sides. (You may have to sear it in batches to avoid overcrowding.) Transfer to a plate.

Heat the remaining 1 tablespoon oil in the same pot. Add celery, carrots, and onion and sauté for 5 minutes, until onions are softened. Add garlic and sauté another 1 minute. Pour in wine, stirring to scrape up the browned bits. Increase heat to high and boil for 5 minutes, until reduced by half.

Pour in stock. Return venison to the Dutch oven, then add bay leaf and thyme. Bring to a simmer, cover, and transfer to the oven. Cook for 1½ to 2 hours, until meat is fork tender.

VENISON IN RED WINE

1 (1-lb) venison roast, cut into 1-inch pieces
Salt and black pepper
2 Tbsp extra-virgin olive oil (divided)
3 stalks celery, diced
2 carrots, diced
1 onion, diced
2 cloves garlic, finely chopped
1½ cups red wine
2 cups beef stock
1 bay leaf
1 Tbsp chopped thyme

1 lb orzo

3 Tbsp extra-virgin olive oil (divided)

8 oz button mushrooms, stems removed and thinly sliced (2 cups)

1 large shallot, finely chopped

1 clove garlic, finely chopped

1 (14½-oz) can diced tomatoes, drained

Salt and black pepper, to taste

1 cup frozen peas

½ cup heavy cream

½ cup freshly grated Parmesan

ASSEMBLY

1 Tbsp grape or pomegranate molasses (see Note)

NOTE Grape molasses and pomegranate molasses are syrupy, tangy fruit concentrates. They can be found in Middle Eastern markets.

TOMATO AND MUSHROOM ORZO When the venison is nearly cooked, bring a large saucepan of salted water to a boil over high heat. Add orzo and cook according to package instructions. Reserve 1 cup of cooking liquid for later use, then drain orzo in a colander.

Heat 2 tablespoons oil in the same pan over medium heat. Add mushrooms and sauté for 5 minutes, until browned. Add the remaining 1 tablespoon oil, shallot, and garlic. Sauté for 2 minutes, or until shallot begins to soften. Add tomatoes, salt, and pepper and cook for 8 minutes, until liquid is mostly evaporated.

Stir in the peas and cream. Add orzo and cook until warmed through. Remove from the heat and stir in Parmesan. If the sauce seems too thick, add enough reserved pasta water to maintain a creamy texture.

ASSEMBLY Remove venison from the oven and stir in the grape (or pomegranate) molasses.

To serve, divide orzo among plates and top with the braised meat.

MCCOLLUM HERITAGE 91

CJ MCCOLLUM
OWNER

REGION
WILLAMETTE VALLEY

When most people stumble on a great glass of wine at a restaurant, they do the predictable thing: order another. But CJ McCollum is not like most people. When faced with a particularly delicious Oregon Pinot from Walter Scott, McCollum didn't just want more, he wanted to know more—about everything: AVAs, soil types, microclimates, clones. He dove deep, tasting all around the region and filling his wine cellar with incredible bottles. But the more he learned, the more he wanted to do. And so, in 2018 he created his own label, McCollum Heritage 91, which he made in partnership with Gina Hennen at Adelsheim (page 32). And in 2021 he became the first active NBA player to own a vineyard.

"I didn't just jump in," he says. "Anything I put my name on, I'm committed to and engaged in the process. If you want to be successful, you have to work hard, ask questions, and recognize what you don't know."

Buying the 318-acre property in the Yamhill-Carlton AVA allowed him to put down roots in Oregon—no matter where his playing career takes him. And, he says, it was the next step in his maturation as a winemaker. "I understood the location, the soil profile, and what I could do with it. A blank canvas gave me time to strategically plan it out and move at my own pace."

So far, he's planting Pinot Noir and Chardonnay, with plans to add sparkling to the lineup of red, white, and rosé. He and his wife, Elise, are planning the build-out of the winery, which will include a tasting room and lots of open space, all with an eye toward sustainability—and inclusion.

"The biggest thing I'm excited about is to be a player in the wine space and figure out ways to bring diversity in all aspects to the way wine is produced, from winemaking to distributing to sommeliers," he says. "The more diverse we are, the better our world will become in the long haul."

HALIBUT TACOS
with Avocado Dressing

CHEF: JOY DARIO

Serves 4

AVOCADO DRESSING

1 avocado
Juice of 2 limes (about ¼ cup)
2 Tbsp mayonnaise
1 tsp garlic powder
Salt and black pepper, to taste
1 Tbsp finely chopped cilantro
1 Tbsp thinly sliced scallions

HALIBUT TACOS

8 small corn or flour tortillas
1 lb halibut fillets, skin and bones removed
2 tsp garlic powder
2 tsp onion powder
2 tsp paprika
2 tsp dried oregano (preferably Mexican)
1 tsp ground coriander
1 tsp ground cumin
1 tsp salt, plus extra to taste
½ tsp black pepper, plus extra to taste
2 Tbsp olive oil
1 Tbsp butter
1 Tbsp lemon juice
2 cups shredded iceberg lettuce
1 large tomato, diced
1 Tbsp finely chopped cilantro
2 limes, cut into wedges, to serve
Hot sauce, such as Tapatío

WINE PAIRING: McCollum Heritage 91 Chardonnay

Lean white fish showered in savory spices takes center stage in these fresh and healthy fish tacos. Chef Joy Dario loves the firmness of halibut for these, but Pacific cod works well, too. Instead of the usual dairy, she uses an avocado to make a creamy dressing that adds lushness without relying on sour cream or crema. The flinty lemon notes in the McCollum Heritage 91 Chardonnay make it a great pairing.

AVOCADO DRESSING In a small mixing bowl, mash avocado and lime juice together with a fork. Stir in mayonnaise and garlic powder, then season to taste with salt and pepper. Fold in cilantro and scallions. Refrigerate until ready to use.

HALIBUT TACOS Preheat oven to 350°F.

Heat a large skillet over high heat. Toast a few tortillas in it in a single layer for about 30 seconds per side, until they take on a little color and smell toasty. Wrap tortillas in aluminum foil and keep warm in the oven. Repeat with the remaining tortillas.

Slice halibut fillets into 8 even strips. In a small bowl, combine garlic powder, onion powder, paprika, oregano, coriander, cumin, salt, and pepper. Season all sides of the fish with the spice mixture.

Heat oil in the large skillet over medium-high heat. Add halibut and sear for 4 minutes, until brown on the bottom. Turn fish over and sear other side for another 4 minutes, until just cooked through and it flakes easily. Remove from heat, then add butter and lemon juice to the pan. When butter is melted, use a spoon to baste the halibut with the mixture.

To serve, divide halibut among warm tortillas, season with salt and pepper, and spoon avocado dressing over. Top with shredded lettuce, tomato, and cilantro. Serve with lime wedges on the side and hot sauce at the table.

OATMEAL CRAN-RAISIN COOKIES

CHEF: JOY DARIO

Makes 2 dozen small cookies

½ cup (1 stick) butter, softened
½ cup packed brown sugar
¼ cup granulated sugar
1 egg
½ tsp vanilla extract
¾ cup all-purpose flour
½ tsp baking soda
¼ tsp salt
½ tsp ground cinnamon
1½ cups rolled oats
½ cup dried cranberries
½ cup golden raisins

WINE PAIRING: McCollum Heritage 91 Rosé

Perhaps the best thing about oatmeal cookies, aside from their deliciousness, is how they're actually pretty good for you—especially this version from CJ McCollum's personal chef Joy Dario. Knowing pro athletes need extra energy, she packs these with extra dried fruit, which has the added benefit of making them even more compatible with the sweet berry aromas and bright fruit notes of McCollum Heritage 91 Rosé.

Preheat oven to 325°F. Line two baking sheets with parchment paper.

In the bowl of a stand mixer fitted with the paddle attachment, cream together butter and both sugars on medium-high speed for 3 minutes, or until light and fluffy. Stop and scrape down the sides of the bowl. Add egg and vanilla and beat until fully combined, stopping to scrape down the sides of the bowl as needed.

In a separate bowl, whisk together flour, baking soda, salt, and cinnamon. With the mixer on low, slowly add dry ingredients to the wet mixture and mix just until fully combined. Stir in oats, cranberries, and raisins.

Scoop heaping tablespoon portions of batter onto the prepared baking sheets, evenly spacing them 2 to 3 inches apart. (At this point, you can freeze them until hard and pack into an airtight freezer bag. Raw cookies will keep for 3 months in the freezer. Bake from frozen for a few minutes longer.)

Bake cookies for 6 minutes. Rotate baking sheets from front to back and from the top to bottom racks and bake for another 6 to 9 minutes, until edges are set and light brown. For softer cookies, underbake slightly.

MONTINORE ESTATE

RUDY MARCHESI
PARTNER

REGION
WILLAMETTE VALLEY

In 1971, Rudy Marchesi filled his station wagon with Zinfandel grapes for $50. He was in Sonoma County for graduate school, studying clinical psychology, and went out for a drive through the surrounding vineyards, seeking comfort and a connection to his Italian roots.

He knew wine grapes would provide that. "I called up my grandfather and said I have the grapes, Pops. Now what do I do?" Like so many of his ancestors who made wine at home in Italy, Rudy made a half barrel of Zinfandel and that was his watershed moment.

Since then, Rudy's had a storied career in wine, but his work in Oregon is where he's made a significant impact and transformed the landscape with his heart and soul. In 2005, he bought Montinore, a 200-acre wine estate that was planted in 1982.

Over the next few years he transitioned to biodynamic farming and winemaking. "The goal is to make the best wine you can," he says. "If you're enhancing that life in the soil, you're making things more interesting and more complex. It's going to show up in the glass."

Today, Montinore is one of the largest producers of certified estate wines made from biodynamic grapes in the country. As his wines continue to become more expressive and distinct, Rudy's motivation to spread the gospel of sustainability deepens. He hosts educational events at Montinore for winemakers, farmers, and other agricultural professionals interested in biodynamic farming. And he's embraced leadership roles on national and international biodynamic organizations.

Ultimately, this deep-seated passion for land circles back to his family. A first-generation Italian American, Rudy's roots are in Lombardia, a mountainous region south of Milan. In this landscape with abundant vineyards, small farms, and alpine preserves, his grandparents found great joy in growing and producing their own food.

Rudy embraces those same values on his farm—his family tends to fruit trees, raises poultry, and grows 90 percent of the vegetables they eat. In his home wine cellar, you'll find batches of prosciutto, salumi, coppa, and sopressata curing—which makes him a very popular dinner guest. "It's how we like to live," he says.

Nonna's Chicken with Farfalle (p. 180)

NONNA'S CHICKEN
with Farfalle

CHEF: RUDY MARCHESI, MONTINORE ESTATE

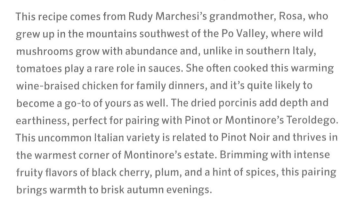

WINE PAIRING: Montinore Estate Teroldego

This recipe comes from Rudy Marchesi's grandmother, Rosa, who grew up in the mountains southwest of the Po Valley, where wild mushrooms grow with abundance and, unlike in southern Italy, tomatoes play a rare role in sauces. She often cooked this warming wine-braised chicken for family dinners, and it's quite likely to become a go-to of yours as well. The dried porcinis add depth and earthiness, perfect for pairing with Pinot or Montinore's Teroldego. This uncommon Italian variety is related to Pinot Noir and thrives in the warmest corner of Montinore's estate. Brimming with intense fruity flavors of black cherry, plum, and a hint of spices, this pairing brings warmth to brisk autumn evenings.

Serves 6 to 8

1 (4- to 5-lb) whole chicken
Salt and black pepper, to taste
½ cup (½ oz) dried porcini mushrooms or a mix of dried shiitake and other wild mushrooms
½ cup extra-virgin olive oil (divided)
4 cloves garlic, chopped
1 yellow onion, chopped
1 Tbsp dried basil
1½ tsp dried thyme
1½ tsp dried marjoram or oregano, plus extra for garnish
1½ cups Pinot Noir
1 lb farfalle pasta
¼ cup grated Parmesan, plus extra for garnish

Cut chicken into parts, separating legs from thighs and quartering the breasts. (Freeze back and wings for another use, such as making stock.) Season with salt and pepper.

Place mushrooms in a small bowl and add just enough hot water to cover. Soak for at least 30 minutes.

Heat ¼ cup oil in a large Dutch oven over medium-high heat. Add chicken skin side down and sear for 8 minutes, or until pieces easily release from the pan. Turn chicken and add garlic, onion, basil, thyme, and marjoram (or oregano) on top. Cook chicken for 5 minutes, until browned.

Lift chicken pieces up and set on top of the onion mixture. Cook for 5 to 7 minutes, until the onion becomes transparent and starts to caramelize.

Pour in wine, scraping up the brown bits at the bottom of the pan. Reduce heat to a simmer and cook, stirring occasionally, for 10 minutes.

Remove soaked mushrooms from water and squeeze dry. Chop, then add to the pan. Pour soaking liquid through a fine-mesh strainer into the pan, taking care to leave any sediment behind in the bowl.

Cover and simmer for 1 hour, stirring occasionally. (If mixture is sticking to the pan, lower heat and add a little water.) Remove lid and simmer for another 10 to 20 minutes, if necessary, until sauce thickens. Season to taste with salt.

Meanwhile, bring a large saucepan of salted water to a boil. Cook pasta according to package instructions. Drain, then transfer to a large bowl. Toss with the remaining ¼ cup olive oil until coated, then the Parmesan.

Divide pasta among bowls and top with braised chicken and sauce. Garnish with a sprinkle of Parmesan and dried oregano.

SWISS CHARD AND RICOTTA MANICOTTI
with Porcini Sauce

CHEF: RUDY MARCHESI, MONTINORE ESTATE

WINE PAIRING: Montinore Estate Reserve Pinot Noir

Serves 8

Manicotti made with crepes, instead of pasta, "is the custom in Northern Italy," says Rudy Marchesi. His version, loaded with sautéed greens and fresh cheese, celebrates the Willamette Valley's wild porcini mushrooms and local Pinot Gris. Montinore's Estate Reserve Pinot Noir offers vibrant acidity to play with the rich and creamy sauce, while notes of black cherry, fig, and cedar enhance the earthy mushrooms.

PORCINI MUSHROOM SAUCE Place dried mushrooms in a medium bowl and cover with 1 cup hot water. Soak for 30 minutes.

Heat oil in a medium saucepan over medium heat. Add onion and sauté for 15 minutes, or until softened and beginning to turn golden. Add sage and cook for 2 minutes. Pour in Pinot Gris, stirring to scrape up the brown bits from the bottom of the pan. Simmer for 5 minutes, until wine has almost evaporated.

Remove soaked mushrooms from the water and squeeze dry. Chop, then add mushrooms to the saucepan. Pour the soaking liquid through a fine-mesh strainer into the pan, taking care to leave any sediment behind in the bowl. Add stock and bring to a boil over high heat. Reduce heat to medium-low, then gently simmer for 30 minutes, or until the sauce is reduced by half.

In a small bowl, mix the flour with ¼ cup sauce to make a paste. Stir into the pot and simmer for 5 minutes, or until thickened. Season with salt and pepper to taste. Set aside until needed.

RICOTTA FILLING Meanwhile, beat eggs in a large mixing bowl. Mix in the ricotta, Parmesan, garlic powder, salt, nutmeg, and lemon zest. Stir in Swiss chard (or spinach) until evenly mixed. Set aside.

PORCINI MUSHROOM SAUCE
1 cup (1 oz) dried porcini mushrooms
¼ cup extra-virgin olive oil
1 large yellow onion, diced
⅓ cup chopped sage
½ cup Pinot Gris
3 cups mushroom stock
¼ cup all-purpose flour
Salt and black pepper, to taste

RICOTTA FILLING
2 eggs
4 cups ricotta
1 cup grated Parmesan
1 tsp garlic powder
1 tsp salt
¼ tsp nutmeg
Grated zest of 1 lemon
Bunch of Swiss chard or spinach leaves, steamed until wilted, squeezed dry, and chopped (1 cup)

CREPES

1⅓ cups all-purpose flour
½ tsp salt
2 cups whole milk
4 eggs
Olive oil, for frying

ASSEMBLY

¼ cup grated Parmesan
Chopped Italian parsley, for serving

CREPES Combine flour, salt, milk, eggs, and 1 cup water in a blender and process until smooth. Set aside to rest for 15 minutes so the flour can hydrate more fully.

Heat a 9-inch nonstick skillet over medium heat. Lightly brush pan with oil. Pour ¼ cup batter into the pan, wait a few seconds, then tilt the pan in all directions to spread batter into an even circle across the bottom and slightly up the sides. Cook for 1 minute until top is dry. Loosen the edges with the tip of a rubber spatula, slide it underneath the crepe, and carefully turn it over. Cook for another 30 seconds, then slide crepe onto a plate. Repeat with the remaining batter, stacking the cooked crepes.

ASSEMBLY Preheat oven to 350°F. Coat the bottom of a 9- by 13-inch baking dish with a little porcini sauce.

Set a crepe on a work surface and spoon ¼ cup of ricotta filling across the middle. Roll up and place seam side down in the dish. Repeat with the rest of the crepes, fitting them tightly together in the pan.

Cover manicotti with remaining porcini sauce. Cover with aluminum foil, taking care not to let it touch the manicotti. Bake for 40 minutes, until bubbling. Remove the foil, sprinkle with ¼ cup Parmesan, and bake until it starts to brown, about 10 minutes more. Sprinkle with parsley and serve.

R. STUART & CO. WINERY

ROB STUART
OWNER AND WINEMAKER

REGION
WILLAMETTE VALLEY

When you're a jet-lagged seventeen-year-old from Buffalo, New York, dropped in front of an English manor house and handed a crystal flute of 1961 Bollinger from a silver tray, that first sip is likely to have a big impact. According to Rob Stuart, "That set me on this journey. I fell in love with champagne."

It was the early 1970s, but Rob didn't know he could make a career out of winemaking until, fresh out of college with a biochemistry degree, he found out about something called enology. He soon jettisoned his job in higher education for the chance to work at a California sparkling winery. He then spent the 1980s and early 1990s making wine in Southern Oregon and rural Yakima, Washington—until his love of Burgundian grapes and a city slicker named Maria prompted a move to the Willamette Valley.

The move would be pivotal for the newlyweds and soon-to-be parents, who would later go on to launch R. Stuart & Co. Winery in an old grain depot in McMinnville in 2002, specializing in Pinot Noir, Pinot Gris, and sparkling wines all made with fruit sourced from some of the best sites in the region. "I've always been interested in working with different growers and the diversity of clones, sites, and soils," says Rob.

But bringing out the best from a diverse group of people was Maria's superpower, as she would go on to become executive director of the International Pinot Noir Celebration (IPNC), and take on many other influential industry roles. Her elevated hospitality and

event-planning skills and deep commitment to community helped support and spotlight a region that was just starting to come into its own.

"For her, the winery was a launchpad to build McMinnville the way she had envisioned," says Rob. "She became so much a part of the community that the winery and the community are intertwined."

Maria passed away in late 2021, leaving behind an indelible legacy and unending gratitude from the many people whose lives she touched. Of her impact, Rob says it best: "I feel blessed to have had the time I did have with this amazing person."

CHICKEN AND CHANTERELLES
Braised in Pinot Noir

CHEF: MARIA STUART, R. STUART & CO. WINERY

WINE PAIRING: R. Stuart & Co. Autograph Pinot Noir

Serves 4

3 lbs boneless skinless chicken
    thighs
Salt and black pepper
3 Tbsp extra-virgin olive oil
    (divided)
1 Tbsp butter
1 lb chanterelles, cleaned and
    chopped
4 cloves garlic, finely chopped
    (divided)
2 tsp herbes de Provence (divided)
1 onion, finely chopped
¾ cup Pinot Noir
½ cup dry Madeira
1 (14½-oz) can diced plum
    tomatoes
2½ cups mushroom stock
1 bay leaf
1½ cups pitted green olives, rinsed
2 tsp cornstarch
1 Tbsp sherry vinegar
2 Tbsp chopped Italian parsley
Polenta or buttered egg noodles,
    to serve

As Maria Stuart's many friends recall, her sublime cooking was rivaled only by her hosting prowess. She loved entertaining guests with warming dishes like this autumnal braise, which can also be made with duck breasts instead of chicken thighs. A dish this classically Oregon deserves a classic Oregon Pinot, and R. Stuart's Autograph Pinot Noir, which blends Rob's favorite single-vineyard lots into one bottle, is an ideal choice.

Season chicken liberally on all sides with salt and pepper.

Heat 1 tablespoon oil and the butter in a large skillet over medium-high heat. Add chanterelles, a quarter of the garlic, and 1 teaspoon herbes de Provence. Sauté for 5 minutes, or until fragrant and mushrooms just begin to brown. Set aside.

Heat the remaining 2 tablespoons oil in a large Dutch oven over medium-high heat. Add enough chicken to fit in the bottom of the pan without crowding and cook for 3 minutes, until lightly browned and the meat easily releases from surface. Repeat on the other side. Transfer to a plate and repeat with the remaining chicken.

Add onion and sauté for 3 minutes, until softened. Add remaining garlic and cook for another minute. Pour in wine and Madeira, stirring to scrape up the brown bits from the bottom of the pan. Bring to a boil and cook for 5 minutes, until liquid is reduced by half.

Stir in tomatoes and their juice, stock, remaining 1 teaspoon herbes de Provence, and bay leaf. Return chicken to pan, along with any juices. Cover, reduce heat to low, and simmer for 25 minutes.

Add olives and chanterelles to the stew. Simmer, partially covered, for another 20 to 30 minutes, until meat is very tender. Transfer chicken to a cutting board and cut into bite-sized pieces. Skim fat off the braising liquid in the pan. Discard the bay leaf.

Boil braising liquid over high heat for 3 minutes until reduced slightly. Dissolve cornstarch in 1 tablespoon water and stir into the sauce. Simmer for 2 minutes, stirring, until thickened. Add chicken and vinegar and season to taste with salt and pepper.

Garnish with parsley and serve over polenta (or buttered egg noodles).

NORTHWEST CIOPPINO
with Savory Cheese Shortbread

CHEF: MARIA STUART, R. STUART & CO. WINERY

WINE PAIRING: R. Stuart & Co. Rosé d'Or Brut

Maria Stuart adapted this dish from a beloved slow cooker recipe, giving it a few of her signature twists and serving it with her mom's cheese shortbread. Feel free to add scallops, calamari, and crab legs for a particularly seafood-rich bowl. The bright, tomato-based seafood stew and savory, cheesy cookies (a lovely appetizer on their own) are just begging for a special glass of fruit-forward bubbly, and the gorgeous and complexly layered R. Stuart Rosé d'Or Brut is just the ticket.

CHEESE COOKIES In a stand mixer fitted with a paddle attachment, combine cheddar, butter, and Worcestershire sauce and beat on medium speed until thoroughly combined. Reduce speed to low and mix in flour, salt, and cayenne.

Turn dough out onto a work surface, gather into a ball, then roll into a log, about 6 inches long and 1½ inches in diameter. Wrap in plastic wrap and refrigerate for 2 to 3 hours (or freeze for up to 2 months). (Tip: To keep the log from developing a flat side, turn it over a few times while it chills.)

Preheat oven to 350°F. Line a baking sheet with parchment paper. Slice log into ¼-inch-thick rounds. Arrange on the prepared baking sheet. Bake for 15 minutes, until edges begin to brown. Cool on the pan for 1 to 2 minutes, then transfer to a wire rack. Makes 25 to 30 cookies. (Leftover cookies can be stored in an airtight container for several days.)

NORTHWEST CIOPPINO Heat oil in a large skillet over medium heat. Add onion and sauté for 5 minutes, until softened. Add garlic and sauté for another minute.

Stir in remaining ingredients except the mussels (and/or clams), fish, shrimp, and black pepper. Bring to a boil over high heat, reduce heat to low, and simmer for 1 to 1½ hours.

Increase heat to high and stir in the mussels and/or clams. Cover and cook for 3 to 5 minutes, or until beginning to open. Add the fish and shrimp, cover, and simmer another 3 minutes until just cooked through. Season to taste with salt and pepper. Ladle into bowls, garnish with thyme, and serve with cheese cookies.

Serves 6

CHEESE COOKIES
1 cup grated sharp cheddar (3 oz)
½ cup (1 stick) butter, room temperature
½ tsp Worcestershire sauce
1 cup all-purpose flour
1 tsp salt
⅛ tsp cayenne

NORTHWEST CIOPPINO
2 Tbsp olive oil
1 onion, chopped
2 cloves garlic, finely chopped
1 cup dry white wine
1 cup full-bodied dry red wine, such as Zinfandel
1 (32-oz) bottle clam juice
1 (28-oz) can Italian plum tomatoes (diced, or chopped if whole)
1 Tbsp (heaping) Better Than Bouillon Lobster Base
1 bay leaf
2 Tbsp chopped Italian parsley
1 to 2 tsp chopped marjoram
1 to 2 tsp chopped thyme, plus a few sprigs for garnish
½ tsp salt, plus extra to taste
¼ to ½ tsp red pepper flakes, or to taste
1 lb mussels and/or clams, cleaned and debearded
1 lb cod or rockfish fillets, cut into bite-sized pieces
¾ lb medium shrimp (21/25), peeled and deveined
Black pepper, to taste

REMY WINES

REMY DRABKIN
WINEMAKER

REGION
WILLAMETTE VALLEY

Many winemakers aim to let the grapes speak for themselves, forgoing any attempts at conformity through additives and manipulations. For Remy Drabkin, this philosophy in the cellar is an extension of her philosophy on life. No matter the prevailing winds, she's unafraid to chart a course that's authentically her own.

Case in point: She's a winemaker in a region dominated by Burgundian grapes, and yet she focuses on northern Italian varieties—grapes like Dolcetto, Lagrein, and Nebbiolo. "I love Italian wines because they are so versatile with food," says Remy. "And the way that Italians interface with food and wine culturally is near and dear to my heart. That's a huge part of it."

Remy grew up in the McMinnville area as Oregon's pioneer winemakers were carving out an industry in the 1980s, and it made

a deep impression. "I was in their cellars from the time I was really young—riding on tractors, making things dirty, getting sticky. And when you're six years old and their kids, today's second-generation winemakers, are sixteen-year-olds talking about becoming winemakers, that's the coolest thing in the world."

So, having aspired to the career since grade school, you'd think she'd be like most other winemakers and focus her efforts on just that—making wine—but Remy commits just as much time and energy to social justice work. "I'm not a person who

limits myself to one thing," she says. She's a committed public speaker, a community organizer, and a public servant—in 2022, she became mayor of McMinnville, no less—who pushes for equity, whether that's through affordable housing, spearheading the LGBTQ+ nonprofit Wine Country Pride, or through diversity and inclusion outreach in the wine industry and beyond.

"We have a lot of work to do, equity work, in Oregon and in the wine industry in general," she says. "It's my goal to stay in public service. I find it very fulfilling."

Moroccan Chicken and Rice with Dates and Olives (p. 192)

MOROCCAN CHICKEN AND RICE
with Dates and Olives

CHEF: MARIA STUART, R. STUART & CO. WINERY

WINE PAIRING: Remy Wines Lagrein

Remy Drabkin comes from a family of serious cooks, but when asked for a dish to include in this book, she immediately thought of her close family friend Maria Stuart (page 184). Growing up, she spent nearly as much time cooking with Maria as she did with her own family. This comforting yet boldly flavored recipe from her beloved friend has become a staple of Remy's harvest meals. Pair it with her full-bodied Lagrein—its berry-cordial-meets-tobacco notes enhance the sweetness of the dates.

Preheat oven to 400°F.

In a large bowl, season chicken thighs generously with salt and pepper. Add 2 tablespoons each of oil and harissa and toss to coat. Set aside.

Heat the remaining 2 tablespoons oil in a large ovenproof skillet over medium heat. Add onion and season with salt. Sauté for 7 minutes, until soft. Add garlic and sauté for another minute. Add cumin and coriander and sauté for 30 seconds. If the skillet looks dry, add another 1 tablespoon oil.

Stir in rice until thoroughly coated. Gently toast, stirring, for 4 to 5 minutes. Stir in dates, olives, and remaining 2 tablespoons harissa.

Using a vegetable peeler, peel zest from the orange in big strips and add to skillet. Cut orange in half and squeeze ¼ cup juice into skillet. Add another ½ teaspoon salt.

Nestle chicken pieces in a single layer on top of the rice. Scrape any leftover harissa from the bowl into the pan. Pour stock around the edge of the pan, taking care not to rinse the harissa off the chicken.

Place pan, uncovered, in the oven and cook for 25 minutes. Stir any exposed rice into the liquid so that it cooks. Cook for another 15 minutes, or until the chicken is golden brown and cooked through.

Remove from the oven, cover with aluminum foil or a lid, and allow to rest for 5 to 10 minutes to steam rice. Sprinkle chopped pistachios on top and serve warm.

Serves 6

6 to 8 bone-in, skin-on chicken thighs
Salt and black pepper
¼ cup extra-virgin olive oil, plus extra if needed (divided)
¼ cup harissa, plus extra to taste (divided; see Note)
1 yellow onion, chopped
2 to 3 cloves garlic, finely chopped
1 Tbsp ground cumin
1 Tbsp ground coriander
1 cup basmati rice, rinsed
6 Medjool dates, pitted and chopped
½ cup good-quality green olives, pitted
1 orange
1½ cups chicken stock
2 Tbsp roughly chopped pistachios

NOTE Harissa is a spiced Moroccan red pepper paste with mild to medium heat. It's available in jars in the international foods aisle at most well-stocked supermarkets.

ITALIAN NUT MACAROONS
(Nuces)

CHEF: REMY DRABKIN, REMY WINES

Makes about 2 dozen cookies

1 (7-oz) package marzipan
¾ cup confectioners' sugar
⅓ cup granulated sugar
2 egg whites
⅔ cup pine nuts
2 cups crushed hazelnuts without
    skins (divided)
Flaky sea salt

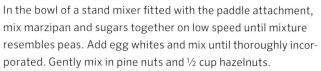

WINE PAIRING: Remy Wines Black Heart Sparkling Wine

Nuces means "nuts" in Latin, a fitting name for a cookie that can be adapted to any kind of nut you prefer. Inspired by the chewy almond macaroons she enjoyed at Italian bakeries in Pittsburgh, where she once lived, Remy Drabkin developed this recipe with Oregon hazelnuts to serve at one of her wine club parties. They're delicious with sparkling wine, dessert wine, or even a robust red wine, especially one prominent with berry flavors. Remy Wines's Black Heart is a perfect fit—and a fundraising wine for the ACLU to boot.

In the bowl of a stand mixer fitted with the paddle attachment, mix marzipan and sugars together on low speed until mixture resembles peas. Add egg whites and mix until thoroughly incorporated. Gently mix in pine nuts and ½ cup hazelnuts.

Turn dough out onto a large sheet of plastic wrap. Gather into a ball, then shape and roll it into a log. Wrap in the plastic, then freeze for at least 1 hour but preferably overnight. The dough should be firm. (Can be made 2 weeks ahead and frozen.)

Preheat convection oven to 350°F (see Note).

Set a small bowl of warm water nearby to clean your hands while you handle the cookies (the dough is sticky). Set another bowl with the remaining hazelnuts nearby. Line two baking sheets with parchment paper.

Cut the dough into slices and roll each into 1½-inch balls. Toss and coat in crushed hazelnuts. Arrange on the prepared baking sheets, evenly spacing them 3 inches apart. Sprinkle lightly with salt. Bake for 15 to 20 minutes, until golden brown and firm. Set aside to cool completely on the baking sheet so they don't stick to the parchment. (Depending on humidity, cookies tend to soften a few hours after baking. They can be stored in an airtight container for up to 3 days.)

NOTE If your oven doesn't have convection, test the timing by baking one cookie first. You may have to rotate the baking sheets from back to front and between the upper and lower racks. They can brown quickly before cooking completely if you're not careful.

REX HILL VINEYARDS

MICHAEL DAVIES
EXECUTIVE WINEMAKER

REGION
WILLAMETTE VALLEY

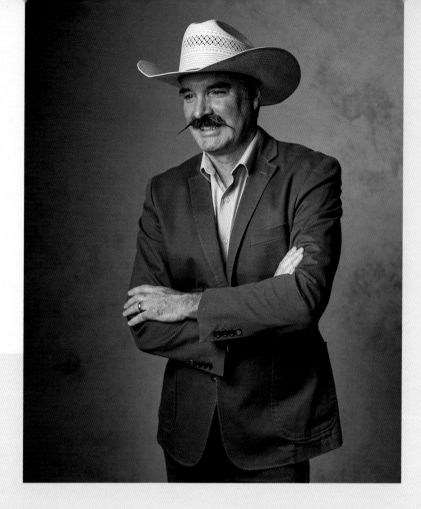

It's an age-old tale. Michael Davies found himself on a plane from New Zealand to Oregon, chasing his future. His choice was to either pursue a gig as a "flying wine-maker" in Spain or follow the love of his life to the Willamette Valley. He picked Cupid.

Twenty years later, he and his wife, also a winemaker, are firmly rooted in Oregon. Since 2007, he's been shaping the wine program at REX HILL, a role he took on right after the legacy winery was acquired by A to Z Wineworks that same year.

He found his path to winemaking during his OE (overseas experi-ence). "It's a rite of passage in New Zealand," explains Michael—a rich tradition that pairs travel with life experience, often in some far-flung locale. "Traveling is always a great education."

He pursued a range of interests, from running a bungee-jumping company to managing youth hostels in Scandinavia and the United Kingdom, and "each job steered me towards winemaking." A profession combining science, nature, people, and creativity.

"In my early years in winemaking, I used to think that there was one right answer to every question, that this is what you did in a situ-ation," says Michael. "And if you knew it, or you're experienced enough, you got ten out of ten on the test."

After twenty-five years in the industry, he realizes there are no absolutes. "My job is to trust my intuition and deliver what I think is a good expression of that site or that year," he says. "Some years it means getting out of the way. And others you've got to risk a little."

The focus at REX HILL is on bou-tique Pinot Noirs and Chardonnays, "which are a wonderful vehicle for individual expression, either for the person, the vintage, or the site," Michael says. Ultimately, his goal is to make wine that people connect to on a personal level. "Like a movie, wine should give different people different things. So that when they're enjoying it together, they can actually appreciate different parts of it."

Grilled Romano Beans with Plum-Miso Dressing and Crispy Shallots (p. 196)

GRILLED ROMANO BEANS
with Plum-Miso Dressing and Crispy Shallots

CHEF: DAVID SAPP, REX HILL VINEYARDS

WINE PAIRING: REX HILL Reserve Pinot Noir

Serves 4

Large and dense, Romano beans are the perfect summer veg to throw on the grill. Here they get tossed with a sweet-tart dressing that marries the juicy fruity taste of plum with complex umami flavors from white miso. Crispy shallots finish the dish with a sweet caramelized flavor and irresistible crunch. REX HILL's Reserve Pinot Noir offers supple cherry flavors to complement this layered side dish, a delicious expression of the season's bounty.

MISO DRESSING

2 red plums, halved and pitted
½ cup red wine vinegar
2 Tbsp white (shiro) miso paste
⅓ cup extra-virgin olive oil

CRISPY SHALLOTS

3 shallots, evenly sliced with a mandoline
½ cup rice flour, plus extra if needed
Canola oil, for frying
Salt, to taste

ASSEMBLY

4 cups Romano beans, trimmed
1 Tbsp extra-virgin olive oil
Salt, to taste
2 red plums, halved, pitted, and thinly sliced
1 cup basil leaves
Miso Dressing (see here)
Crispy Shallots (see here)

MISO DRESSING Preheat oven to 350°F. Line a baking sheet with parchment paper.

Place the 4 plum halves, face down, on a prepared baking sheet. Roast for 5 to 10 minutes, until skin pulls away from flesh and plums are tender. Using tongs, pull skin from plums while still hot and discard. Set plums aside to cool.

In a blender, combine roasted plums, vinegar, and miso paste and blend until smooth. With the blender running, slowly add oil in a thin stream until emulsified. (Dressing can be made up to 3 days ahead and refrigerated.)

CRISPY SHALLOTS In a medium bowl, combine shallots and rice flour and toss to coat evenly, making sure the rings are all separated. If the shallots seem too sticky, add more rice flour.

Heat 1 inch oil in a heavy-bottomed saucepan over medium heat until it reaches 250°F.

Place shallots onto a wire skimmer and shake off excess flour. Gently lower into the oil and fry for 8 minutes, lightly stirring and monitoring the oil temperature until they turn a light tan color. Using the skimmer, remove shallots from the oil and transfer to a paper-towel-lined plate. Season well with salt.

ASSEMBLY Preheat a grill to medium-high heat (350°F to 400°F). In a large bowl, combine beans, oil, and salt and toss well. Lay beans on the grill perpendicular to the grill grates so they won't fall in and grill for 3 to 4 minutes, until charred on both sides. Transfer to a large bowl.

To serve, add sliced plums to the bowl of beans. Drizzle with miso dressing to taste and toss to coat. Tear basil leaves into the bowl and add half of the crispy shallots. Season to taste with more dressing or salt and toss again. Transfer to a large platter. Scatter the remaining shallots on top and serve.

PAN-SEARED HALIBUT
and Roasted Corn Succotash with Sea Beans

CHEF: DAVID SAPP, REX HILL VINEYARDS

WINE PAIRING: REX HILL *Seven Soils Chardonnay*

Serves 4

4 (4- to 5-oz) halibut fillets,
    skin removed
Salt
2 ears corn, in husks
6 Tbsp extra-virgin olive oil
    (divided)
1 shallot, finely chopped
1 small zucchini, diced (1 cup)
1 cup shelled fava beans (from
    about 1½ pounds in the pod;
    see Note)
1 heirloom tomato, chopped
½ cup sea beans or chopped
    Castelvetrano olives
3 Tbsp butter
1 Tbsp apple cider vinegar
Black pepper, to taste
High-quality extra-virgin olive oil,
    for drizzling

NOTE To prepare fava beans,
remove the fuzzy outer
pods and cook the beans in
a saucepan of salted, boiling
water for 30 seconds. Plunge
beans into cold water to stop
the cooking. Squeeze to slip off
the waxy skin and pop out the
tender bean inside. Shelled fava
beans will keep refrigerated for
several days.

This riff on Southern succotash uses Oregon ingredients like fava beans and sea beans, which bring a briny saltiness to the dish. If you are unable to source sea beans where you live, feel free to experiment with chopped Castelvetrano olives or fried capers. This dish is a colorful celebration of summer, and perfect alongside pan-roasted halibut and REX HILL's Seven Soils Chardonnay, with its bouquet of ripe apple and lemon verbena followed by a silky finish.

Preheat oven to 375°F. Pat the halibut dry and generously season all sides with salt. Set aside for 10 minutes.

Roast corn in their husks directly on the oven rack for 12 to 18 minutes, until fragrant and tender. Set aside until cool enough to handle, then remove husks and silk. Increase oven temperature to 400°F.

In a large skillet set over medium-high heat, or over the flame of a gas grill, char corn until the kernels begin to blacken slightly. Set aside to cool, then shave corn kernels and put into a large bowl.

Heat 2 tablespoons oil in a large ovenproof skillet over medium-high heat until it begins to smoke (add more oil if needed to cover the bottom). Lay halibut, prettier side down, in pan. Sear for 2 to 3 minutes. Gently turn the fillets over and place the pan in the oven. Roast for 4 to 6 minutes, until center of fish is just warm. (Tip: Gauge the temperature by placing the tip of a knife into the center of each portion and then hold it against the bottom of your lower lip to see if it's warm.) Transfer halibut to a plate, tent with aluminum foil, and set aside to rest.

Heat the remaining ¼ cup oil in a large skillet over medium-high heat until shimmering. Add shallot, season lightly with salt, and sauté until softened, stirring frequently to prevent burning. Add zucchini, fava beans, and roasted corn. Season lightly with salt and sauté for 3 minutes, until vegetables begin to soften.

Add tomato and sea beans (or olives) and sauté for 1 minute, then reduce heat to medium. Add butter and vinegar, stirring slowly until creamy. Season to taste with salt and pepper.

To serve, spoon succotash onto four warmed plates in a small mound slightly off-center. Lean a portion of halibut onto the succotash, drizzle high-quality olive oil on top, and finish with a little more pepper.

SOKOL BLOSSER WINERY

ALEX SOKOL BLOSSER
CO-PRESIDENT
AND WINEMAKER

REGION
WILLAMETTE VALLEY

Alex Sokol Blosser grew up right alongside the Oregon wine industry itself. His parents, Bill and Susan Sokol Blosser, were part of the pioneering wave of winegrowers in Oregon, planting their first vineyard in 1971, just a few years before Alex was born. They opened Oregon's first tasting room in 1978, and led the way in sustainability, too, as Sokol Blosser eventually became the first winery to be Salmon-Safe certified in 1996.

Thanks in part to their hard work, the wine industry grew along with their winery, and Alex had a front-row seat to it all. How could he not join the family business? Try as he might to get away, he was always lured back to the grape.

"I love wine. It's a beautiful thing," he says. "There's no consistency, and that is what's so awesome and beautiful about making it."

Alex thrives on the challenge of making wine despite Oregon's unpredictable weather, fascinated by the promise that each harvest brings. "A lot of winemaking is getting lucky," he says. "When the vintage is right, you can make a wine that keeps going and makes you think."

Over the decades, he has worked in nearly every role at the winery, becoming co-president with his sister (and winery CEO) Alison Sokol Blosser in 2008 and taking on the head winemaker role in 2013. The siblings and their eldest brother, Nik, now encourage the third generation to dip their toes into each role, in hopes that someday they'll take over the family business.

But before then, Alex has work to do. "You only get one shot a year to make wine, and every year is a different year. I've got another ten to fifteen tries to make that great Pinot from our estate. It's a game of continuous improvement. The hope is, before I hand over the baton, there's a great Pinot in me."

WATERMELON AND ROASTED BEET SALAD

CHEF: TRAVIS BIRD, SOKOL BLOSSER WINERY

WINE PAIRING: Sokol Blosser Estate Rosé of Pinot Noir

Serves 6 to 8

Make this salad in the height of summer, when exceptionally juicy watermelons begin hitting the market. There's something deeply satisfying about the combination of fruity melons marinated in honey and rosé with earthy-sweet beets, nutty-crunchy quinoa and pepitas, and salty cheese. Sokol Blosser's chef Travis Bird uses a cow's milk cheese from neighboring Briar Rose Creamery, but traditional feta works as well. Pairing this with Sokol Blosser's Rosé, with its fresh-melon fruitiness, is the essence of summer.

Preheat oven to 400°F. Wrap each beet individually in aluminum foil and set on a baking sheet. Roast for 50 to 60 minutes, until tender enough to be easily pierced with a fork all the way through. Set aside to cool, then peel and cut into ½-inch cubes. Makes about 3 cups. Chill the beets until needed. (Can also be made 2 days ahead and refrigerated.)

Bring 1 cup salted water to a boil in a medium saucepan over medium-high heat. Add quinoa, then reduce heat to medium and cook for 12 minutes, until tender. Drain using a fine-mesh strainer and set aside for 2 to 3 minutes so all water runs through.

Line a baking sheet with paper towels and spread quinoa evenly over it to air-dry, or toss in a paper-towel-lined bowl.

Heat vegetable oil in a large skillet over medium heat. Add quinoa and sauté for 2 to 4 minutes, until golden brown and crispy. Using a spoon, transfer quinoa to a paper-towel-lined bowl and toss several times, replacing the towels as needed, until most of the oil has been removed from the quinoa. Season to taste with salt. Let the quinoa come to room temperature. (Crispy quinoa can be made 5 days ahead and stored in an airtight container.)

In a medium mixing bowl, combine chilled beets and toasted pepitas. Season with ½ teaspoon salt, drizzle in the Arbequina olive oil, and toss to coat.

In another medium mixing bowl, whisk together rosé, honey, and ½ teaspoon salt. Add watermelon and gently toss to coat. Set aside to marinate for 10 minutes, mixing occasionally.

To serve, arrange watermelon on your favorite serving platter in an even layer. Top with beets and pepitas. Generously sprinkle the crumbled cheese over. Top with crunchy quinoa. Tear basil leaves into bite-sized pieces and scatter over dish. Drizzle with aged balsamic vinegar (or saba) and serve.

2 lbs beets, scrubbed, tops removed
Salt
½ cup tricolor quinoa
2 Tbsp vegetable oil
½ cup toasted pepitas (see Note)
2 Tbsp Arbequina extra-virgin olive oil
4 oz Sokol Blosser Rosé
2 Tbsp raw honey
1 (4-lb) seedless watermelon, rind removed and cut into 1-inch cubes (5 to 6 cups)
8 oz feta cheese, such as feta-style Briar Rose Fata Morgana, crumbled
½ cup basil leaves
Aged balsamic vinegar or saba, for drizzling

NOTE To toast pepitas, arrange on a baking sheet and bake in a 350°F oven for 5 to 10 minutes, or until lightly golden.

SEARED SALMON

with Confit New Potatoes, Kale, and Beurre Blanc

CHEF: TRAVIS BIRD, SOKOL BLOSSER WINERY

WINE PAIRING: Sokol Blosser Dundee Hills Chardonnay

Serves 4

Beurre blanc, or white wine butter sauce, is one of the most classic of French sauces—its bright, buttery flavor is a simple yet luxurious way to liven up fish and vegetables. In this version, Sokol Blosser's executive chef Travis Bird uses the winery's signature Dundee Hills Chardonnay, which makes wine pairing a cinch. But even without including it in the sauce, the wine's silky mouthfeel and notes of delicate pear and toast make it a natural with fish and cream sauces alike. Here, you get both. Make the confit potatoes ahead of time and this elegant meal comes together in under an hour.

CONFIT NEW POTATOES
2 lbs new potatoes
1 head garlic, halved horizontally
½ bunch thyme
1 to 1½ cups extra-virgin olive oil
Salt and black pepper, to taste

CONFIT NEW POTATOES Preheat oven to 375°F.

In a 9-inch baking dish or Dutch oven, combine all ingredients, adding enough oil to just cover the potatoes. Season with salt and pepper. Bake for 40 minutes, until potatoes are fork tender. When cool enough to handle, cut in half. Set aside, reserving oil and garlic. (Can be made 3 days ahead and refrigerated.)

4 (4- to 6-oz) salmon fillets
Salt and black pepper
Confit New Potatoes (see here)
½ cup Sokol Blosser Chardonnay
2 cloves garlic, finely chopped
½ large shallot, finely chopped
Juice of 1 lemon
¼ tsp white pepper
6 Tbsp cold butter, cut into cubes
½ bunch tarragon, chopped
1 Tbsp chopped Italian parsley
1 Tbsp grapeseed or vegetable oil
1 lb kale, ribs removed and chopped

ASSEMBLY Preheat oven to 400°F. Pat salmon dry and season with salt and black pepper. Set aside at room temperature for 20 minutes.

Place confit potatoes cut side down on a baking sheet with some of the garlicky oil (reserve the rest for another use) and roast in the oven for 15 to 20 minutes until golden on the bottom. Add the confit garlic cloves and roast a few minutes longer, until heated through.

Meanwhile, make the sauce. In a medium saucepan over medium heat, combine wine, garlic, and shallot. Cook for 5 to 7 minutes, until shallot is translucent and wine has reduced by two-thirds. Add lemon juice, pinch of salt, and white pepper and cook for another minute.

Remove from heat. Whisk in cold butter, cube by cube, until emulsified and creamy, briefly returning to low heat as needed until all butter has been melted. Add tarragon and parsley and season with salt and pepper. Remove from heat and keep warm. (Tip: The sauce can break and become greasy if overheated or allowed to get cold. Keep it warm in a thermos if you won't be using it right away.)

Heat oil in a large skillet over medium-high heat until oil begins wisping light smoke. Place salmon skin side up in the pan. Sear, untouched, for 4 to 5 minutes, until a golden brown crust forms and flesh is opaque halfway up the sides. Carefully flip salmon and cook for another 4 to 5 minutes, until fish is opaque and easily flakes. Transfer to a large plate.

Add kale to skillet, increase heat to high, and sauté for 90 seconds. Season to taste with salt and black pepper.

To serve, divide roasted confit potatoes and garlic and the sautéed kale among plates. Place salmon on top of potatoes and generously spoon beurre blanc sauce on top.

SOTER VINEYARDS

CHRIS FLADWOOD
WINEMAKER

REGION
WILLAMETTE VALLEY

In 2004, Chris Fladwood was a twenty-one-year-old soldier deployed in Iraq. When he received a care package with a book about winemaking, he started reading, even though he didn't drink wine. One day, his squad leader spied the title of the book—he absolutely loved wine—and thereafter, on patrols, began sharing his vinous tales. "It fascinated me," says Chris. "He planted the seed that wine was like art; people collect it and pass it down."

Once he returned stateside, a series of fortunate coincidences set Chris on an unexpected path—"a reminder that the universe works in mysterious ways," he says. After graduating with a degree from WSU in viticulture and enology, he spent a few years spinning the globe, working harvests in Washington State, Bordeaux, and New Zealand.

He got his first full-time wine industry job in 2009 at Soter Vineyards, one of Oregon's most prestigious wineries, founded by Tony and Michelle Soter in 1997. "Tony has been a phenomenal mentor for over a decade," says Chris, who worked his way up from cellar master to winemaker.

The estate, known as Mineral Springs Ranch, is a gorgeous 240-acre biodynamic farm, vineyard, and tasting room. Their commitment to regenerative farming guarantees idyllic vistas, with resident chickens, cows, sheep, pigs, turkeys, donkeys, and goats grazing on different parts of the property throughout the year.

"Farming the way we do allows the vines to express themselves more fully," says Chris. "We unlock a bit more personality and, as a result, we can make wines that are more interesting."

While Soter is known for exquisite Pinot Noirs, their legendary Brut Rosé (which debuted in 1997) is consistently deemed one the Willamette Valley's most compelling and coveted wines.

Chris shares how the grapes for that sparkling wine have a tiny window for picking to get the nuanced cherry expression they want. "That moment is fleeting," he says. "So during harvest, we walk the vines and taste the grapes every single day, multiple times a day, to best understand and estimate when that opportunity will arise."

CREAMY MATSUTAKE SOUP

CHEF: CLAYTON ALLEN, SOTER VINEYARDS

Serves 2 to 4

½ cup (1 stick) butter

2 large leeks, white and light green parts only, sliced ¼-inch thick

1 lb matsutake mushrooms, cleaned and roughly chopped

1 cup whole milk, plus extra if needed

1 cup heavy cream

2 cups chicken or vegetable stock

Salt, to taste

Briar Rose Brebis cheese or chèvre, for garnish

Salad burnet leaves, torn lovage leaves, or celery leaves, for garnish

Crunchy baguette, to serve

WINE PAIRING: Soter Vineyards Mineral Springs Brut Rosé

Prized for their earthy, spicy, piney flavor, matsutakes are among the most sought-after mushrooms growing in Oregon's forests. They're pricey if you don't forage them yourself, but since this soup is puréed you don't have to buy pristine specimens.

Soter's signature sparkling Mineral Springs Brut Rosé offers an elegant counterpoint to the soup with fine bubbles and cherry blossom aromas followed by sun-soaked raspberries on the finish.

When matsutakes are out of season, use half shiitakes and half portobellos for a robust version of the soup that goes great with Pinot Noir.

Melt butter in a stock pot or Dutch oven over medium-high heat. Add leeks and sauté for 5 to 7 minutes, until slightly browned and caramelized. Add mushrooms and cook for 10 minutes, until softened.

Add milk, cream, and stock. Season with a large pinch of salt. Bring just to a boil, then reduce heat to low and simmer for about 20 minutes, until mushrooms and leeks are very soft. Turn off heat and let soup cool slightly. Transfer to a blender and blend until smooth. (Cooling it down first prevents the steam from building up under the lid.) Strain through a fine-mesh strainer and discard any solids. Season to taste with salt and add more milk if you prefer a thinner texture.

Garnish with crumbled cheese and greens. Serve with sliced baguette.

CARAMELIZED FENNEL
with Manchego, Chili, and Almonds

CHEF: CLAYTON ALLEN, SOTER VINEYARDS

WINE PAIRING: Soter Vineyards Mineral Springs Ranch Pinot Noir

For this hearty side dish, Soter executive chef Clayton Allen uses ingredients he gleans from Soter's farm and preserves for the long winter, like tomatoes canned during the height of summer and slightly spicy dried chilies with deep, dark flavors ground into powder. "It's a simple dish that lets its ingredients do all the legwork," he says. The caramelized fennel gets topped with Manchego and almonds for an almost luxurious nuttiness that's perfect with earthy sausages like merguez. Soter's Pinot Noir brings a balance of dark red fruit and a dusting of earth and spice flavors to this ode to autumn.

Melt butter in a large cast-iron skillet over medium heat. Stir in fennel and a large pinch of salt. Cover and reduce heat to medium-low. Sauté for 15 to 20 minutes, until soft. Add stock, wine, and tomatoes. Cook for 30 to 45 minutes, until reduced and thickened.

Preheat oven to 400°F.

Sprinkle fennel with cheese, almonds, and chili powder. Bake for 15 minutes, until fennel is bubbling and cheese is golden.

Serves 4

½ cup (1 stick) butter
3 large bulbs fennel, tops removed, cored, and cut into ½-inch-thick slices
Salt
1 cup chicken stock
½ cup red wine, such as Pinot Noir
1 (8-oz) can crushed tomatoes
1 cup shredded aged Manchego cheese (5 oz)
½ cup Marcona almonds, chopped
1 Tbsp ancho chili powder

STOLLER FAMILY ESTATE

KATE PAYNE BROWN
WINEMAKER

REGION
WILLAMETTE VALLEY

Kate Payne Brown thought she had her career all planned out. Fresh out of college with a bachelor's in biology and chemistry, she was on track to becoming an optometrist when a chance encounter with a wine consultant awakened her inner nomad. "I thought, 'He gets to travel the world drinking wine and consulting on grapes. I'd like to travel the world drinking wine, too.'"

So she did just that, enrolling in the prestigious Master of Viticulture and Oenology program at Australia's University of Adelaide. When she graduated, she and her new husband, who also took the plunge into the wine industry while down under, planned on staying in Australia, but realized they had found their place and their people after working a harvest in Oregon. "Because of the climate, it takes an adventurous spirit to make wine here in Oregon. And because of that, it draws people who are interested in continuing to learn and experiment," she says.

But the region's proclivity for sparkling wine is really what sealed the deal. "Anyone who knows me knows I adore sparkling wine, and Oregon is known as a perfect place to grow the holy trinity of sparkling grapes: Pinot Noir, Pinot Meunier, and Chardonnay."

Her winemaking dreams came true in 2016, when she joined Stoller Family Estate and was invited to head the sparkling wine program. Best of all, Stoller's slightly warmer vineyard site offered her the opportunity to get creative about her approach. "What's great about my science background is it laid a strong foundation to color outside the lines and know where I can move beyond the textbook."

Kate says she probably would have been perfectly happy as an optometrist, but the work wouldn't have captured her heart the way winemaking has. "I see myself as a storyteller. Wines are a time capsule, or like visiting an old friend. The making of it is tied to memories of people and of a time and place. It's personal and nostalgic, and so beautiful in that way."

STEAK TARTARE

CHEF: BECCA RICHARDS, STOLLER WINE GROUP CULINARY DIRECTOR

Serves 4

16 oz quality beef tenderloin
Salt and black pepper, to taste
2 shallots, finely chopped (about ⅔ cup)
3 Tbsp non-pareil capers, drained but not rinsed, roughly chopped
1 Tbsp thinly sliced scallion
1 Tbsp chopped Italian parsley
1 tsp finely chopped chives
½ tsp grated lemon zest
2 Tbsp Dijon mustard
2 tsp sherry vinegar
2 tsp Worcestershire sauce
¼ cup flavorful extra-virgin olive oil
4 egg yolks
Flaky sea salt
Espelette pepper or chili flakes of your choice
Kettle chips, to serve

WINE PAIRING: Stoller Family Estate Reserve Pinot Noir

Chef Becca Richards is exacting about the freshness of her ingredients, which is why she can confidently serve dishes with minimal intervention, like this steak tartare. The only secret to making this at home is sourcing high-quality beef tenderloin or top sirloin from a butcher shop. She also recommends farm-fresh, pasture-raised eggs for their rich, flavorful yolks. "Some people like it mustardy, some folks like it with more capers. The beauty of this recipe is that the final flavor profile is all up to you."

Steaks aren't often paired with Pinot because, once cooked, the flavor can get big, fatty, and overwhelming. But when uncooked and lightly dressed, the flavor remains clean and fresh—perfect for enhancing the elegant profile of Stoller's Reserve Pinot Noir.

Cut beef into strips and freeze for 10 to 15 minutes to firm up. Dice into ⅛-inch cubes. If beef warms and softens while cutting, return it to the freezer for a few minutes to chill and firm back up.

In a mixing bowl, mix beef with a pinch of salt and pepper. Add shallots and capers and gently stir. Add scallion, parsley, chives, and lemon zest. Gently stir. Add mustard, vinegar, and Worcestershire sauce. Stir again and adjust taste with more flavorings. Add olive oil and season again to taste.

Place a 3- to 4-inch ring mold in the center of a plate (or fashion one out of aluminum foil). Spoon tartare mixture into the mold, gently packing it. (Don't press too hard, or juices will squeeze out onto the plate.)

Using the back of a spoon, make a divot in the center of the tartare and add egg yolk (remove the globule-like chalazae if still attached). Garnish with a pinch of flaky salt and Espelette pepper (or chili flakes). Repeat with the remaining plates. Serve with kettle chips for scooping.

Shellfish Platter with Mignonette and Cocktail Sauce (p. 212)

SHELLFISH PLATTER
with Mignonette and Cocktail Sauce

CHEF: BECCA RICHARDS, STOLLER WINE GROUP CULINARY DIRECTOR

WINE PAIRING: Stoller Family Estate LaRue's Brut Rosé

Serves 4

Few things are more stunningly impressive and as perfectly suited to sparkling wine as a great shellfish platter. For this version, chef Becca Richards offers a trio of sauces, including a mignonette with a splash of sparkling rosé that adds fun effervescence with every slurp. Every element but the oysters can be prepped ahead, so when guests arrive all you have to do is shuck and serve.

COCKTAIL SAUCE In a small mixing bowl, combine all ingredients. Cover and refrigerate at least 1 hour or up to 3 days.

SPARKLING ROSÉ MIGNONETTE In a small mixing bowl, combine all ingredients except the rosé. Cover and refrigerate at least 1 hour or up to 2 days. When ready to serve, mix in the rosé.

YUZU, SHISHITO, AND CUCUMBER SAUCE In a small mixing bowl, combine all ingredients. Cover and refrigerate at least 1 hour or up to 2 days.

POACHED SHRIMP In a large saucepan, combine all ingredients except the shrimp, including both halves of the juiced lemon, and add 2 cups water. Bring to a boil. Set a large bowl of ice water nearby.

Add shrimp and cook for 3 to 4 minutes, just until pink. Remove shrimp from poaching liquid and plunge into ice water to stop the cooking. Discard poaching liquid. Drain shrimp and refrigerate until cold. (Can be made 1 day ahead.)

ASSEMBLY Using a sturdy knife or kitchen shears, split shells of crab legs to make meat extraction easy for your guests.

Rinse oysters in a bowl of ice water with baking soda. Make sure to agitate them to help purge the grit. Place cleaned oysters in a second bowl filled with ice to keep them cold.

Put a bed of crushed ice on a serving platter. As you shuck oysters, arrange them in a ring around the outside so the point of the shell goes inward and the cups face the edge. Check shucked oysters for shell fragments and make sure they smell fresh and clean. (If not, throw away.)

COCKTAIL SAUCE
¾ cup ketchup
1 Tbsp Worcestershire sauce
1 Tbsp prepared horseradish
¾ tsp black pepper
½ tsp salt
Grated zest and juice of ½ lemon

SPARKLING ROSÉ MIGNONETTE
¼ cup finely chopped shallot
2 Tbsp champagne vinegar
¾ tsp black pepper
Pinch of granulated sugar
Pinch of salt
2 Tbsp sparkling rosé

YUZU, SHISHITO, AND CUCUMBER SAUCE
1 shishito or jalapeño pepper, seeded if desired, thinly sliced
3 Tbsp peeled, seeded, and finely diced cucumber
1 Tbsp finely chopped shallot
1½ tsp granulated sugar
½ tsp black pepper
¼ cup rice wine vinegar
2 Tbsp yuzu juice (see Note)
2 Tbsp lime ponzu (see Note)

NOTE Yuzu juice is very sour and made from the juice of the yuzu fruit, which tastes like a cross between lemons, limes, and grapefruits. Lime ponzu is a sweet-sour sauce made with lime juice, soy sauce, and sugar. Find both at Asian markets or online retailers.

4 sprigs Italian parsley

2 sprigs thyme

3 cloves garlic, gently smashed

1 bay leaf

3 Tbsp salt

1 tsp black peppercorns

1 cup Stoller Family Estate Reserve
    Chardonnay

Juice and rinds of 1 lemon

12 sustainably sourced giant
    tiger prawns or colossal shrimp
    (U/15), shelled, tails on,
    and deveined

ASSEMBLY

1 lb cooked Dungeness or king
    crab legs

12 oysters (see Shucking
    Instructions)

Pinch of baking soda

Crushed ice, for serving (ask your
    fishmonger)

Lemon wedges, for serving

Horseradish root, for garnish

Finely chopped chives, for garnish

Next, make an inner ring of crab legs with lemon wedges arranged intermittently between. Place shrimp in the center of the platter. Top shrimp with a little grating of horseradish root and finely chopped chives.

Just before serving, add sparkling rosé to your mignonette so guests can see the effervescence. Dip poached shrimp in the cocktail sauce and enjoy the crab with a squeeze of fresh lemon. For the oysters, try both sauces.

SHUCKING INSTRUCTIONS

Once oysters are cleaned, fold a kitchen towel lengthwise into thirds. You'll be using it to brace the oyster and, most importantly, to protect your hand. Put the largest part of the shell, belly side down, on the folded towel with the hinge point (not the curve) facing out. Fold the towel over the top of the oyster to hold with your non-dominant hand. Place your oyster knife between the top shell and the belly shell at the pointy part facing out of the towel. Then, wiggle the knife slightly into that space until you feel the hinge.

When you feel that pressure point, lever the knife tip upward to pop the hinge—it may take a wiggle or even a slight twist of the oyster knife. Drag the knife blade across the top shell for the cleanest opening. When the top shell is off, use your finger and sweep out any grit, sand, or mud in the cup surrounding the oyster.

At this stage, it's essential to check the oyster for anything that could be off; smell is a huge indicator. If it smells bad when you open it, it is bad. There can be shell fragments and (rarely) tiny crabs inside the oyster. If you see one, it doesn't mean the oyster is bad; just remove them and toss the top shell, shell fragments, and the little crabs away.

To finish shucking, wipe the blade of your knife clean and sweep it under the oyster to cut through the foot (or adductor) that anchors it to the shell so your guests can pick up the oyster and slurp without having to loosen it themselves. Once that is all completed, grab your next oyster and repeat.

TROON VINEYARD

NATE WALL
WINEMAKER

REGION
ROGUE VALLEY

"What can we do next?" is a question that's transformed Troon Vineyard since new ownership took the reins in 2016. That's why when you arrive at the wine farm in the Applegate Valley, you'll find a grove of newly rooted cider apple trees, a botanical garden with almost a hundred different species of native plants, and a robust plot of heirloom vegetables.

You'll also spy a herd of sheep for natural mowing, a boundless pollinator habitat, and biodynamic apiaries for native bee species. The belief here is that biodiversity makes for better wines—a mantra swiftly gaining traction across the region.

"I joined right as they started the shift from conventional to biodynamic agriculture," says winemaker Nate Wall. "It was an opportunity I couldn't pass up." Before Nate found his way to wine, he had an established career in microbiology and environmental engineering, a natural segue into the world of studying complex soil microbial communities.

Like many winemakers, he was drawn to biodynamic agriculture for pragmatic reasons: the best wines he tasted were from biodynamic vineyards. "It gives wines a unique voice," he says. "I can taste that this wine has something to say—it's not a background wine."

Over the past few years, he's worked with the team at Troon as they've implemented biodynamic practices along with regenerative agriculture in the vineyard, working to rebuild soil health. "What I value most about regenerative agriculture is that it doesn't just sustain, it goes beyond and repairs and improves."

In 2021, Troon Vineyard became the second winery in the world to become Regenerative Organic Certified (ROC), a newer designation that encompasses three pillars— soil health, animal welfare, and social fairness—and the rally to "farm like the world depends on it."

As for the wines? Nate finds a purity to the fruit, a deeper expression of place. The estate plantings lean mostly to Rhône varieties including Syrah, Grenache, and Mourvèdre, but there's also a smattering of unusual grapes such as Tannat, Négrette, and Vermentino.

"One grape that's absolutely thriving is Vermentino," he says. "It's clearly meant to grow right here."

Pastrami Beet Reuben (p. 216)

PASTRAMI BEET REUBEN

CHEF: CARL KRAUSE, WILDER COOKING AND EARNEST BAKING COMPANY

WINE PAIRING: Troon Vineyard Estate Syrah

A heady blend of spices and a stint on the smoker transform humble beets into little flavor bombs that are so good you won't miss the meat. With melty Swiss cheese, tangy sauerkraut, and a generous slather of homemade Russian dressing, these grilled sandwiches are well worth the time investment. The black pepper notes in Troon's Estate Syrah play off the pastrami spices in a delightful way. This is a popular pairing at winery events and the chef's personal favorite. "It's fun to take a pretty humble vegetable and treat it like the star of the show," he says.

BEET BRINE Preheat oven to 300°F.

Place all ingredients in a Dutch oven and pour in 4 cups water. The liquid should almost cover the beets completely. Bring to a boil over high heat. Cover, then transfer to the oven. Cook for 1½ to 3 hours, depending on the size of the beets, until they are tender enough to be easily pierced with a fork. Remove from the brine and set aside to cool. Refrigerate, uncovered, overnight.

PASTRAMI RUB Preheat a smoker to 200°F and add a handful of soaked wood chips such as alder wood. (Alternatively, preheat the oven to 200°F. This will make "corned" beets rather than pastrami beets, as smoke is the only difference.)

Mix all ingredients in a large bowl. Add the brined beets and toss to coat. Arrange beets on a rack in the smoker or a baking sheet in the oven and cook for 3 hours. (Beets will keep in the refrigerator for 5 days.)

Serves 4

BEET BRINE
4 to 6 medium beets, trimmed and peeled (about 1½ lbs)
4 cloves garlic, crushed
3 cardamom pods, crushed
3 Tbsp salt
3 Tbsp packed brown sugar
2 Tbsp honey
2 tsp pickling spice
2 tsp juniper berries
1 tsp coriander seeds
1 tsp mustard seeds

PASTRAMI RUB
2 Tbsp ground coriander
1 Tbsp salt
1 Tbsp garlic powder
1 Tbsp packed brown sugar
2 tsp black pepper

1 small shallot, finely chopped

½ cup mayonnaise

¼ cup ketchup

2 Tbsp relish

2 tsp prepared horseradish

2 tsp lemon juice

1 tsp Dijon mustard

½ tsp paprika

ASSEMBLY

Pastrami Beets (see here),
   thinly sliced

1 cup drained and rinsed sauerkraut

8 slices Swiss cheese

8 slices rye sandwich bread

¼ cup (½ stick) butter, softened

1 cup Russian Dressing (see here)

RUSSIAN DRESSING Mix all ingredients in a small bowl. Makes 1 cup. (Can be made 1 week in advance and refrigerated.)

ASSEMBLY Preheat oven to 350°F.

Divide sliced beets into 4 piles on a parchment-lined baking sheet. Spread each into mounds of similar dimensions as the bread. Divide the sauerkraut among each mound and place 2 slices of Swiss cheese over each. Bake for 5 minutes, or until the cheese starts to melt.

Meanwhile, preheat a cast-iron skillet over medium-high heat. Spread one side of each bread slice with butter. Add 2 slices of bread to the pan, buttered side down, and toast until golden. Remove and repeat with the remaining bread slices.

Slather untoasted sides of the bread with 2 tablespoons dressing. Place a stack of beets, sauerkraut, and cheese on 4 slices, then place the other toasted slices on top. Fry each sandwich in the skillet over medium-high heat for 1 minute on each side to re-crisp. Cut in half and serve.

ROASTED VEGETABLES
with Baked Tofu, Brown Rice, and Herbed Tahini Sauce

CHEF: NATE WALL, TROON VINEYARD

WINE PAIRING: Troon Vineyard Kubli Bench Estate Vermentino

Winemaker Nate Wall loves to fuel up with veggie-packed bowls. He roasts a garden's worth of vegetables, then piles them on brown rice with flavorful baked tofu and zesty, nutty tahini sauce. Pair this with Vermentino, a Corsican grape with a slightly saline touch that's quite versatile and phenomenal with shellfish. Troon's rich and textural version pairs perfectly with bright herbs, light sauces, and all those hard-to-match vegetables.

BAKED TOFU Cut tofu into 1-inch-thick slabs. Arrange in an even layer on a clean, lint-free dish towel or paper towels and place another towel on top. Set a cutting board on top and weight with a heavy pan or cans for 30 minutes. (Pressing tofu gives it a firmer texture and allows it to absorb flavors better.)

Preheat oven to 400°F. Line a baking sheet with parchment paper.

In a mixing bowl, combine the remaining ingredients. Cut pressed tofu slabs into 1-inch cubes, add to the bowl, and toss to coat.

Arrange tofu in an even layer on the prepared baking sheet. Bake for 25 to 30 minutes, tossing halfway through, until golden brown around the edges.

Serves 4

BAKED TOFU
1 (12- to 15-oz) block organic
    extra-firm tofu, drained
1 Tbsp extra-virgin olive oil
1 Tbsp soy sauce or tamari
1 Tbsp cornstarch or arrowroot
    starch
½ tsp ground ginger
½ tsp garlic powder

ROASTED VEGETABLES

5 cloves garlic

3 small sweet potatoes, peeled and cut into ¾-inch chunks

2 carrots, peeled and cut into ¾-inch chunks

1 red onion, cut into 1-inch chunks

1 large red bell pepper, seeded, deveined, and cut into 1-inch chunks

½ small head cauliflower or broccoli, cut into florets

8 oz cremini mushrooms, ends trimmed and halved if large

¼ cup avocado oil or other high-heat oil

1 Tbsp dried Italian seasoning

1 Tbsp porcini powder or umami seasoning blend

Salt and black pepper, to taste

HERBED TAHINI SAUCE

½ cup tahini

Grated zest and juice of 1 lemon, plus more to taste

½ cup packed Italian parsley

½ cup packed cilantro

½ tsp red pepper flakes

½ tsp garlic powder

Salt, to taste

ASSEMBLY

5 cups steamed brown rice

ROASTED VEGETABLES Preheat oven to 450°F.

In a large mixing bowl, combine garlic, vegetables, and oil and toss to coat. Add seasonings and toss again. Season generously with salt and pepper.

Transfer vegetables onto two baking sheets and spread out in even layers. Roast for 20 to 30 minutes, flipping vegetables over halfway through, until lightly browned.

HERBED TAHINI SAUCE Combine all ingredients in a blender or food processor, add ⅓ cup water, and blend until creamy and smooth, occasionally stopping to scrape down the sides. Add more water if needed to reach desired consistency. Adjust taste with more lemon juice and/or seasonings.

ASSEMBLY Divide rice among bowls, top with roasted vegetables and baked tofu, and spoon herbed tahini sauce on top.

VALCAN CELLARS

JUAN PABLO VALOT
OWNER AND WINEMAKER

REGION
WILLAMETTE VALLEY

For many, wine is a universal language. That's certainly true for Juan Pablo "JP" Valot. JP grew up in Rivadavia, a city outside the province of Mendoza, Argentina. Many of his relatives, including his grandfather and father, worked in Argentina's thriving wine industry. Inspired by his roots, JP graduated from college in 2001 with a degree in agricultural engineering and a focus on vineyard management and winemaking.

As he was pursuing internships, fate—or rather fortune—stepped in. Instead of heading to Europe, where he was exploring options in either Spain or Italy, a twist of timing landed him in Oregon. "It was so clean and green and beautiful," he says. He quickly fell in love with the evergreens, the wine community, and the food.

JP worked for Soter (page 204) and Willamette Valley Vineyards (page 226) before moving to Eugene where he joined Silvan Ridge Winery in 2005 and is now the head winemaker. As he put down roots, he kept thinking about his dad's dream of a family winery. "His dream became my dream," says JP. And as an ode to his heritage, he launched Valcan Cellars in 2012. The name is a portmanteau, blending his last name with that of his wife, Doris Cancel. "We created the business as a legacy for our children," he says. For his small-batch wines, JP sources Pinot Noir, Pinot Gris, and Chardonnay from the Willamette Valley. He also works with grapes from the Rogue Valley in Southern Oregon, including Tempranillo, Syrah, Petit Sirah, Malbec, and Barbera.

But his calling card is Malbec, a wine he makes to be balanced and approachable with juicy plum and dark fruit flavors. "Malbec keeps me connected to Mendoza, it's the bridge to my roots in Argentina."

JP's creative spin on the grape includes a Malbec rosé, a white Malbec, and a red sparkling Malbec. For the latter two, he's the first winemaker in the U.S. to release wines made in that style. The inspiration? "I just love Malbec!" he says.

ENSALADA DEL HUERTO
with Yuzu Vinaigrette and Quinoa Crackers

CHEF: NATHAN HARDING, ANDINA

WINE PAIRING: Valcan Cellars White Malbec

This Peruvian salad pops with bright colors from roasted corn and bell peppers and bright flavor from a tangy yuzu vinaigrette. Crispy quinoa crackers add a welcome touch of earthiness and crunch.

The first white Malbec released by an American winery, this bottle from Valcan Cellars spurs great dinner party conversations. The crisp melon and citrus flavors stand out and the brisk acidity makes it an ideal match for the lively layers in the salad.

ROCOTO YUZU VINAIGRETTE Combine all ingredients in a jar and shake until emulsified. (Can be made 5 days ahead and refrigerated.)

QUINOA CRACKERS Purée all ingredients in a blender or food processor. With the machine running, slowly add ¼ cup water and process until a dough forms. Set aside to rest at room temperature for 30 to 60 minutes.

Preheat oven to 400°F. Set a sheet of parchment paper on a work surface.

Roll out the dough on the parchment paper until very thin, about 1⁄16 inch. Transfer the parchment with the rolled-out dough to a baking sheet. Bake for 15 minutes, until browned around the edges. Cut into quarters, turn the pieces so the middle areas are now on the outside edge, and bake 5 minutes more until fully golden. Set aside to cool, then break into 3- or 4-inch pieces.

Serves 4 to 6

ROCOTO YUZU VINAIGRETTE
1 clove garlic, finely chopped
1 small shallot, finely chopped
2 Tbsp rice wine vinegar
2 Tbsp Kewpie mayo
2½ Tbsp yuzu juice (see Note)
1 Tbsp honey
2½ tsp Dijon mustard
2 tsp aji rocoto (hot pepper purée; see Note)
¼ cup extra-virgin olive oil
Salt, to taste

QUINOA CRACKERS
1 cup all-purpose flour, plus extra for dusting
¾ cup cooked quinoa
1 Tbsp chopped huacatay (see Note)
1 tsp salt
1 tsp black pepper
⅓ cup extra-virgin olive oil

NOTE Yuzu juice can be found at Asian markets or online retailers.

Aji rocoto is a Peruvian chile pepper with a bright fruity heat like a habanero but with a much fleshier texture. You can find jars of the purée at Latin and Caribbean markets or online retailers like Amazon.

Huacatay, also called black mint, is a Peruvian herb with a savory mint flavor. If you can't find it, a mix of cilantro and mint is a good substitute.

2 ears corn, shucked and broken
    in half
1 red bell pepper, seeded,
    deveined, and quartered
1 orange bell pepper, seeded,
    deveined, and quartered
1 Tbsp extra-virgin olive oil
2 plums, diced
1 cup Riesling grapes or other
    sweet white grapes
1 avocado, cut into ½-inch cubes
½ small red onion, thinly sliced
    and soaked in ice water for
    10 minutes
1 cup crumbled queso fresco
Rocoto Yuzu Vinaigrette (see here),
    for drizzling
Salt and black pepper, to taste
Cilantro, for garnish

ENSALADA DEL HUERTO Preheat broiler.

Bring a large saucepan of water to a boil and set a bowl of ice water nearby. Add corn to the pan and cook for 1 minute. Transfer to the bowl of ice water to stop the cooking.

Place corn and bell peppers on a baking sheet. Drizzle with oil and toss to coat. Broil for 10 minutes, turning corn regularly, until corn and peppers are lightly charred.

When cool enough to handle, dice peppers and shave corn kernels off the cob. In a mixing bowl, combine corn, peppers, plums, grapes, avocado, onion, and queso fresco. Add just enough vinaigrette to lightly coat. Season to taste with salt and pepper.

Divide among bowls, garnish with cilantro leaves and serve with quinoa crackers on the side.

LOMO SALTADO
with Papas Fritas

CHEF: NATHAN HARDING, ANDINA

WINE PAIRING: Valcan Cellars El Torero Tempranillo

Serves 4

Deeply savory, with a mild glow of heat, these tender cubes of marinated beef are served on garlicky steamed rice for maximum deliciousness. At Andina Restaurant in Portland, this Peruvian dish also comes with crispy papas fritas (aka french fries), so don't be shy about grabbing a bag of your favorite frozen fries to go with it. This dish calls for a robust red, and Valcan Cellars's El Torero Tempranillo, with deep blackberry flavors and layers of cedar and spice, is the perfect partner.

MARINATED BEEF Combine all marinade ingredients in a mixing bowl. Add beef and marinate for 30 minutes at room temperature.

GARLIC RICE Rinse rice in several changes of water.

Heat oil in a medium saucepan over medium heat. Add garlic and gently cook for 2 minutes, until softened and fragrant but not browned. Stir in rice, salt, and 1¾ cups water. Bring to a simmer over medium-high heat, then reduce heat to low. Cover and cook for 15 minutes. Remove from heat and set aside, covered, for 5 minutes. Fluff with a fork.

ASSEMBLY Heat oil in a large cast-iron skillet over high heat. Remove beef cubes from bowl, reserving marinade. Working in batches to avoid overcrowding, add beef to the pan in an even layer. Sear until nicely browned and the meat easily releases from the pan. Turn and repeat on the other sides. Transfer to a plate. Repeat with the rest of the beef.

Add more oil to the pan if needed and add the onion. Sauté for 5 minutes, or until softened. Add pisco (or wine) to deglaze the pan, stirring to scrape up the browned bits. Add tomatoes and aji limo (or habanero) and sauté 1 minute. Add seared beef and reserved marinade and cook on high heat, until liquid is slightly reduced. Remove from heat, move beef and vegetables over to the side, and whisk in cold butter to create a creamy sauce.

Divide garlic rice among bowls, place beef and pan sauce on top, and garnish with cilantro. Serve with a handful of papas fritas (french fries).

MARINATED BEEF
6 cloves garlic, finely chopped
½ tsp ground cumin
½ tsp dried oregano
½ cup low-sodium soy sauce
2 Tbsp red wine vinegar
1 Tbsp tomato paste
1 Tbsp lime juice
10 oz beef tenderloin or sirloin, cut into 2-inch cubes

GARLIC RICE
1 cup jasmine rice
2 Tbsp extra-virgin olive oil
3 cloves garlic, finely chopped
1 tsp salt

ASSEMBLY
1 Tbsp vegetable oil, plus more as needed
1 large red onion, halved and thickly sliced
1 Tbsp pisco or white wine
3 Roma tomatoes, seeded and quartered
1 aji limo or habanero pepper, seeded, deveined, and cut into matchsticks
2 Tbsp cold butter
Cilantro leaves, for garnish
Papas fritas (cooked french fries), to serve

WILLAMETTE VALLEY VINEYARDS

JIM BERNAU
FOUNDER
AND CEO

REGION
WILLAMETTE VALLEY

Willamette Valley Vineyards was established in 1983 when Jim Bernau planted an overgrown pioneer plum orchard in the Salem Hills with Pinot Noir, watering his vines with seventeen lengths of seventy-five-foot garden hose.

While the vines grew, Jim focused on helping other Oregon winegrowers by seeking the state's help to create a full-fledged industry. "We were a ragtag group from different walks of life," he says. "Engineers, urban planners, dentists, physicians. We could all meet in each other's homes."

That work included pushing for new laws so they could ship their wines to other states and policies that protected vineyard lands but also allowed wineries to offer food and hospitality to the growing number of tourists. Later, his work helped establish the Oregon Wine Board. And his personal gift to Oregon State University created

the first professorship for fermentation science in the nation. These things, pivotal to the growth of the industry, are taken for granted now, but they wouldn't have happened without an outside-the-box thinker who is also a passionate winemaker.

Jim took the same innovative approach as founder and CEO of Willamette Valley Vineyards, growing it into a world-class winery and a leading producer of Pinot Noir. He paved the way for community funding for small businesses when he built his winery by conducting the first "crowdfunding" in the nation, obtaining permission from the Securities and Exchange Commission in 1988. Today, Willamette Valley Vineyards has grown to more than 24,000 wine enthusiast

shareholders and is listed on the NASDAQ under the symbols WVVI and WVVIP.

And he's done it all through a lens focused on sustainability. Willamette Valley Vineyards and Jim personally have been recognized for environmentally responsible wine-growing by LIVE (Low Impact Viticulture and Enology) and received the Sustainable Standard-Setter Award from the Rainforest Alliance for their use of FSC-certified cork. In 2014, Jim was honored with the Los Heroes de Salud! award for his contributions to providing health care to Oregon's vineyard workers. "Willamette Valley Vineyards is a vehicle by which we can develop and innovate better ways of stewardship," he says.

Chicken and Seafood Paella (p. 228)

CHICKEN AND SEAFOOD PAELLA

CHEF: DJ MACINTYRE, WILLAMETTE VALLEY VINEYARDS

WINE PAIRING: Willamette Valley Vineyards Bernau Block Chardonnay

Serves 6 to 8

Chef DJ MacIntyre at Willamette Valley Vineyards says this is a great recipe for large gatherings—just double the ingredients and cook it outdoors in a twenty-two-inch paella pan. You'll get a classic hint of smoky flavor that way, too. "But have all the ingredients prepped and ready before you start," he says, "as the process is quick." The shellfish makes this an ideal pairing with a crisp glass of chilled Willamette Valley Vineyards Bernau Block Chardonnay.

Season chicken with 1½ teaspoons of salt and 1½ teaspoons pepper.

Heat oil in a 15- to 18-inch paella pan or large skillet over medium-high heat until hot. Add scallops and shrimp and sear for 90 seconds per side. Transfer to a plate.

Add chicken to the pan in an even layer without crowding and sear for 1½ minutes per side. Transfer to a plate.

Add peppers, onion, bay leaves, paprika, chili threads (or pepper), and bouillon powder. Cook for 2 minutes, until vegetables begin to char.

Add tomatoes and garlic and sauté until tomatoes blister. Stir in rice and chicken. Pour in wine, stirring to scrape up the browned bits. Add saffron water, 4 cups stock, and remaining 1 tablespoon each salt and pepper. Reduce heat to medium and cook for 12 to 15 minutes, stirring occasionally to keep the rice evenly submerged, until almost al dente.

Nestle clams and mussels in the rice and add remaining 1½ cups stock. Do not stir from this point on. Arrange scallops and shrimp on top. Cook for 5 minutes, until the clam and mussel shells open up. (Discard any that don't.)

Remove pan from the heat, lightly tent with foil, and allow to rest for 5 minutes to let the remaining liquid absorb. Garnish with parsley and lemon wedges.

½ lb boneless, skinless chicken thighs, cut into ¾-inch cubes

1½ Tbsp salt (divided)

1½ Tbsp black pepper (divided)

¼ cup canola oil

¾ lb dry-packed sea scallops, side muscle removed if necessary (see Note on page 143)

½ lb large white shrimp (16/20), shelled, tails on, and deveined

1 red bell pepper, seeded, cored, and sliced into 2-inch strips

1 yellow bell pepper, seeded, cored, and sliced into 2-inch strips

½ white onion, diced (1 cup)

2 bay leaves

1½ Tbsp smoked paprika

1½ tsp red chili threads (see Note on page 92) or use Espelette or Aleppo pepper

3 chicken bouillon cubes, crushed into a powder

12 cherry tomatoes

3 cloves garlic, finely chopped

2¼ cups bomba rice (1 lb)

2 cups dry white wine

¾ tsp saffron threads, mixed with 2 Tbsp hot water

5½ cups warm chicken stock (divided)

¼ lb Manila clams, cleaned

¼ lb mussels, cleaned and debearded

2 Tbsp chopped Italian parsley, for garnish

2 lemons, cut into wedges, for garnish

FLANK STEAK
with Currant and Walnut Stuffing

CHEF: DJ MACINTYRE, WILLAMETTE VALLEY VINEYARDS

Serves 4

¼ cup walnuts, chopped
3 Tbsp butter
¼ small onion, diced (about ¼ cup)
1 Tbsp finely chopped garlic
1 stalk celery, diced (½ cup)
2 cups coarse breadcrumbs
1½ tsp dried thyme
1 tsp dried savory
½ tsp grated lemon zest
¼ to ½ cup warm chicken stock
    (divided)
¼ cup black, red, or white currants,
    thawed if frozen
Salt and black pepper
½ tsp granulated garlic
½ tsp onion powder
1 (1½- to 2-lb) flank steak
1 Tbsp extra-virgin olive oil

WINE PAIRING: Willamette Valley Vineyards Elton Pinot Noir

This elegant entrée, ideal for special occasions, has deep roots in chef DJ MacIntyre's family. "As a child, I remember every holiday season climbing up on a stool and helping my father chop and prep the ingredients. I still make this recipe with my family today." The savory stuffing, which must be made a day ahead, is studded with walnuts and fresh currants. It echoes the earthy berry notes in Willamette Valley Vineyards's Elton Pinot Noir, allowing the rich flank steak to pair beautifully with the wine.

Preheat oven to 350°F. Spread walnuts evenly on a baking sheet and toast for about 5 minutes, until golden and fragrant.

Melt butter in a medium skillet over medium heat. Add onion and garlic and sauté for 4 to 6 minutes, until onion is softened. Set aside to cool to room temperature.

In a large bowl, combine celery, breadcrumbs, walnuts, thyme, savory, and lemon zest. Stir in the onion-garlic mixture.

Add ¼ cup stock. Gently mix until butter and stock have completely integrated with breadcrumbs, breaking up any large chunks. Add a little more stock, 2 spoonfuls at a time, until stuffing can hold its shape for 5 to 6 seconds before crumbling. (You want it to be just moist enough, but not too moist or it will become dense after it absorbs the juices of the cooked meat.) Fold in currants and season to taste with salt and pepper. Transfer to an airtight container and refrigerate overnight to let the ingredients meld.

In a small bowl, combine 1½ tsp salt, 1 tsp pepper, granulated garlic, and onion powder. Lay flank steak on a baking sheet. Using a sharp knife, gently score one side of the meat and then season both sides with the spice mixture. Allow the steak to sit at room temperature for 30 minutes.

Preheat oven to 400°F. With scored side up, mound as much stuffing as will fit lengthwise down the middle of the steak. Pull sides up and over the stuffing like a long tube. Tie with butcher's twine or use short metal skewers to pin sides together.

Pack ends with more stuffing. Brush the steak with olive oil. Place on a rack inside a roasting pan or on a foil-lined baking sheet. Roast for 10 to 20 minutes, until steak temperature (not the stuffing) reads 130°F for medium-rare. Set aside meat to rest for 7 minutes. Slice crosswise with a sharp knife and serve.

WINDERLEA VINEYARD AND WINERY

DONNA MORRIS AND BILL SWEAT
OWNERS

REGION
WILLAMETTE VALLEY

For Donna Morris and Bill Sweat, exploring the tiny wine shops in Boston's Beacon Hill and North End on their first dates was the start of their wine story. It was the 1980s and they were both working in the financial services industry and loved learning about wine.

"We eventually found our way to Burgundy and it was all over from there," jokes Bill. They became avid wine lovers, traveling to wine regions around the world for vacation. After working in Japan for a few years, the time abroad inspired them to explore a significant life change. "We always came back to wine and vineyards," says Donna.

A quick scan of their cellar confirmed their love of Pinot Noir, especially Oregon's delicate, elegant wines. "Our favorite wines were from the Dundee Hills," says Bill. In 2004, they traveled to the Willamette Valley multiple times, walking thousands of acres of

vineyards to find the perfect site. "We are big believers in serendipity," he says.

Almost two years later, they found their dream property, a twenty-acre vineyard in the Dundee Hills. Planted in 1974, the historic vineyard was located where Oregon's international recognition for great Pinot Noir took root. It was kismet.

As the couple built out their business plan, they prioritized sustainability. "It was part of the ethos we grew up with and we wanted to create a winery with that foundation," says Bill. They immediately pursued organic and biodynamic certifications for the vineyard

along with plans for an eco-friendly, energy-efficient tasting room that includes solar-integrated architecture.

Winderlea is also one of a handful of wineries that comprise the Oregon Wine Country EV Byway, with two electric car chargers out front. In 2015, the winery became a certified B Corp.

Most recently, the couple welcomed a flock of sheep to their vineyard, natural mowers for weed control. With salt-and-pepper fluffs speckled across the vineyard, "The view just keeps getting better," says Bill.

SALAD OF LUSCIOUS FRUITS
with Creamy Burrata and Aromatic Herbs

CHEFS: JARET FOSTER AND MONA JOHNSON, TOURNANT

Serves 4

3 lbs mixed ripe summer fruits,
    such as heirloom tomatoes,
    peaches, plums, figs, grapes,
    and/or melon

Flaky salt

White balsamic vinegar,
    for drizzling

Orange blossom water

8 oz burrata

High-quality extra-virgin olive oil,
    for drizzling

1 cup torn aromatic herbs,
    such as anise hyssop, shiso,
    bronze fennel, and/or any
    variety of basil

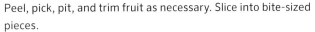

WINE PAIRING: Winderlea Chardonnay

Every meal from Tournant showcases the season, not only because they often happen outdoors in the most spectacular settings, but also because chefs Jaret Foster and Mona Johnson build their menus around the freshest ingredients available at that particular moment. This salad is a perfect example of that philosophy. Best of all, it has a secret ingredient: orange blossom water, available at spice shops and Middle Eastern markets. Pour some in an atomizer and spritz it over the salad, or just sprinkle a tiny bit on. Too much and it can taste perfumey, but a whisper tastes magical and enhances the lovely orange blossom and stone fruit notes of Winderlea's silky Chardonnay.

Peel, pick, pit, and trim fruit as necessary. Slice into bite-sized pieces.

    Arrange decoratively on a serving platter, then sprinkle with a bit of flaky salt and drizzle with vinegar. Very sparingly, sprinkle a hint of orange blossom water over the fruit.

    Tear burrata into pieces over salad. Drizzle liberally with oil. Sprinkle again with flaky salt and scatter herbs on top.

233

LAVENDER HONEY-GLAZED PORK BELLY
with Ratatouille, White Beans, and Basil

CHEFS: JARET FOSTER AND MONA JOHNSON, TOURNANT

WINE PAIRING: Winderlea Vineyard Estate Pinot Noir

Serves 4 to 6

Tournant's immersive, farm-to-fire dinners, retreats, and workshops in the forests and along the shores of the Pacific Northwest are nothing short of a celebration of place, and when summer comes, this lovely meal often takes center stage. For maximum color, aim for a mix of eggplant and squash varieties. Winderlea's Estate Pinot Noir, with its bright and juicy red fruit notes and supple texture, offers a harmonious pairing.

PORK BELLY Season pork belly generously with salt, cover, and refrigerate overnight.

Preheat oven to 300°F.

In a Dutch oven, combine stock, wine, garlic, thyme, celery (or fennel), bay leaves, fennel seeds, and coriander seeds and bring to a boil over medium-high heat. Season to taste with salt. Add pork belly, cover with a tight-fitting lid, and transfer to the oven. Braise for 2½ to 3 hours, until very tender.

Transfer pork belly to a rack over a baking sheet and chill, uncovered, in the refrigerator for at least 2 hours or overnight. Strain and reserve braising liquid, discarding solids.

In a small saucepan, bring honey to a boil without browning. Remove from heat and carefully pour in vinegar, as it will bubble up. Add lavender, then return to low heat and simmer for 15 minutes, until slightly reduced and syrupy. Strain and reserve.

If pork belly is rectangular, keep whole. If square, cut in half.

Heat oil in a large cast-iron skillet over medium-high heat. Add chilled pork belly and sear for 2 minutes per side, until nicely browned and warmed through. Add honey glaze and a splash of reserved braising liquid, turning until all sides are well coated. Cook for another 2 minutes, turning pork often, until sauce is reduced to a sticky glaze. Remove from heat and allow to rest for 5 to 10 minutes. Slice into thick slices.

PORK BELLY

1 (1½-lb) center-cut pork belly, preferably rectangular, skin removed

Salt

3 cups chicken or pork stock

1 cup dry white wine

4 cloves garlic, crushed

4 sprigs thyme

2 stalks celery or 1 small fennel bulb, roughly chopped

2 bay leaves

1 tsp fennel seeds

1 tsp coriander seeds

½ cup honey

¼ cup apple cider vinegar

1 Tbsp dried lavender

2 Tbsp neutral oil, such as grapeseed

Extra-virgin olive oil, for frying

1 small globe eggplant, cut into
  ½-inch cubes (4 cups)

Salt

2 small Japanese eggplants, halved
  lengthwise and sliced ½ inch
  thick (4 cups)

1 yellow onion, diced

4 cloves garlic, sliced

2 small zucchinis, halved
  lengthwise and sliced ½ inch
  thick

2 small yellow crookneck squash,
  sliced ½ inch thick, "necks"
  reserved whole

1 cup dry white wine

2 large ripe tomatoes, grated on a
  box grater and skins discarded

3 sprigs thyme

2 cups cooked white beans,
  such as flageolet

1 cup multicolored cherry
  tomatoes, halved (divided)

½ cup green and purple basil
  leaves, torn if large (divided)

ASSEMBLY

Extra-virgin olive oil, for drizzling

Flaky salt

2 squash blossoms, torn into petals
  (optional)

RATATOUILLE Heat a large Dutch oven over medium-high heat. Add enough olive oil to cover the bottom, then add globe eggplant. Sauté for 8 to 10 minutes, until tender and lightly browned. (Add more oil if needed.) Season with salt and transfer to a medium bowl.

Repeat with Japanese eggplants and sauté for 6 minutes, or until tender and lightly browned. Season with salt and add to the bowl of globe eggplant.

Heat another 1 tablespoon oil. Add onion and a pinch of salt and sauté for 5 to 7 minutes, until softened. Add garlic and cook for another minute. Add zucchinis and squash and sauté for 3 to 5 minutes, until softened. Season with salt, then stir in eggplant.

Add wine and cook for 5 minutes, or until most of the liquid has evaporated. Add tomato, thyme and a big pinch of salt and bring to a simmer. Add beans and cook for 5 to 10 minutes, stirring occasionally, until flavors are melded, vegetables are tender, and tomato has reduced to coat vegetables. Season to taste with salt and stir in half of the cherry tomatoes and basil.

ASSEMBLY Spoon ratatouille into a large shallow bowl or onto a rimmed platter. Scatter remaining tomatoes over ratatouille. If desired, use a mandoline to thinly shave reserved squash necks over the dish.

Arrange braised pork belly slices on top of the ratatouille. Drizzle dish with oil and sprinkle with flaky salt. Garnish with remaining basil leaves and squash blossom petals, if using.

WINTER'S HILL ESTATE

RUSSELL GLADHART
OWNER AND MANAGER

REGION
WILLAMETTE VALLEY

In 2004, Russell Gladhart was living in Beaune, the wine capital of Burgundy, studying enology. His wine epiphanies, however, were discovered on hikes, after he came across a guidebook of walking trails for the Côte d'Or. "Every weekend, we'd explore vineyards," he says.

"After walking through different places, day after day, those lines on the map start to make sense." He became attuned to soil, slope, elevation, and myriad other factors influencing the hierarchy of wines in one of the world's foremost wine-growing regions.

Almost twenty years later, he's still walking vineyards—these are just closer to home. On what was originally a grass seed and crimson clover farm, Russell's parents established Winter's Hill Estate in 1990. Set on a hilltop with breathtaking views, the hundred-acre property includes oak savanna,

woodlands, native plants, and pollinator habitats.

In 2015, Russell took on the winemaking role, where the focus is on estate-grown Pinot Noir, Pinot Gris, Chardonnay, and Pinot Blanc. "Growing our own grapes and working with the same vineyard year after year provides real benefits and opportunities to learn," he says.

One of their signature wines is Pinot Blanc, a grape known for bright, crisp flavors. It's usually fermented in stainless steel tanks to capture the fresh varietal characteristics. "And it's delicious,"

says Russell. But he opts to ferment and age their Pinot Blanc in barrels or puncheons. "I like that extra complexity you can get with the barrel fermentation."

Overall, Russell aims for longevity. "Our wines consistently age well and have consistently good structure," he says. "And it's always been the vineyard first, because that's how our business started." Which reminds him, if you're ever in the area, stop by for a hike. He still thinks it's one of the best ways to learn about wine.

Sunflower Seed and Orange Bread (p. 238)

SUNFLOWER SEED AND ORANGE BREAD

CHEF: EMILY GLADHART, WINTER'S HILL ESTATE

Makes 2 loaves

This seedy bread with a kiss of citrus can easily do double duty as an AM or PM treat. Toast it and top with store-bought artichoke bruschetta topping (a marinated artichoke spread you can find in the olive aisle) and enjoy with a glass of Pinot. For a deluxe variation, sprinkle the topping with Parmesan and briefly broil. It's also wonderful for breakfast or as part of a brunch buffet with butter and honey. Emily Gladhart of Winter's Hill says her grandson even likes it with melted aged cheddar cheese as an after-school snack. It's no wonder she always doubles the recipe and keeps a loaf on hand in the refrigerator or freezer. The round loaves fit perfectly in gallon-size ziptop bags.

Preheat oven to 350°F. Spread sunflower seeds in a single layer on a baking sheet and toast for 15 minutes, or until fragrant.

Heat 2 cups water to 105°F to 110°F. In a large mixing bowl, combine warm water, yeast and 2 tablespoons of sugar. Set aside for 5 minutes, until yeast is foamy.

Add whole wheat flour, mix well, and allow to rest for 45 minutes in a warm place. This is the sponge.

To the sponge, add the remaining ⅓ cup sugar and the oil, salt, orange zest, and sunflower seeds. Mix well with a spoon. Slowly add all-purpose flour. When dough becomes too stiff to mix with a spoon, continue to knead it by hand in the bowl. Turn dough out onto a lightly floured surface and knead for 10 minutes, until dough is smooth and elastic. Add more flour if necessary.

Wash and dry the bowl and coat with olive oil. Place dough in the bowl, turn to coat, and cover with a lid or dish towel. Set aside to rise for 1½ to 2 hours in a warm place, until doubled in size.

½ cup shelled sunflower seeds (2½ oz)
2 Tbsp active dry yeast
⅓ cup plus 2 Tbsp granulated sugar (divided)
3 cups whole wheat flour (13 oz)
¼ cup extra-virgin olive oil, plus extra for greasing
1 Tbsp salt
Grated zest of 1 orange
3 cups all-purpose flour (13 oz), plus extra for dusting and as needed
1 Tbsp milk or 1 beaten egg white
Store-bought artichoke bruschetta, for serving
Microgreens, for garnish

Turn dough out onto the work surface and knead lightly to allow air bubbles to escape. Divide dough in half. Shape dough into 2 rounds and set on a lightly oiled baking sheet, or shape into loaves and place in lightly oiled loaf pans.

Lightly oil the surface of the dough, then set aside to rise again in a warm place for 40 minutes.

Preheat oven to 350°F.

With a sharp knife, score an "x" on top of each round loaf and brush tops and sides with milk (or egg white). If baking loaves in pans, score the top lengthwise and just brush the top. Bake for 35 to 45 minutes, until golden brown. Cool completely on a wire rack, then slice. Toast slices until golden, top with artichoke bruschetta, and garnish with microgreens if desired.

VARIATION

Omit sunflower seeds and orange zest. Mix together 1 tablespoon each of the following seeds: sesame, poppy, fennel, caraway, sunflower, and flax. Or skip some of the seeds and double up on others. Knead seeds into the dough, or mist the shaped loaves with water and roll them in the seeds.

SCALLOP CRUDO
with Chili-Ginger Ponzu Sauce

CHEF: ERIK ENGLUND, FLYING FISH

WINE PAIRING: Winter's Hill Estate Pinot Blanc

The success of scallop crudo—thinly sliced raw scallops—depends entirely on the quality of the scallops themselves. So, first order of business: visit a reputable fishmonger, like Portland's Flying Fish, where you can get day boat or diver scallops brought to shore the same day, and where this delicious dish originates. It's topped with finely diced Granny Smith apple and cucumber, making it a gorgeous match with the apple and melon notes in the Pinot Blanc from Winter's Hill.

THAI CHILI OIL Heat oil and chiles in a small saucepan over medium heat, until it reaches 300°F. Set aside to cool to room temperature.

When cooled, pour into a blender or food processor and blend until chiles are completely pulverized. Strain through a fine-mesh strainer into an airtight container. Discard solids. (This makes more oil than you need, so the extra can be refrigerated for several weeks.)

CHILI-GINGER PONZU SAUCE Mix all ingredients in a small bowl. Refrigerate until ready to use. (Can be made 5 days ahead.)

SCALLOP CRUDO Lay scallops, slightly overlapping, on a chilled plate. Dress with enough chili-ginger ponzu sauce to completely coat. Sprinkle apple, cucumber, fried shallots, and shiso on top. Garnish with lemon zest.

Serves 4

THAI CHILI OIL
1 cup grapeseed oil
1 oz dried Thai chiles (about 5 whole dried chiles, often found in a pack)

CHILI-GINGER PONZU SAUCE
¼ cup Thai Chili Oil (see here)
¼ cup yuzu ponzu sauce (see Note)
¼ cup toasted sesame oil
1 (¾-inch) piece ginger, peeled and grated (about 1 Tbsp)

SCALLOP CRUDO
8 very fresh, dry-packed day boat or diver scallops, side muscle removed if necessary, thinly sliced into ¼-inch-thick rounds (see Note on page 143)
Chili-Ginger Ponzu Sauce (see here)
1 tart Granny Smith apple, peeled, cored, and very finely diced
1 English cucumber, seeded, peeled, and very finely diced
1 cup fried shallots (see Note)
5 shiso leaves, thinly sliced
Grated zest of 1 lemon

VARIATIONS

For a quick weeknight meal, you can sub Thai chili oil with your favorite storebought chili oil.

You can also make the scallop crudo with sashimi-grade salmon instead.

NOTE Yuzu ponzu sauce can be found at Asian markets. Fried shallots can be found at Asian markets. Or see page 196 to make your own.

METRIC CONVERSION CHART

VOLUME

Imperial or U.S.	Metric
⅛ tsp	0.5 mL
¼ tsp	1 mL
½ tsp	2.5 mL
¾ tsp	4 mL
1 tsp	5 mL
½ Tbsp	8 mL
1 Tbsp	15 mL
1½ Tbsp	23 mL
2 Tbsp	30 mL
¼ cup	60 mL
⅓ cup	80 mL
½ cup	125 mL
⅔ cup	165 mL
¾ cup	185 mL
1 cup	250 mL
1¼ cups	310 mL
1⅓ cups	330 mL
1½ cups	375 mL
1⅔ cups	415 mL
1¾ cups	435 mL
2 cups	500 mL
2¼ cups	560 mL
2⅓ cups	580 mL
2½ cups	625 mL
2¾ cups	690 mL
3 cups	750 mL
4 cups /1 quart	1 L
5 cups	1.25 L
6 cups	1.5 L
7 cups	1.75 L
8 cups	2 L
12 cups	3 L

WEIGHT

Imperial or U.S.	Metric
½ oz	15 g
1 oz	30 g
2 oz	60 g
3 oz	85 g
4 oz (¼ lb)	115 g
5 oz	140 g
6 oz	170 g
7 oz	200 g
8 oz (½ lb)	225 g
9 oz	255 g
10 oz	285 g
11 oz	310 g
12 oz (¾ lb)	340 g
13 oz	370 g
14 oz	400 g
15 oz	425 g
16 oz (1 lb)	450 g
1¼ lbs	570 g
1½ lbs	670 g
2 lbs	900 g
3 lbs	1.4 kg
4 lbs	1.8 kg
5 lbs	2.3 kg
6 lbs	2.7 kg

LIQUID MEASURES

(for alcohol)

Imperial or U.S.	Metric
½ fl oz	15 mL
1 fl oz	30 mL
2 fl oz	60 mL
3 fl oz	90 mL
4 fl oz	120 mL

CANS AND JARS

Imperial or U.S.	Metric
6 oz	170 g
14 oz	398 mL
19 oz	540 mL
28 oz	796 mL

LINEAR

Imperial or U.S.	Metric
⅛ inch	3 mm
¼ inch	6 mm
½ inch	12 mm
¾ inch	2 cm
1 inch	2.5 cm
1¼ inches	3 cm
1½ inches	3.5 cm
1¾ inches	4.5 cm
2 inches	5 cm
2½ inches	6.5 cm
3 inches	7.5 cm
4 inches	10 cm
5 inches	12.5 cm
6 inches	15 cm
7 inches	18 cm
10 inches	25 cm
12 inches (1 foot)	30 cm
13 inches	33 cm
16 inches	41 cm
18 inches	46 cm
24 inches (2 feet)	60 cm
28 inches	70 cm
30 inches	75 cm
6 feet	1.8 m

TEMPERATURE

(for oven temperatures, see chart in next column)

Imperial or U.S.	Metric
90°F	32°C
120°F	49°C
125°F	52°C
130°F	54°C
140°F	60°C
150°F	66°C
155°F	68°C
160°F	71°C
165°F	74°C
170°F	77°C
175°F	80°C
180°F	82°C
190°F	88°C
200°F	93°C
240°F	116°C
250°F	121°C
300°F	149°C
325°F	163°C
350°F	177°C
360°F	182°C
375°F	191°C

OVEN TEMPERATURE

Imperial or U.S.	Metric
200°F	95°C
250°F	120°C
275°F	135°C
300°F	150°C
325°F	160°C
350°F	180°C
375°F	190°C
400°F	200°C
425°F	220°C
450°F	230°C
500°F	260°C
550°F	290°C

BAKING PANS

Imperial or U.S.	Metric
5- × 9-inch loaf pan	2 L loaf pan
9- × 13-inch cake pan	4 L cake pan
11- × 17-inch baking sheet	30- × 45-cm baking sheet

ACKNOWLEDGMENTS

OREGON WINE + FOOD grew from a Zoom conversation we had with publisher Chris Labonté in the middle of the pandemic. At that time, we could only dream of impromptu dinner parties with friends and spending golden afternoons in hilltop tasting rooms overlooking a sea of vineyards. We had faith that someday we could put the isolation of the pandemic behind us, and we found comfort in working on a book that celebrated the many reasons to bring people together around the table.

So, first and foremost, a sincere thank you to Chris for believing in this project and the crew at Figure 1 for shepherding it through: Managing Editor Lara Smith, who wrangled chaos into order with cheerful calm; Publishing Coordinator Aleisha Smith, who kept all of the dizzying details in check; Creative Director Naomi MacDougall, who provided the all-important vision; Senior Designer Teresa Bubela, who turned words and pictures into art; and Director of Marketing Mark Redmayne for his dedication to spreading the word.

We dare not even think about what we would have done without the exceptional and meticulous work by our editing team: Michelle Meade, Pam Robertson, and Renate Preuss. We've never met more careful and enthusiastic editors and proofreaders and will be grateful to them for all time!

Our team of recipe testers also earns our undying gratitude for generously offering their time and expertise to test the recipes in this book: Karen Bridges, Ericka Carlson, Jodie Chase, Ted Farthing, Sandi Francioch, Polly Luthro, Keely Murphy, JoAnna Rodriguez, and Kevin Tangen. Their hard work ensures each recipe is dinner-party ready.

This book couldn't have happened without the talent and dedication of John and Theresa Valls, the photography dream team. Not only are they skilled at capturing the spirit of people and places through their photos, they brought so much joy to this project. And we feel so lucky to have had food stylist extraordinaire Andrea Slonecker on board, cooking all the recipes with precision and transforming them into stunningly beautiful plates with the help of her assistant Tess Paterson.

Special thanks goes to the talented chefs who created recipes for this book. Working with them was a reminder of our creative, generous, and beautifully connected culinary community. The book wouldn't be complete without their inspired contributions. And their fabulous food was further elevated by gorgeous, locally made tableware courtesy of Martina Thornhill, Wolf Ceramics, Justin Caraco, and Notary Ceramics + Home.

A few big bottles of bubbly are in order for these magic-makers who never failed to answer our late-night emails and share their expertise: Melissa Broussard, Kayt Mathers, Sarah (Sally) Murdoch, Emily Petterson, and, of course, our lead cheerleader Julien Perry, the author of *Washington Wine + Food*. The unconditional support of these smart and savvy women got us through the tough times.

And, above all, thank you to the Oregon wine community. We are fortunate to live in a state where wine represents so much more than an agricultural product. Here, the commitment to make wine that is a true expression of place is only matched by the dedication to make a difference and bring meaning to the table. It was an honor to share your stories. Salud!

DANIELLE CENTONI is a food, drink, and travel writer and a cookbook author based in Portland, Oregon. In her two-decade career, she has written and developed recipes for a wide range of publications, including *Better Homes & Gardens*, *Conde Nast Traveler*, EatingWell, and The Kitchn. *Oregon Wine + Food* is her seventh cookbook, and she has contributed editorial work to several others.

KERRY NEWBERRY has been a food and lifestyle writer for more than fifteen years. She's a contributing writer for *1859 Magazine*, and her work appears in numerous publications including *Travel Oregon, Sunset, Forbes, Fodor's Travel Publications, Wine & Spirits* magazine and *Civil Eats*. She holds a master's degree in Educational Leadership for Sustainability from Portland State University and has studied with the Wine & Spirit Education Trust.